THE MULTILINGUAL SUBJECT

Published in this series

The Multilingual Subject

What Foreign Language Learners Say about their Experience and Why it Matters

CLAIRE KRAMSCH

OXFORD
UNIVERSITY PRESS

OXFORD
UNIVERSITY PRESS

Great Clarendon Street, Oxford OX2 6DP

Oxford University Press is a department of the University of Oxford.
It furthers the University's objective of excellence in research, scholarship,
and education by publishing worldwide in

Oxford New York

Auckland Cape Town Dar es Salaam Hong Kong Karachi
Kuala Lumpur Madrid Melbourne Mexico City Nairobi
New Delhi Shanghai Taipei Toronto

With offices in

Argentina Austria Brazil Chile Czech Republic France Greece
Guatemala Hungary Italy Japan Poland Portugal Singapore
South Korea Switzerland Thailand Turkey Ukraine Vietnam

OXFORD and OXFORD ENGLISH are registered trade marks of
Oxford University Press in the UK and in certain other countries

ISBN: 978 0 19 442478 3

Printed in China

To Madame Boyer
In Memoriam

Acknowledgments

This book has been a long time in the making. The difficulty of writing objectively about an experience that I had lived through myself as a foreign language learner and the fear of being misunderstood, together with the recent proliferation of publications on the subjective experiences of language learners—all made me procrastinate longer than usual in the completion of this book. Surely everything had already been written on the topic! Yet I only had to talk to my fellow foreign language teachers and my colleagues in applied linguistics to see why the book still needed to be written and why perhaps it was not quite as superfluous as I perceived it to be. I am all the more grateful for the encouragements and nudges received over the years.

First and foremost my greatest thanks go to Henry Widdowson, whose intellectual rigor and generosity have shepherded this book since its inception, not the least during a memorable brainstorming week in July 2002 at his and Barbara Seidlhofer's country home in Maigen, Austria. I wish to thank the many colleagues who throughout our informal conversations helped me conceptualize the framework for the book: Robert Blake, Martin Bygate, Chris Candlin, Guy Cook, Rick Donato, Patsy Duff, Fred Genesee, Bill Hanks, Diane Larsen-Freeman, Tony Liddicoat, Jo LoBianco, Jim Lantolf, Allan Luke, Tim McNamara, Bonnie Norton, Alastair Pennycook, Ben Rampton, John Schumann, Ron Scollon, Elana Shohamy, Dick Tucker, Leo van Lier, Johannes Wagner, Ruth Wodak. I am grateful to many of them for inviting me to discuss my ideas at their universities. Sincere thanks are owed to the many colleagues in France, Germany, and the UK, in particular Hans Barkowski, Lothar Bredella, Michael Byram, Adelheid Hu, Ulrike Jessner, Hans Jürgen Krumm, Karen Risager, Christine Schwerdtfeger, Geneviève Zarate, Danielle Lévy, Bernd Rüschoff, and their students for providing me with a forum to discuss the ideas contained in this book. These ideas were inordinately enriched by an unforgettable meeting with Ben Rampton's research team at King's College in London in January 2007.

My sources of inspiration have come not only from the social sciences, but also from the humanities. Many thanks go to my colleagues on the Modern Languages Association Ad Hoc Committee for Foreign Languages, in particular Michael Geisler, Peter Patrikis, and Mary Louise Pratt, for our discussions on the notion of translingual and transcultural competence. At UC Berkeley, I wish to thank my colleagues at the Berkeley Language Center, Mark Kaiser and Rick Kern, as well as the UC Berkeley foreign language teachers with whom I have exchanged ideas over the years, in particular Rutie

viii   *Acknowledgments*

Adler, Lisa Little, Karen Moller, and Sonia Shiri. Linda von Hoene remains one of the best conversational partners on matters of teacher development at the college level. I would not have remained honest if I hadn't had the unwavering critical support of my present and former doctoral students: Julie Belz, Meg Gebhard, David Gramling, Tes Howell, Shlomy Kattan, Eva Lam, David Malinowski, Steve Thorne, Greta Vollmer, Paige Ware, Chantelle Warner, Chad Wellmon, Tim Wolcott, Anne Whiteside. Many of them have become professors themselves and are now helping their students become multilingual subjects. They have all contributed to this book with their enthusiasm and their criticisms. Some of them, impatient for the book to come out, have suggested in jest that I give it the title: 'The Forever Emergent Subject'. They and the many graduate students whose emails I received last year will be happy to know that *The Multilingual Subject* is indeed coming out and we can at last talk about something else.

Finally, I wish to thank the readers of the final manuscript, especially Aneta Pavlenko, whose astute assessment of its intended readership gave the introduction its final shape. The production of this book owes a great deal to the encouragements of both Cristina Whitecross and Catherine Kneafsey at OUP and to the keen eyes of Sylvie Jaffrey and Ann Hunter. I am most grateful for their support.

Beside my own biography, the impetus for this book comes from my two sons Olivier and Christophe, who each in his own way has lived the multilingual experience to the full: Olivier, a cultural geographer, with his passion for borders of all kinds; Christophe, a medical doctor, with his constant reminder that 'Maman, there is more to life than words!' I have dedicated the book to Madame Boyer, my philosophy professor, who in the 1950s taught me about the symbolic power of myth to understand the relation of language and culture, especially with regard to the multilingual subject.

C.K.

Berkeley, California
15 June 2009

Contents

Introduction

The subjective dimensions of language

In the summer of 2000, a participant in a seminar on intercultural communication described her experience as follows:

> Over the course of five days, tears often streamed down my face for reasons outside my consciousness. My back went into spasms several times a day although I had not had any back problems to date. One of the course participants was a young Swedish professional married to an American living in the Midwestern part of the US. She said to us 'My sister is coming to visit this summer, so I guess I will have to get back into my Swedish self to prepare for this.' She was clearly very aware of this multidimensional aspect of her identity, both linguistically and culturally. I then asked myself 'Do you have a Persian self?' In spite of using Persian on a daily basis as a language of communication in my home (English is my first language) since 1979, raising a bilingual child, and teaching courses routinely on intercultural communication for language educators, it had never occurred to me to consider that I might have a 'Persian self'. When I shared this anecdote with several Persian colleagues who teach in the social sciences and/or education areas, they laughed and said 'You do too. We see you switch all the time. You speak much more loudly in Persian than in English'. When I thought about their comments, I realized they were right and the tears I was shedding along with the pain in my lower back were somatic connections to identity issues I had not begun to resolve. Am I a different person when I speak Persian? Absolutely. Would I have answered this question affirmatively five years ago? Absolutely not.[1]

Testimonies like these are easily recognizable by people who know several languages and associate very personal memories and experiences with each one of them. Whether they sojourned abroad, emigrated to a foreign country, married a foreign national, raised their children in a foreign tongue, or simply experienced the language in the confines of a classroom, they often describe the experience as one that engages their emotions, their bodies, and the most intimate aspects of themselves.

In its attempts to elucidate how people learn and use various languages, second language acquisition (SLA) research has traditionally given more attention to the processes of acquisition than to the flesh-and-blood individuals who are doing the learning. It has separated learners' minds, bodies, and social behaviors into separate domains of inquiry and studied how language intersects with each of them. Some researchers have thought of language acquisition as a kind of cognitive grafting of language on a pre-existing mind; others have conceived of language as a social scaffolding for the development of the mind in interaction with others; yet others have viewed it as a communication tool for the achievement of social tasks or the expression of culturally specific emotions. In all these cases, not only has language been studied separately from its affective resonances in the bodies of speakers and hearers, but it has been viewed as a transparent and neutral tool for the formulation of thought, for interpersonal communication, and social interaction. In part because of the rationality of its grammar and the logic of its vocabulary, language has been taught and learned mostly as a tool for rational thinking, for the expression and communication of factual truths and information, and for the description of a stable and commonly agreed-upon reality. It has not been taught as a symbolic system that constructs the very reality it refers to, and that acts upon this reality through the categories it imposes upon it, thereby affecting the relation between speakers and the reality as they perceive it. The emotional upheaval experienced by the seminar participant quoted above is not just a bout of childhood nostalgia triggered by the memory of a family language; it is the sudden realization that by knowing another language, she has access to another reality, and that the world in English is not the only reality possible. Her everyday world acquires a different meaning by being named differently. Indeed, the very sense of who she is can be very different in English and in Persian.

The recent interest in ecological theories of language has prompted researchers to view the use of another symbolic system as a semiotic, historically and culturally grounded, personal experience. As a sign system, language elicits subjective responses in the speakers themselves: emotions, memories, fantasies, projections, identifications. Because it is not only a code but also a meaning-making system, language constructs the historical sedimentation of meanings that we call our 'selves'. In our times of increased migrations and displacements, when globalization enhances what Pratt (1999) calls the 'contact zones' and the 'traffic in meaning' (2002) among individuals and communities, it is important that we look in richer detail at the lived experiences of multiple language users.

1 Yet another book on the multilingual subject?

In the past several years the market has been flooded with monographs and collections on the subjective experiences of bi- and multilingual individuals.

There has been a plethora of language-learning biographies by bilingual writers and scholars who, having emigrated or lived abroad or experienced being minority speakers in their own country, have recounted the trials and tribulations they underwent acquiring another language and living in a country other than their own or that did not feel like their own (see Rodriguez 1982; Hoffman 1983; Lvovich 1997 and the testimonies collected in Benson and Nunan 2004; Franceschini and Miecznikowski 2004; Burck 2005 among many others). Literary authors have reflected on what it means to write in a second or in several languages: Gustavo Perez Firmat (2003), for example, analyzes in moving detail his relationship to Spanish and English in his writings. Bilingual writers Shirley Geok-Lin Lim, Ariel Dorfman, Sylvia Molloy, and Eva Hoffman reflect on their use of English vis-à-vis their other languages (de Courtivron 2003). The English Canadian Nancy Huston and the Algerian writer Leila Sebbar exchange views on how writing in French enriches their literary creativity (Huston and Sebbar 1986).

Based on these biographical accounts, scholars in applied linguistics have conceptualized the experiences of bilinguals and second language learners: how they perform who they are in two languages (Wolf 2006; Koven 2007), how they develop multilingual identities (Burck 2005; Block 2007), and the relation between emotions and subjectivity (Pavlenko 2005, 2006). Others have given in-depth analyses of bilingual authors like the ones we will encounter in this book. For example, Mary Besemeres (2002: 278) has analyzed the life writings of such 'life migrants' as Eva Hoffman in her cross-cultural autobiography *Lost in Translation,* as has Richard Rodriguez in his quest for his own language, *Hunger of Memory.*

While this research and the literary biographies that have inspired it have had a tremendous impact on the field of applied linguistics and developmental bilingualism in particular, they have not changed much of what is going on in foreign/second language and literature classrooms that are attended by developmentally mature students. There, psycholinguistic and sociocultural SLA research has had a much greater influence on foreign language curricula, pedagogic practices, and teaching materials than research on bilingualism.[2] Most language instruction strives to develop communicative competence as exchange of information and the fulfillment of communicative tasks. Foreign language instruction is meant to prepare students to read literature in the upper-level classes. They are taught how to read monolingual foreign language texts without any consideration of the other language(s) the students might bring to the classroom. These texts are discussed mostly for their thematic content, on which the students are then asked to write essays that are evaluated for their grammatical correctness and the clarity of their ideas. In short, students are taught a standardized linguistic system with which they are expected to approximate a monolingual native speaker and reader. Yet, below the radar of tasks and exercises, the students discover in and through the foreign language subjectivities that will shape their lives in unpredictable ways.

This book explores these subjectivities in adolescents and young adults who acquire another language in institutional settings.[3] We are fooling ourselves if we believe that students learn only what they are taught. While teachers are busy teaching them to communicate accurately, fluently, and appropriately, students are inventing for themselves other ways of being in their bodies and their imaginations. Success in language learning is an artifact of schooling, of the need by institutions to demarcate those who know from those who don't, but the language-learning experience itself is neither successful nor unsuccessful. It can be lived more or less meaningfully and can be more or less transformative, no matter what level of proficiency has been attained. Without an understanding of what they associate with the music of the new language, its sounds and rhythms, shapes and syntaxes, we cannot grasp the identities students are constructing, consciously or unconsciously, for themselves.

It is often believed that, unlike learners who acquire a language in natural settings and often because of economic necessity, foreign language learners do not construct new identities for themselves. David Block (2007: 144), for example, has argued that 'in the FL setting, there is usually far too much first language-mediated baggage and interference for profound changes to occur in the individual's conceptual system and his/her sense of self in the TL'. Pavlenko (2005: 9) has suggested that because 'classroom learning results in subordinate representation—mapping of new linguistic items onto the pre-existing conceptual system' learners are much too attached to their original sense of self to undergo any major transformation. Moreover, those who study foreign languages are generally perceived as being part of the elite, secure in their identity and eager to increase their cultural capital. No doubt knowing another language in an ideologically monolingual society can give someone a profit of distinction and even sometimes extra pay. But the testimonies presented in this book show that there is much more to foreign language study than that. Precisely because they learn the foreign language in isolation from the real world, these youngsters project onto it their dissatisfactions with their own and their dreams of a better world. Language for them is not just an unmotivated formal construct but a lived embodied reality. It is not simply an agglomeration of encoded meanings, that are grasped intellectually, cognitively internalized, and then applied in social contexts; rather, it is the potential medium for the expression of their innermost aspirations, awarenesses, and conflicts.

There are many reasons why people set out on the arduous task of learning another language in school. Some, out of desire or necessity, strive to approximate as much as possible the native speaker they encounter (or imagine encountering) on the streets of London, Paris, or Beijing. Some want to be able to communicate with business partners or other professionals. Others, who grew up in a bilingual family, want to reconnect with the language of their ancestors. Yet others want to read literary works in the original or fulfill academic requirements. And of course there are always the polyglots, who collect languages like others collect butterflies. For young people who are seeking to define their linguistic identity and their position in the world, the language class is often the first time they are consciously and explicitly confronted with the relationship between their language, their thoughts, and their bodies. Engaging with a different language sensitizes them to the significance of their own and of language in general. Those who just sit out the language class as a boring but necessary step towards graduation find themselves vindicated in their monolingual selves. Later, they will say with pride, 'I have had six years of French and I can't even order a cup of coffee in French.' Others will start having thoughts they never had in their mother tongue. The experience of the foreign always implies a reconsideration of the familiar.

But how do we gain access to subjective aspects of language acquisition that, by definition, elude objective observation? How do we document the subjective effects of language on the embodied perceptions, memories, and emotions of speakers like the one cited at the beginning of this introduction, that give them the feeling they are another person when they speak another language? The data used in this book will be taken from language users themselves, who encode their experience in testimonies written in one or the other language, or even sometimes in a mixture of languages. Because of the importance of their choice of words, I have chosen mostly speakers and writers of the European languages that I know and am able to analyze and interpret. For the languages I don't know, such as Korean or Japanese, I have sought the help of native speakers. Three kinds of data will be used. First, published testimonies and language memoirs of former language learners writing about their experiences in their acquired language. They report such subjective aspects as: heightened perceptions and emotions, awareness of one's body, feelings of loss or enhanced power, together with imagined identities, projected selves, idealizations or stereotypes of the other. These phenomena seem to be central to the language-learning experience, but they are difficult to grasp within the current paradigms in SLA research. They are not exhausted by motivation studies or social psychological theory, neurobiological appraisal theory, or even sociocultural theory, as they are not amenable to traditional psycholinguistic or sociolinguistic modes of inquiry. Because they appear in the form of written accounts, they have to be read as *ex post facto* reconstructions of events that were often lived in a much more confused manner at the time. Moreover, they have been cast into specific narrative genres and their authors are often experienced literary writers. This is not to say that language memoirs should be disregarded as unreliable data, but the subjective truths they reveal can only be accessed through alternative modes of inquiry that take into account their metaphoric and literary nature. Language memoirs present a challenge to traditional SLA research, as they require new ways of apprehending and accounting for experience—ways, one might say, that aim at understanding rather than explanation.[4]

The second source of data will be spoken and written data from language learners such as testimonies from learners' journals (Chapter 1), discourse completion surveys (Chapter 2), oral interviews on their language-learning experiences and transcriptions of classroom discourse (Chapter 4) as well as first- or third-person essays on what it means to be multilingual (Chapter 5). This kind of data will be analyzed like sociolinguistic data within their context of production and reception, taking into account the markers of subjectivity displayed in the discourse and the intertextualities or intersubjectivities that they reveal (see section 4 below). Like the first set of data, these too will have to be taken to reveal contingent truths and emergent theories of the self, co-constructed between writer and reader, interviewer and interviewee. The third source of data will be online data from language learners using networked computers in electronic chat rooms, telecollaboration projects, or text messaging exchanges (Chapter 6). We will have to approach such data with analytical and interpretative caution, as behind the words on the screen the computer remains an influential, albeit invisible, presence that calls for the kind of analysis used by postmodern sociolinguistics.

In order to interpret these data, I will be drawing from research that has conceptualized the link between symbolic forms and symbolic power on the one hand, perception and desire on the other in the construction of the subject and, ultimately, a subject's sense of self. But first I have to define some of the terms I have just used, as they will be central to my argument.

2 Language as symbolic form

Any language teacher knows that letters, sounds, and words are symbols or signs that denote, that is, refer to objects and events in the real world, as in: 'the word *tree* is a linguistic symbol'. When we say that 'language is a symbolic system', we mean that it is made of linguistic signs that are related to one another in systematic and conventional ways. Non-linguistic signs include, for example, a flag as a national symbol, or a green light as a symbol for 'go ahead'. Even though for monolingual speakers linguistic signs have become so attached to their referents that they seem to be part of the object itself, for multilinguals or newcomers to a language, the fact that the same object is called tree in one language, *Baum* or *arbre* in another, makes it evident that the linguistic sign as symbolic form is quite arbitrary, even though it is used in non-arbitrary ways.

We may focus on two aspects of symbols. On the one hand, symbols are conventional in nature, they refer to and represent the social and psychological reality of a speech community. As signs shared by a social community, symbols derive their meaning from the force of social convention. Learners of a foreign language have to adhere to the grammatical and lexical conventions of the symbolic system they are learning and to the social conventions of its use. By conforming to these conventions they are given the symbolic power to enter a historical speech community and be accepted as members of that community. However, such membership has its price: grammaticality, social acceptability, and cultural appropriateness put limits on what an individual may say or write.

On the other hand, the use of symbols triggers subjective resonances both in the users and in the receivers. It reproduces a speaker's sense of self and enables him or her to act upon the symbolic order of the speech community. Because each speaker's experiences are different, each speaker inflects conventional symbolic forms with personal, often idiosyncratic, meaning. For non-native speakers, the power that comes from being able to sound like or even to pass for someone else, to put one's own experience into someone else's words, to speak English but to feel Persian or speak German with an American sensibility, creates new symbolic power relations that enable learners to break with conventions and to bring about other symbolic realities. The social and cultural meanings given to events by a given speech community can generate for speakers who don't belong to that community a new sense of self. For example, I am writing this in Paris, where I hear on French TV President Bush addressing the American people and commemorating September 11, 2001. The American president speaks in English but I hear him in French through the French telecaster's translation. For the first time, I see and hear the 9/11 events through the eyes and the language of someone else—an astonishing metamorphosis: September 11 becomes a historical rather than an ideological event, Bush's words cease to address me, as a fellow American; they address 'them', the Americans, commemorating 'their' traumatic event on the evening news. The French language frees me to hear the American president with French ears, that is, with empathy but with the distance afforded by a different position in space and time. In a second, my view of reality and of my own position has changed, as it does when I look at a European map of the world where the world revolves not around North America, but around Europe. French words, French maps are all symbols that mediate for me a different reality and a different subject position.

As we shall see in this book, these new subject positions are not just social or psychological realities, but, rather, they are symbolic, that is, created through the language user's engagement with and manipulation of symbols of a very concrete, material kind, such as vowels and consonants, nouns and verbs, sounds and accents, as well as maps and televised images. The word 'symbolic', when applied to entities such as 'symbolic reality', 'symbolic self', or 'symbolic power', refers not only to the *representation* of people and objects in the world but to the *construction* of perceptions, attitudes, beliefs, aspirations, values through the use of symbolic forms. In this book we will encounter the term 'symbolic' in these two meanings of the word: language use is symbolic [1] because it mediates our existence through symbolic forms that are conventional and represent objective realities, and [2] because symbolic forms construct subjective realities such as perceptions, emotions, attitudes, and values.

How can symbolic forms like the sound of a word, the shape of a letter, an intonation contour, or a sudden switch of linguistic code construct attitudes, beliefs, and other psychological realities? How does symbolic *power* emerge through the use of symbolic *form*? This question is rarely discussed explicitly in language classes, even though it is easily responded to by politicians, marketing strategists, preachers, and language teachers themselves, who all wield symbolic power to influence people's desires and move people to action—through language. For learners and users of several languages, the question is: what is the nature of the symbolic power that is potentially associated with the knowledge and use of multiple languages? I examine in turn various ways in which language as symbolic power has been theorized in linguistics (Austin 1962), sociology (Bourdieu 1991), and semiotics (Barthes 1957).

3 Language as symbolic power

3.1 The power of the performative

When linguists refer to language as symbolic power they refer to the power of language users not just to say things correctly and appropriately, but to 'do things with words'. For language educators, this well-known phrase by John Austin (1962) is usually taken to refer to a speaker's ability, given the right conditions, to bring about a change of reality through words: to marry or christen or vote or graduate, acts that come to pass by the sheer performance of appropriate words by the appropriate person. Indeed, these utterances are a prime example of the symbolic power of performatives. Ultimately, Austin suggested that all utterances have a performative dimension, as they all have what speech act theory calls a perlocutionary effect, that is, they act upon reality through the very performance of the words uttered.

But where does symbolic power come from? Is it to be found in special formulaic rituals like those found in fairytales, or in everyday phrases like 'let's do lunch', or in the intention and the social status of the speaker as Austin posited? Should it be traced back to the institution that gives the speaker the legitimacy and the authority to speak and be listened to? Some scholars such as Bourdieu (1991) argue that it is ultimately the power of history that gives words their symbolic power. But history is made up of little daily speech acts that can both sediment through time in the form of tradition and subvert the tradition when the conditions are right.

More recently, philosophers of language such as Judith Butler (1997, 1999) and linguistic anthropologists such as Alexei Yurchak (2006), interested in the relation of language and symbolic power, have looked less to large entities for the source of symbolic power than to the language users themselves and what they do with language to uphold or subvert the power of dominant institutions. Drawing on the work of Jacques Derrida, Butler points out that between a speech act and its perlocutionary effect there is a timelag or semiotic gap that can be used to give the speech act a meaning other than the one intended.[5] Her analysis of the way sexist or racist insults can be resignified by those to whom these insults are addressed, or Yurchak's study of the way Soviet citizens repurposed the political phrases they were expected to produce in the last decades of Soviet rule show that symbolic power is more equally distributed than we think. An insult, whose symbolic power comes from the history of domination of one group over another, may be turned against its author when the conditions are right. Political slogans and euphemisms can be uttered in quotation marks, thus distancing the speaker from the words uttered, according to the needs of the moment. As we shall see, those who can express themselves in more than one language have greater semiotic resources to draw on to redress the balance of symbolic power. Politicians and marketing strategists are well aware of that power and they use it to win votes and influence people. But everyday language users as well as language learners are not helpless recipients or imitators. They too experience the language both for what it states and what it does, and can wield the power that comes from using a whole range of symbolic forms to be who they want to be.

3.2 The power of ritual

As Bourdieu eloquently demonstrated in *Language and Symbolic Power* (1991), the exercise of symbolic power can also take the form of rituals, that is, uses of language that, rather than contest convention, reinforce dominant values. This is the case with the advertisements on American television that are broadcast day after day before the evening news and have become as much of a daily ritual as is the watching of the news. Because their goal is not just to inform or entertain but ultimately to sell products, their value is to exercise the symbolic [2] power of ritual to promote their commercial interests. Besides marketing ads, rituals can also be of a more modest kind. They can range from what Clark calls 'ostensible' communicative acts of verbal politeness (Clark 1996: 378) such as 'Hi, how are you?'—'Fine, how are you?' to the mindless use of current euphemisms such as 'empowerment' or 'partnership'. These rituals do not carry any particular referential meaning, their purpose is rather to wield subjective and social symbolic power by upholding the conventional ethos of friendly interaction and democratic opportunity.

Ritualized speech fills the vagaries of daily life with the soothing, predictable little verbal practices that mirror and uphold the larger social order. Besides advertising jingles and patriotic slogans, it can be found also in any uses of language that appeal to the emotions by exploiting the resources of memory and identification, for example in the forced narratives of self, called 'personal statements' or 'statements of purpose' required for college admission or scholarship applications at US colleges and universities. The identities that applicants have to display in these statements have to fit into the dominant ideology of the self-made person, who against all odds has pulled herself up by her bootstraps and seized the opportunities on the road to success. This is not to say that these uses of language don't have a communicative purpose, but that purpose is less to inform than to impress, less to represent reality than to use the right buzzwords in order to elicit a certain subjective effect in the reader or the listener. Like emblems, totems, and ciphers, language here is a vehicle for impression management and, sometimes, ideological manipulation.

The emphasis in language teaching is on language as reference and representation rather than on language as symbolic power. For example, the American phrase 'let's do lunch' is taught as an informal and friendly way of inviting someone to lunch. Learners of English who first hear a native speaker say at the end of an encounter 'let's do lunch' might at first be seduced by the informal generosity of what they understand literally to be a casual invitation to lunch. For them, the words have connotations of American friendliness and generosity, raising the expectation of future friendly encounters. However, for native speakers this might not be a true invitation, but just an attempt to give an impression of friendliness while taking leave. For them, the words have become a convenient ritualistic phrase, uttered in order to placate the interlocutor and make leave-taking easier. The words construct a social reality, but not the one expressed by the literal meaning of the utterance. Rather than mean 'I invite you to lunch in the next few days', it might be a cipher for 'it was nice meeting you' or even 'I don't intend to see you again'. The symbolic force of the utterance does not derive from the intention of the speaker, but from a general communication culture that strives to avoid conflict and keep everybody happy. Non-native speakers might find the American quite impolite for not following up on the invitation; they might be disappointed to find out that the statement was nothing but an empty ritual. Learners of English who have not learned the symbolic value of 'let's do lunch' are left to conclude that Americans are pretty indifferent or insincere, while the latter are convinced they have been particularly friendly. How can one know ? One of the dilemmas of human communication is that words at the same time represent and manipulate, and that speakers always have an alibi in language.

3.3 The power of myth

To understand the link between symbolic form and symbolic power, it is useful to go back to a little essay that the French semiologist and literary critic Barthes published in 1957 under the title *Myth Today* shortly after the first large-scale American exhibition of photographs 'The Family of Man' opened its doors in Paris after World War II. For Barthes it was clear that, after five years of a war that had killed millions of human beings, such a theme was less a representation of facts than a way of making a symbolic statement. The phrase 'Family of Man' did not refer to a real family, it was a metaphor for a deeper truth, namely, that irrespective of nationality, race, age, and occupation we are all humans and we should get along together. In this exhibition, language and photographs contrived to represent and perform a post-World War II reality of world peace and harmony. Barthes gave the use of these symbolic forms (words, pictures, photographs) that transformed the referent 'family' into a larger entity 'Family of Man', the name 'myth'. He did not mean to say that such a phrase was false, only that it transformed the multiple historical realities of real people giving birth, growing up, working, and dying into one big metaphor, that of a Happy Family.

Barthes went on to characterize in the same way many of the metaphors, slogans, and advertisements of his day such as ads for wine or publicity for a French bicycle race, whose message went beyond their referential meaning and that were used to deliver a deeper message. What the Tour de France, red wine, or *bifteck-pommes frites* had in common in the French imagination, he said, was an additional layer of meaning that not only superimposed itself on the referential meaning, but replaced it with a very specific ideological message that was made to seem totally natural. *Red wine*, for example, had ceased to be an alcoholic beverage made of grapes, but had become the very essence of Frenchness. The *Tour de France* no longer denoted a bicycle race around a geographical territory called France, associated with athletic feats and yellow shirts for the winners, but had become a logo of national pride and identification, that could be exploited—and exported—by corporations and governments for commercial and political purposes. Myth, he said, empties words and images of their historical context and fills them with timeless ideological content that serves the interests of its creators.[6] Barthes argued that the press and the media created and disseminated many such myths. Today the use of myths by politicians and marketing strategists to influence public opinion is matched by the ease with which such myths are recirculated in the language of everyday life. They influence our way of thinking and the way we see ourselves.[7]

Myth highlights the fact that language makes meaning not only by referring to or standing for things in the world, but by evoking or indexing them. In its indexical capacity, myth is, however, ambiguous. On the one hand, it can bring to the fore what we have called the realm of the symbolic [2]. It can take the form of narratives that reveal essential truths about the human condition even if the events they relate are fictional. Parables, fairy tales, bedtime stories, are often allegories of real events, they enact the deeper meaning of phenomena beneath an entertaining plot. For example, *The Little Engine that Could* teaches American children that youth and determination can save the day, while *The Cat in the Hat* reminds them that pranks and the temporary questioning of authority can be fun and need not lead to anarchy. Myth in this case fulfills a creative, imaginative function that can break the stale conventions of society and open up untold scenarios of possibility. We return to the beneficial aspects of myth at the end of Chapter 3.

On the other hand, myth can be a form of speech in which the symbolic order [1] has been highjacked and replaced by the subjective realm of a symbolic order [2] that masquerades as a symbolic order [1]. It is a way of using language less for its objective truth value than for the subjective beliefs and emotions that it expresses, elicits, and performs. In other words, beyond its referential meaning, mythic speech focuses on the aesthetic, that is, perceptual, aspects of words and on the affective impact of their connotations, and the way they shape the relationship between addresser and addressee. It then transforms subjective connotation into objective denotation as if it were a conventional meaning that everybody agrees upon. Because it condenses a variety of historically contingent meanings into one timeless symbol, myth often functions as a 'condensation symbol' (Rothenbuhler 1998: 17; see also Sapir 1934/49: 565–6). One such condensation symbol is the American landscape as used in the TV ads for Toyota in the US. The camera offers an initial shot of an early morning mist in a mountain-surrounded valley in one of the most remote parts of the American countryside. The shot then fades into a breathtaking view of the Pacific ocean and the wide open spaces of a California beach, following a lone biker right into a sparkling new Toyota assembly plant, while a mellifluous male voice recites in American English: 'From the foothills of West Virginia to the Pacific Ocean…we do our small part to add to the landscape of America'. Through a condensation symbol in which American landscapes stand for freedom itself, Toyota not only informs the viewer about the cars that the Japanese corporation is selling in the US, it creates and reinforces the fundamental myth of the American entrepreneurial spirit as expressed through its wide open landscapes. Day after day before the evening news, by using an American voice to sell Japanese cars, Toyota constructs its identity as a Japanese corporation that blends in naturally with American interests.

Myth, then, is a use of symbolic forms (verbal or visual) that is not primarily meant to refer or inform, but to act upon listeners' or readers' sensibilities and influence their perceptions. As the subjective dimension of language, myth encompasses the imagined, emotional resonances that people associate with the language they speak and hear. It expresses both conventional, socialized ways of thinking, and creative, subjective beliefs and idealized realities. It is when these idealized realities are imposed as objective or are taken as conventional ones, that is, it is when subjective beliefs are made to look as if they were natural, that myth distorts and manipulates. Because myth is anchored in an imagined reality that does not operate in chronological, historical time, it has been called 'a-historical' (Barthes 1957). One of the antidotes against this use of myth is what Bakhtin (1981, 1986) called the 'heteroglossia' of language, that is, the multiplicity of voices that constitutes language in discourse. The notion of heteroglossia points to the fact that language is plural, not only because it is made of multiple linguistic codes, registers, and styles but because of the multiplicity of potential meanings expressed by these codes in the course of history.

In sum, the use of symbolic forms carries with it symbolic power both through the informational content they convey and through the emotional impact they exert on the senses. Words uttered are both symbols, whose meaning can be found in the textbook or the dictionary, and ciphers for other meanings: performatives, rituals, myths that index larger, factual or imagined realities and that are inserted into a social context in order to act upon that context by the sheer power of their enunciation. For foreign language learners, the symbolic nature of language is enhanced as connotations multiply across codes and additional meanings thrive in the interstices of different linguistic systems.

3.4 Symbolic power and subjectivity in language

Even though native and non-native speakers alike go beyond the truth value of language and draw on its subjective potential, L2 learners, like poets and advertisement designers, are particularly prone to do so. Primary socialization in one's native language encourages the referential use of signs and the expectation that 'words mean what they say and say what they mean'. Indeed, children are socialized into believing that words and the world are one. By contrast, in the early stages of second language acquisition, especially as it occurs in classrooms or in settings far removed from communities of native speakers, signs are dislocated from their natural context of occurrence. The referential relation between signs and their objects is not (yet) perceived as natural and necessary, and the symbolic possibilities of the sign are much more evident than at later stages.

When we consider adolescent language learners, who, unlike children, have been socialized in a different language and whose imagination in the new language may therefore work in non-conventional ways, we have to take into consideration this hidden layer of imagined meanings, idiosyncratic representations, ritualized verbal behaviors, that accompany the use of symbolic forms. Beginning learners and non-native speakers who have not been socialized in the target culture make quite different associations, construct different truths from those of socialized native speakers. Newcomers to the language apprehend the linguistic system in all its fantastic dimensions: the sounds, the shapes, the unfamiliar combinations, the odd grammatical structures. And they give meaning to all: French nasals are construed as 'sexy', Italian vowels are heard as 'romantic', German sounds are apprehended as 'harsh', Arabic script is seen as 'mysterious'. Learners' imagination can be heavily at work, building imagined communities of native speakers endowed with timeless attributes that are projected onto the language itself. No doubt these projections are stereotypes, that exoticize and essentialize the speakers of those languages, but stereotypes—good and bad—fulfill an important emotional function as non-native speakers try to make sense of the new symbolic system.

Those who are learning the language of their ancestors as their linguistic and cultural heritage experience its symbolic value in particularly acute ways. Even if it is a language that they heard growing up but never really mastered or never spoke at all, it has nevertheless left emotional traces of childhood in their memory. For example, Armenian terms of endearment such as *sakis* (honey), *hokis* (my soul), interspersed with English in an Armenian grandmother's speech to her American granddaughter have acquired a symbolic value. Like the spells in fairytales, they have the performative power of enacting and instituting family membership and ethnic solidarity. The American granddaughter who then decides to learn Armenian in a classroom context is likely to be disappointed when confronted with the referential meanings of words severed from their subjective dimensions. This demythification of language can be painful for heritage language learners and requires particular sensitivity on the part of the teacher.

Indeed, pedagogies that reduce language to its informational value, be it grammatical, social, or cultural information, miss an important dimension of the language-learning experience. Many heritage language learners abandon learning the language of their ancestors because they don't recognize their grandmother behind the dry declensions and conjugations. Many who return from a lived experience abroad can't identify with the language they find in the classroom and drop out of the game altogether. The challenge for the teacher is how to use myth wisely, in a way that will not only corral the learners into conventional ways of speaking, but awaken the subjective relevance the language can have for them.

4 Perception and desire

The first thing one notices when reading the testimonies of foreign language users is the intensity of their multilingual experiences. Some SLA research has tried to determine what conditions are favorable to the construction of a new social identity in a foreign language, but, by focusing on language mostly as a means to an end, that is, as a tool for the achievement of pragmatic goals or for social acceptance by a group, it has bypassed a large domain of what makes us human, namely, the need to identify with another reality than the one that surrounds us. This need for identification with the Other, be it another person such as a native speaker or another image of oneself, is so strong that Kristeva (1980) called it 'desire'. Desire in language is the basic drive toward self-fulfillment. It touches the core of who we are. Anyone who has spent some time learning a foreign language while studying or working abroad knows the thrills and frustrations of desire.

In language learning, desire is first of all escape—the urge to escape from a state of tedious conformity with one's present environment to a state of plenitude and enhanced power. Many adolescents find in a foreign language a new mode of expression that enables them to escape from the confines of their own grammar and culture. At an age when they are conscious of their bodies, they rebel against the limitations imposed on them by the constraints of their social environment. In the same manner as teenage slang subverts canonical ways of speaking, the foreign idiom can challenge the monopoly of the language(s) spoken in the environment and offer a distinction that others don't have. For example, Korean-Americans cherish the French they learn in college as a way of circumventing the family pressure to learn the language of their ancestors. The children of Chinese immigrants use Chinglish (a mixture of Chinese and English) in Internet chat rooms as a secret language that their Anglo-American peers don't understand. English, that is associated by many around the world with freedom and economic opportunity, can serve to rebel against the traditional hierarchies of family and society, while for others, German, with its multiple historical and political connotations, might serve to problematize the meanings expressed by the English language in today's media.

But desire can also be the urge to survive and to cling to the familiar. Some may have a deep desire not to challenge the language of their environment but to find in the foreign words a confirmation of the meanings they express in their mother tongue. Thus they might claim that learning a language is nothing more than giving other labels to the familiar furniture of their universe. Their resistance to the language is at the measure of the threat it poses to their integrity as subjects. What drives them to learn the forms but retain their own accent and grammar is a deep desire to preserve what is theirs.

In the same manner as the subject comes into being in interaction with others (see below), desire, as positive or negative identification with the Other, is by essence dialogic and intersubjective. The Other is an imagined other, an idealized representation, even if this representation is triggered by a flesh-and-blood native speaker. Cultural studies scholars have suggested that in this age of migration, diaspora, and Internet communication, identification and ways of belonging have become more important than stable identities, attached to fixed places on the map.[8] When we talk about desire in language learning, we talk about exploring various possibilities of the self in real or imagined encounters with others.

Desire is not just a question of striving to be someone else or clinging to whom one is. As Taylor (1992: 49) would say, it is the drive for 'subjectivation', that is, the construction of an 'inwardly generated identity', a quest for a horizon of significance larger than the self. For many language learners, desire is the need for a language that is not only an instrumental means of communication, or a means of identification with some native speaker, but a way of generating an identity for themselves, of finding personal significance through explicit attention to articulation and meaning. Many adolescents and young adults are not satisfied with the convenient answers given by the slogans that surround them in their mother tongue, nor by the ready-made identities offered by the marketing industry. Like poetry and creative writing in one's own language, the acquisition of a foreign language can reveal unexpected meanings, alternative truths that broaden the scope of the sayable and the imaginable.

One example was given recently by Sylvia Molloy (2003: 73–4), an Argentinian raised in Spanish and French and now living in New York. In 'Bilingualism, Writing, and the Feeling of Not Quite Being There', she writes:

One always writes from an absence, the choice of a language automatically signifying the postponement of another. What at first would seem an imposition—why does one have to choose—quickly turns into an advantage. The absence of what is postponed continues to work, obscurely, on the chosen language, suffusing it, even better, contaminating it with an *autrement dit* that brings it unexpected eloquence…I wrote the word 'alterity' which brings to my mind the French for satisfying one's thirst, *désaltérer*. The writing of a bilingual writer, I would venture, is of need always altered, never 'disaltered'; always thirsty, always wanting, never satisfied. And is also, in another sense, *alterada*, in the way I used to hear the Spanish term used by my mother, my aunts, when referring to somebody who was slightly off, who could not control her thoughts, her voice.

For someone who has a choice of several languages, the language she chooses to express herself at any given time can bear traces of the sounds, shapes, and meanings of the others. These unused potential meanings shape her imagination, nourish her intimate memories, and suffuse her understanding of events. They give her the feeling of being both there and not quite there.

For language learners, the construction of an inwardly generated identity is not the same as psychic empathy or general feelings of sympathy for the other. As we shall see in this book, subjectivation is always mediated through symbolic systems, be they verbal, musical, or visual, that give meaning to what the senses perceive. Seduced by the foreign sounds, rhythms, and meanings, and by the 'coolness' of the language as it is spoken by native speakers, many adolescent learners strive to enter new, exotic worlds, where they can be or at least pretend to be someone else, where they too can become 'cool' and inhabit their bodies in more powerful ways. As such, desire is close to affect, but in a more concrete sense than just emotional reactions or metaphysical illuminations of the soul. Because it is firmly grounded in perception, desire is indissociable from aesthetic attention to and identification with symbolic form. It is triggered by learners' apprehension and use of new verbal sounds and shapes, and the subjective meanings they attach to them. One could say that desire in language is the perceptual disturbance and realignment experienced by the language user, whose identity is constitutive of and constituted by the foreign symbolic system itself.

5 Subjectivity, intersubjectivity, subject position

Up to now I have used terms such as 'language learner' or 'non-native speaker' to characterize the user of a foreign language, and 'self' or 'identity' to refer to the way such language users sees themselves and become aware of the subjective dimensions of language learning. It is time to explain what I mean by subjective and subjectivity.

5.1 Subjectivity

While the term 'subjective' in everyday language is often negatively equated with bias and unreliabilility—the opposite of 'objective'—it is also used to characterize the affective aspects of the language experience and is positively associated with the cognitive and emotional development of the self. In the social sciences, the term 'subject' evokes subjection to, domination by someone else, as when we speak of being subject to the constraints of a foreign grammar, or when we refer to language learners being the subjects of psycho- or sociolinguistic experimentation. The word 'subject' here will refer roughly to a learner's experience of the subjective aspects of language and of the transformations he or she is undergoing in the process of acquiring it. One of the main themes of this book is that, as a symbolic system, language creates and shapes who we are, as subjects.

For the purposes of the present discussion, I shall distinguish the subject from the individual, the person, and even the self. The *individual* is usually taken to be distinct from the group or collective community. It is a socio-logical or political entity that is guaranteed rights and obligations under a democratic constitution and a certain social and cultural identity. The *person* is a moral, quasi-metaphysical entity whose integrity needs to be safeguarded and nurtured. In contrast, the *self* is a psychological entity that is given to each human being at birth and is to be discovered, respected, and maintained. The *subject* is a symbolic entity that is constituted and maintained through symbolic systems such as language. It is not given, but has to be consciously constructed against the backdrop of natural and social forces that both bring it into being and threaten to destroy its freedom and autonomy, as will be discussed in Chapter 6.

Under 'multilingual' subject, I include people who use more than one language in everyday life, whether they are learning a foreign or second language in school, or speaking two or more languages in daily transactions, or writing and publishing in a language that is not the one they grew up with. In most cases, they will have acquired one or several languages as a child, and learned the others in various formal or informal settings. They might not know all these languages equally well, nor speak them equally fluently in all circum-stances, and there are some they used to know but have largely forgotten. I also include the many people who are able to understand a family language but can't really speak it, those who were forbidden to speak the language of the home and whose only language is now the language of the school, and those who used to speak a language but, because of past painful experiences, now refuse to do so. These silenced speakers can also be, to some degree, multilingual subjects.

In all these cases, by focusing on the symbolic nature of the multilingual subject, I leave open the possibility of viewing language learning as the con-struction of imagined identities that are every bit as real as those imposed by society. This is not an exercise in romanticism or a return to the touchy-feely pedagogies of the 1960s. At a time when multinational corporations are turning their attention away from the production of commodities in saturated markets towards creating and selling dreams and identities (see the Toyota ad above), language is being put to the service of a globalized economy that requires the total engagement of bodies, hearts, and minds and that thrives on symbols of 'power' and perceptions of 'empowerment'. Knowledge of other languages is often seen as an 'asset' in the pursuit of economic profit and material success. I will argue that learning a foreign language is indeed a means of empowerment, but perhaps of a different kind than is often envisaged. By rallying the body, heart, and mind connection, the foreign language experience can open up sources of personal fulfillment that might be foreclosed by an exclusive emphasis on external criteria of success.

Our ability to recognize and accept ourselves as subjects, with emotions, feelings, memories, and desires, is the prerequisite to developing our sense of self. Subjectivity, as I will use the term, is our conscious or unconscious sense of self as mediated through symbolic forms.[9] It is the symbolic meaning we give to ourselves, to our perceptions, reactions, and thoughts that orients our relationship to others. This meaning can come from our interpretation of events or from the interpretation given by others. That is because subjectivity involves both the conscious mind and the unconscious body's memories and fantasies, identifications and projections, that are often the product of our socialization in a given culture. While selfhood can be as unconscious as the drumbeat of life itself and as self-conscious as thoughts and memories, subjectivity, as the creation and maintenance of a subject, emerges and develops through the use of symbolic forms. This is not to say that the subject creates itself anew. Our subjectivity is constituted and shaped in interaction with our environment through the discourse of others—a subjectivity-in-process (see Chapter 3). We only learn who we are through the mirror of others, and, in turn, we only understand others by understanding ourselves as Other. The term 'subjectivity', then, does not mean narcissistic indulgence, or arbitrariness and lack of objectivity, but as Bakhtin (1981) would say, a responsibility to signify, that is, to use and interpret signs, to respond to and 'reaccentuate' signs, to pass judgment and take moral decisions.[10]

In this sense, subjectivity is indeed, as Taylor noted, a process of subjectivation that feminists and post-structuralist critics call 'decentering' (Threadgold 1997: 5).[11] It is a process in which the speaking subject, as subject of enunciation, strives to see itself and others in their full range of historical possibilities—hearing and seeing not only what they say and do, but what they could have said and done in the past, and what they could say and do in the future given the appropriate circumstances. One could say that becoming a subject means becoming aware of the gap between the words that people utter and the many meanings that these words could have, between the signifiers and the possible signifieds, between who one is and who one could be. This gap has been viewed by artists, philosophers, and feminist scholars as the very essence of life, change, and renewal.

5.2 Intersubjectivity

The term 'intersubjectivity' is used with a different focus in discourse analysis and ethnomethodology on the one hand, and in post-structuralist feminist linguistics on the other. The two traditions merge in the ecological perspective adopted in this book.

Discourse analysts and ethnomethodologists who study language as social interaction define intersubjectivity as a social accomplishment through the structural features of conversation.[12] It characterizes the way 'separate individuals are able to know or act within a common world, [i.e. the way] members of a society negotiate or achieve a common context' (Duranti and Goodwin 1992: 27) through turns-at-talk, conversational routines, and interpretative strategies. Duranti and Goodwin comment, 'Ethnomethodologists argue that both intersubjectivity and the social order visible in coordinated action are accomplished through ongoing, moment-by-moment social and cognitive work: participants display to each other their understanding of the events they are engaged in as part of the process through which these very same events are performed and constituted as social activities (ibid. 28). For example, in the early stages of primary socialization mother and child create an 'intersubjective pool of shared knowledge' (Wells 1981: 53) by first achieving joint attention', then by using 'socially shared symbols' (Tomasello 1999: 106) that make social interaction possible. Similarly, Gumperz shows how the concept of intersubjectivity, as the sharing of interpretative systems, links meaning, context, culture, and society together through specific linguistic features that index the larger context and that he called 'contextualization cues', such as pronouns, code-switching, and prosodic features of speech.

> Specific linguistic features invoke the very context of interpretation to be employed. Since sharing this context of interpretation, and sharing knowledge of the signs by which it is invoked, is dependent on cultural transmission and a history of cooperation in shared networks, and is the prime guarantor of intersubjectivity, it can be argued that in some sense … socialization into this system constitutes socialization into the society itself.
> (Gumperz 1996: 361)

Intersubjectivity can be achieved only if subjects can anticipate one another's behavior and thus trust one another. In this discourse analytic tradition, intersubjectivity is achieved on the basis of how participants orient to one another and to the here-and-now context of an interaction. However, with speakers and learners of several languages, who have been socialized in multiple cultural contexts, intersubjectivity is more difficult to achieve. Thus we turn to post-structuralist theories of language in interaction.

When used by post-structuralist scholars, the term 'intersubjectivity' goes beyond what is achieved in daily encounters between speakers. Subjectivity, they say, is produced discursively, that is, we are formed as subjects through the symbols we create, the chains of signification we construct, and the meanings we exchange with others, but intersubjectivity is not just located in the here-and-now. It is to be found in the shared memories, connotations, projections, inferences elicited by the various sign systems we use in concert with others. In this sense intersubjectivity is synonymous with intertextuality (see Chapter 3)—*text* standing for any stretch of discourse, in whatever modality, produced at whatever point in time and in whatever place.

> A system of intertextual resources—multi-medial, understood to be differentiated according to the subject's location in the social and cultural space, limited or constrained by the habitus of daily life, by class, race and gender—is put in the place of the linguist's system of language. Texts are now understood to be constructed chunk by chunk, intertextually, not word by word, and there can thus be no link between text and context except through the intertextual resources of this discursively produced subjectivity. (Threadgold 1997: 3)

What post-structuralist approaches to subjectivity add to the social interactionist approach is a symbolic and historical dimension. What people say is both more and less than they intend to say. Nor is what a person says necessarily a reply to a previous speaker's utterance in a given interaction. As Goffman (1981) noted, it might be a 'response' to some remembered or imagined or anticipated utterance, it might be a mythic, ritualistic, phatic, or ostensible statement. Bakhtin's (1986: 95) notion of *addressivity* captures the fact that any utterance is a response to past utterances by now living or no longer living individuals, and that it addresses, that is, calls for a response from, others.

5.3 Subject position

As we shall see in Chapter 1, the subject's internal sense of coherence and continuity over time is socially constructed via the symbolic system and the idealized cognitive models available in the community. It is the family, the school, the community that enable children to give meaning to their feelings, their experiences, their memories, in particular through language and through narratives of the self. The term *subject position* refers to the way in which the subject presents and represents itself discursively, psychologically, socially, and culturally through the use of symbolic systems. It comes from a view of the subject as decentered, historically and socially contingent—a subject that defines itself and is defined in interaction with other contingent subjects. Feminist writings 'recognize that "identity" is discursively produced, and that it is *not one*; that it is a network of multiple positions, constructed in and through many chains of signification, always realized in texts, enacted and performed, read and written, heard and spoken, in verbal, visual, graphic, photographic, filmic, televisual and embodied forms, to name just some' (Threadgold 1997: 5). In this book, I shall use the term 'subject position' to characterize the way speakers position themselves in discourse, well aware that multilingual speakers can occupy many positions simultaneously depending on which language they choose to use, with whom, on which topic, and depending on the different memories evoked by different codes as well as the different expectations each of these codes raises in their interlocutors or in their readers. For instance, we shall encounter in Chapter 1 the Siberian writer Andrei Makine writing in French about the Paris district, Neuilly, being at the turn of the century a mere *village* (Excerpt 1.10). What was his subject position as a narrator? As a writer, he was undoubtedly positioning himself as a French narrator, but his Siberian imagination positioned him as a Russian speaker for whom *village* evoked cows, forests, and wooden izbas. In addition, his imagination was clearly reactivating the statement his French grandmother had made about Neuilly some decades earlier: '*Oh! Neuilly, à l'époque, était un simple village* [Oh! At the time Neuilly was just a village]' Thus Makine's subject position as a narrator is multilayered in both time and space. It emerges as a complex time-space at the intersection of several encodings and re-encodings: his French grandmother's original utterance in French, re-encoded in the bilingual child as a French utterance with Russian meaning, and now his own utterance as a French narrator writing in French for a French readership but with a Russian sensibility. This complex subject position was rendered even more complex by the fact that Makine, who by then was living in France, had a notoriously difficult time finding a publisher. He finally decided to submit the manuscript as 'translated from the Russian'. The publisher accepted it with great enthusiasm and...requested to see the Russian original. So Makine had to translate a few of his own chapters from French into Russian to satisfy his publisher. He was thus positioned (and marketed) by his publisher as a Russian writer writing in Russian and translated into French. His different subject positionings are clearly the result of various negotiations of a larger social, cultural, and political nature.

The negotiation and power struggle that surround subject positions in published work as well as in private written or spoken communication are not special to the multilingual subject. Every language variety, dialect or sociolect, carries with it memories of personal experiences attached to each of its variations, and for every author, positioning oneself within a discipline, a field, or across readerships, is a challenge. But multilingual and multicultural situations increase exponentially the semiotic resources available—as well as the risks of miscommunication.

At a time when the ability to speak more than one language is not only useful but often the very condition of social and economic survival, and when multilingualism is a hot topic of research and a political necessity, it is appropriate to pause and reflect on what it means, both for people and for societies, to be multilingual. Halliday (2002) distinguishes 'glossodiversity', the plurality of linguistic codes, from 'semiodiversity', the plurality of meanings, and argues that in a globalized world the first is no guarantee of the second. It is not because we speak different languages that we mean different things, or vice versa, it is not because we all speak English that we mean the same thing. Semiodiversity is a good thing, he says. A danger of our increasingly globalized world of instant telecommunication and social and political displacements is that we all start thinking the same. Multilingual subjects deal with linguistic diversity differently from monolingual subjects and we need to know more about how they do this. Do they really think differently in different languages? Are they really different persons in each of the languages they speak or are they just occupying different subject positions? What about the relation between these subject positions and the way multilingual subjects view themselves and others, and the way monolinguals expect them to act?

This book has been written for foreign/second language teachers and researchers, but also for the growing number of college students interested in conceptualizing their experience of learning and using a foreign language. As applied linguists make their way into foreign language and literature departments, they have an important role to play in acquainting students with the field of applied linguistics—a field that can provide bridges between the study of language and the study of literature in their department. If the book ends with a plea to give greater consideration to the aesthetic aspects of language learning, it is because adolescents and young adults, who constitute the majority of foreign/second language learners around the world, are turning right now to all forms of artistic expression to make sense of the sometimes puzzling, contradiction-ridden world that surrounds them. While they are less and less interested in studying a foreign literature for its own sake, they are as fond of poems and prose fiction as they are of writing blogs and entering virtual narratives. As foreign languages are being instrumentalized to serve the needs of global economic competitiveness and national security (Kramsch 2005), language learners are drawn to less utilitarian horizons of imagined power. To survive linguistically and emotionally the contradictions of everyday life, multilingual subjects draw on the formal semiotic and aesthetic resources afforded by various symbolic systems to reframe these contradictions and create alternative worlds of their own. This book is an attempt to listen to what they say.

6 Organization of the book

The book has seven chapters. The first four chapters use short learner testimonies of adolescents and adults learning a foreign or second language as a stepping-stone to explore theories of the self and of social symbolic action that can illuminate the multilingual experience expressed in these testimonies. The last three chapters consider more complex case studies of language use as communicative practice. They draw on data taken mostly from multilingual adolescents and adults who use their languages for communicative or reflexive purposes in various modalities.

Chapter 1 considers the signifying practices of apprentice language learners and draws on linguistic and semiotic theories to explain the power of signs to act upon sign users and receivers. Chapter 2 considers the effect of foreign sounds, shapes, rhythms, intonations on the embodied self of the language learner. It discusses how the use of another symbolic system affects and channels our memories, our perceptions, and the way we conceptualize reality differently from the way we have been socialized in our native language. It lays the ground for the semiotic/symbolic distinction made in the next chapter. Chapter 3 discusses the often-recurring reference to Self and Other in the testimonies of language learners. These learners are conscious of learning not just another code, but the language of the Other. What is their relationship to this Other? In Chapter 4 we examine how the subject emerges in interaction with others in social and cultural contexts. We analyze and interpret four cases where speakers of a language that is not their own manipulate the language to position themselves symbolically vis-à-vis more powerful others.

Chapter 5 analyzes the way professional writers and undergraduate students narrate their multilingual experiences in writing. Chapter 6 examines data taken from electronic chat rooms and computer-mediated exchanges between language learners across national divides to find out how multilingual individuals create virtual subject positions for themselves in online networks. Chapter 7 is an attempt to resignify the notion of the language learner's 'third place' (Kramsch 1993) as symbolic competence within an ecological perspective. It considers what all this means for teaching foreign/second languages in institutional settings.

Notes

1   I thank an anonymous reader for this personal communication. The seminar in question, titled 'Developing Intercultural Consciousness', was conducted by Milton Bennett and Ida Castiglione at the Intercultural Communication Institute in summer 2000.

2   Some foreign language educators have included in their teacher-training-seminars the work of SLA researchers such as Schumann (1997) who has staked out the neurobiological bases of affect in SLA, Norton (2000) who has researched the link between language learning and the construction of social identity, and Pavlenko and Lantolf (2000) who studied the process of '(re)construction of self' that immigrant language learners undergo when learning the language of the host country. The recent surge of interest in heritage language learners acquiring the language of their ancestors (Campbell and Christian 2003) is foregrounding aspects of language learning that have been neglected up to now in heritage language instruction: links between language and cultural identity, subjective attachment to present, past, or imagined communities. And sociolinguistic research on multilingualism has provided insights into the way language choice intersects with issues of symbolic power and identity, especially during study abroad (Kinginger 2004a; Block 2007: Chapter 6). But because foreign and even heritage languages are taught in relative isolation from any surrounding speech community and have to rely on the imagined communities evoked by the symbolic forms themselves, this research does not fully address the concerns of the thousands of students around the world who learn a foreign language in institutional classrooms.

3   Even though English has become a global language, of which second language learners are encouraged to 'take ownership' (Widdowson 1994), I would argue that in many parts of the world it is still 'someone else's language' because of its strong adherences to a colonial past, a capitalistic present, and the dream of a

global future—aspects of English that are not necessarily espoused by all those who grew up with a language other than English.

4   I am grateful to Henry Widdowson for this insight (personal communication).

5   In an article on Austin titled 'Signature Event Context' (1971), Derrida rejects the idea that there is one appropriate way of realizing speech acts—the serious, native speaker way, and that all the other ways, such as play, display, acting, rehearsals, are parasitic. All language is parasitic, he argues. The rules of the performative, rather than constraints to be deplored, are the very conditions of possibility of speech; they are meant to be both obeyed and transgressed. In order to be spoken at all, an utterance must be performable, and thus distortable. Derrida called this performability *iterability*, i.e. 'the capacity to be reused, which also invariably involves the capacity to be misused, misperformed, changed or twisted in some new way' (Robinson 2003: 19). In his famous essay 'La Différance' (1972), Derrida rejects the notion of a fixed meaning established by a fixed speech community. Meaning is constantly renewed, remade in every individual utterance. Derrida coined the term *différance* (with an *a*)—a combination of the French words for 'difference' and 'deferral' (derived in French from the same verb *différer*, which means both to differ and to defer), to express the fact that language ceaselessly both differentiates and postpones meaning, precisely because of its iterability. It is through this 'movement' or gap between the form of the language and its meaning that history or change enters the picture, and that language learners can inflect the language and make it their own.

6   In his Commentary to *Language Ideologies*, Silverstein (1998: 128) remarks that ideology is an immanent feature of the indexical nature of all language use. 'That people have ideologies of language...is a necessary entailment of the fact that language, like any social semiotic, is indexical in its most essential modality' (ibid. 130). He deplores the lack of attention paid to totemism in everyday language use, thus making an implicit link between language ideology and what I call here 'myth'.

7   There has recently been quite a bit of interest in myth, even though researchers have given it other names. In historical studies, Benedict Anderson (1983: 185) has studied the transformation of maps, names, and words into empty, contextless, memorable, and infinitely reproducible logos that served to build the mythic imagination or 'imagined communities' of colonial powers. In philosophy, Ian Hacking shows how such phrases as 'child abuse', once coined, become reified *categories* or kinds that construct a mythic social reality extending far beyond the actual facts of violence done to children (Hacking 1999). In sociolinguistics, Cameron (2000) discusses the uses of language in a communication culture where words such as 'communication' or 'authentic self' have become commodified on the market of desirable myths. Fairclough (1992: 239), echoing Foucault, refers to the way discourse has become technologized, i.e. transformed into a skill that people can be trained in (to a certain extent, one could say with Barthes that language drills and mechanical instructional practices mythify language). Rampton (2002, 2003) has described the stylized language used by high school adolescents to resist the authority of their teachers or to cross ethnic boundaries on the school grounds. LePage and Tabouret-Keller (1985: 236) document cases in which the language of one group becomes totemized, like the French of Île de France, and made into an icon or totem for all the other groups (see the cultural myth that the French language represents for the French). Yurchak (2006) has documented how language

in the last decades of the Soviet Union had incurred a performative shift, whereby people performed the politically correct routines in order to go on with their lives. Logoization, categorization, commodification, technologization, stylization, totemization, performativity, are all processes by which language becomes myth, i.e. an ahistorical, decontextualized way of using language in order to achieve other purposes than communicating information. Some of these purposes might be: achieving visibility, managing one's image, influencing people, or deriving symbolic benefit from the performance of language itself.

8 See Grossberg (1997).

9 Some scholars have used subjectivity and identity interchangeably (Norton 2000). Here I distinguish the two: identity refers to the identification with a social or cultural group, while subjectivity focuses on the ways in which the self is formed through the use of language and other symbolic systems, both intrapersonally and interpersonally. As individuals participate in multiple symbolic exchanges, themselves embedded in vast webs of social and power relations, subjectivity is conceptualized dynamically as a site of struggle and potential change. For excellent discussions of identity and subjectivity, see Ivanic (1998) and Pennycook (2001).

10 By re-accentuation, Bakhtin (1986: 87) refers to the fact that whenever we speak we use the words of others and give them our own particular meaning (or accent) adapted to our own situation, intention, and style. This idea converges with Derrida's notion of iterability (see Note 5): we make our own subjective meanings through the word definitions given to us (artificially) by the dictionary.

11 The post-structuralist notion of a decentered self, living at the intersection of multiple voices and timescales, has been elaborated by such literary scholars as Bakhtin (1981) and Kristeva (1986), and by postmodern sociolinguists such as Blommaert (2005).

12 See discourse analysts Wells (1981); Duranti and Goodwin (1992); Gumperz (1996); Ochs (1996); and ethnomethodologists Schutz (1967, 1970, 1973); Garfinkel (1967); Schegloff (1991); Sacks (1992); and others.

I

The signifying self

In her memoir, *French Lessons* (1993), the American scholar Alice Kaplan recalls her excitement learning French as a teenager in Geneva.

> Excerpt 1.1
> Every morning those sounds woke me up. I understood more and more until I could anticipate the morning greeting of the Swiss news, and lip synch, word for word, the standard formulae...I always had five or six new words on a personal in-progress list. Each time I heard one of the words on my list, I would notice the context and try to figure out the meaning. When I thought I had the meaning I would wait for the word to come up again, so I could check if my meaning was still right. Finally, I'd try the word out to see if a strange look came over the face of the person I was talking to. If it didn't, I knew I was home free. I had a new word.
> (ibid. 48)

What Kaplan experiences is familiar to many foreign language learners. She learns to distinguish the sounds of French from other surrounding sounds; she then recognizes individual words and learns to anticipate them; she catches their meaning from their surrounding context—a meaning that is standard enough that she can recognize it again in a different context; she knows that words can not only represent things and events but also address people and act on them; with these words, she elicits responses— 'strange looks' or smiles; finally, she gains an awareness of her own power to make and communicate in French a meaning that is accepted by native speakers. What she describes is clearly more than just learning new words. The emotional aspect of the experience and the anxiety involved are captured by her final statement: 'I was home free', which means, depending on the dictionary, 'safe', 'secure', 'out of danger', or 'out of harm's reach'. Behind the poised and well-wrought sentences, we sense the anxiety of the beginning learner.

We find a somewhat different testimony in Richard Watson's *The Philosopher's Demise: Learning French* (1995). Watson, who, as a philosophy professor, was confident reading French, finds himself violently resisting speaking French when taking classes at the Alliance Française in Paris. His account of his 'demise' is cast in hyperbolic terms. The threat to his sense of self is palpable and so is his panic.

Excerpt 1.2

Why did I resist [French] so? Because, I think, all my life I have been trying to learn to write. These new French [spoken] forms threatened to destroy what little progress I had made so far. Not only did I use English forms in speaking French, I was appalled to find myself using French forms when I was writing English. French was undermining my very being! My personality was in danger of disintegrating! A great clanging of alarm bells was set in my deep unconscious, irritated by these alien influences seeping down from above.

(ibid. 57 cited in Schumann 1997:147)

Such testimonies show that beginning learners can have deep personal reactions to the foreign language. Kaplan is excited at learning new words, and is amazed when the sounds she utters make sense to others and are responded to in ways that make sense to her. Watson feels physically overwhelmed by 'alien influences' that 'undermine' his very being. The difference between the two experiences cannot be solely attributed to the natural versus the instructional setting. After all, both are learning French in a francophone environment, at the same time as they are taking classes there. The intensity of their feelings seems to have deeper roots. They both depict beginning language learning as a kind of magic, where language acts upon people and events as if of its own authority.

In this chapter I explore the ways in which learners experience the 'magic' of acting and being acted upon through symbolic forms. Much of this experience is a perceptual one, born of the sounds, shapes, and rhythms of utterances heard and read, and of the apprehension of one's own body voicing new sounds, and drawing new forms on the page.

1 Perception: the neglected dimension in language learning

In much language teaching research and practice, language is seen as a set of labels applied to a well-known reality. Non-native speakers are assumed to dutifully learn new labels for things in the real world and to combine forms and sounds to refer to real-world events. By putting their thoughts into these new word combinations they can communicate them to others who recognize them because they presumably share the same real world to which these words refer. Non-native speakers are supposed to ultimately become like native speakers, who see *through* language to a stable, objectively verifiable reality. If, at the beginning stages, learners look *at* language, this is seen as only temporary: in time, it is believed, they will acquire the automaticity and the fluency that will ultimately enable them to use language as a transparent tool of reference. Too much reflection on language itself is often seen as detrimental to the development of communicative fluency.

Underlying this view of the language learner is the still frequent assumption that the non-native speaker is an empty receptacle for the rules of usage and the rules of use that govern the language practices of native speakers. It is acknowledged that the non-native speaker is already the native speaker of an L1 and a member of an L1 speech community, and so is not strictly speaking a blank slate, but the L1 connection has been studied mostly as a source of interference with the acquisition of the L2 and socialization into the L2 speech community. Overall, the language is seen as a transparent conduit for the practice of conventional meaning-making and the expression of standard meanings. In short, individuals are reduced to being actual or aspiring members of speech communities that impose on them their standards of grammaticality and conventions of appropriate use, either in the L1 or in the L2.

Most of all, many researchers and teachers still consider language learners as talking heads that have to be taught from the neck up, so to speak. They are made to exercise their vocal chords, shape their mouths, purse their lips, and tune their ears in different ways; they are taught to recognize their interlocutors' intended meanings through their vocabulary, their grammar, their intonation, and their facial expressions; they are encouraged to structure or restructure their thinking mainly through the synapses of their brains. From most of the descriptions given in SLA research, one would think that learning a language was predominantly an intellectual, disembodied exercise in problem-solving and strategic thinking, accomplished inside the head or between two or several heads in concert with one another.

The signifying practices of Kaplan and Watson offer a different picture. I examine below excerpts from other language memoirs by Yoko Tawada, Eva Hoffman, Andrei Makine, and Claude Esteban and compare them to the multilingual journals written by language learners in a German class at college level in the US.

Tawada, a Japanese writer now living in Hamburg, writes and publishes both in German and in Japanese. In her language memoir *Talisman* (1996), written in German, she recounts her experience learning German in Germany when she was 14 years old.

Excerpt 1.3
When I came to Hamburg, I knew all the letters of the alphabet, but I could look for a long time at the individual letters without grasping the meaning of the words. For example, I looked every day at the posters at the bus station and never read the names of the products. I only know that on one of the prettiest posters the letter S occurred seven times...I repeated the S-sounds in my mouth and noticed that my tongue suddenly tasted foreign. I didn't know up to now that the tongue could taste of anything.
(ibid. 39, my translation)

Every foreign sound, every foreign sight, every foreign taste had a
disagreeable effect on my body, until my body changed. The Ö-sounds for
example drilled deep into my ears and the R-sounds scratched my throat.
There were also idioms that gave me goose pimples, like, for example
'to get onto someone's nerves', to 'have it up to here', or 'to sh—in one's
pants'.

   Most of the words that came out of my mouth did not express what I
was feeling. That's where I noticed that there was no word in my mother
tongue either that expressed what I was feeling... I had not felt that way
before I started to live in a foreign language.
(ibid. 41 my translation)

For the teenager Tawada, already literate in Japanese, an alphabetical language such as German is first an object of aesthetic perception. She finds the
posters at the bus stations all the 'prettier' as the letter *s* occurs in them seven
times, even though she doesn't understand a word of what they say. But the
sounds of German are the cause of a pain she can only express through metaphors: her tongue started tasting 'foreign', German sounds 'drilled deep' into
her ears, 'scratched' her throat, idioms gave her 'goose pimples'. We have here
not just thoughts and ideas, but heightened perceptions of taste, sight, touch,
sound, triggered by the material nature of the language itself. They affect the
way the learner feels in her living body, indeed in her apprehension of 'life in a
foreign language'. In another passage, she shows how this experience is akin
to the way children apprehend the world.

Excerpt 1.4
Children take the language at its word. Every word acquires a life of
its own, that makes it independent of its meaning within the sentence.
There are even words that are so full of life that they can, like mythical
characters, develop their own autobiographies.
(ibid. 13 my translation)

[The word I liked particularly] was *Heftklammerentferner* [staple
remover]. Its wonderful name embodied my desire for a foreign language.
This small object, that reminded me of a serpent's head with four fangs,
was illiterate... It could only remove staples. But I favored it because
the way he separated the stapled pages worked like magic... In the
mother tongue, words are stapled... Thoughts are stapled to words to
such an extent that neither can fly freely. In a foreign language, you have
something like a staple remover: it removes everything that is stapled
together and sticks together.
(ibid. 15)

The physical nature of Tawada's encounter with the German language, her
perceptual apprehension of ordinary shapes and sounds, her animistic view
of the signs on the page, show how her relationship with the language goes
beyond what the language refers to. 'Every word acquires a life of its own',

it becomes 'independent of its meaning within the sentence'. For the child, as for the adult now writing these lines, words are not always bound by denotation nor by reference in context. It is as if she had made the language her own by ascribing it her own subjective meanings. In the foreign language, she suggests, words are no longer 'stapled' to things; they can 'fly freely', like 'magic'.

These subjective meanings do not just supplement the objective, conventional signs referring to objects in the real world, they transform them in new, enchanted ways. The new meaning Tawada gives a trivial 'staple remover' is not just a nice metaphorical way of representing her experience; it is, for the 14-year-old learner of German, part and parcel of the referential meaning of the word and its emotional resonances. Under Tawada's pen, the subjective connotations of the word have become a new denotation, that is, a device to 'remove the staples' that attach thoughts to words in her first language. Combined with the emotional resonances of the German word, a 'staple remover' has been turned into the very 'embodiment of her desire for a foreign language', that 'removes everything that is stapled together and sticks together' in the mother tongue. The word 'staple remover' now means: 'what a foreign language means for me'. Barthes would say that for her the staple remover has become a myth.

But, the reader might argue, how do we know what the 14-year-old really meant by the word *Heftklammerentferner*, since this symbolic form was available for her to use either with its conventional or with its subjective meaning? Surely, the more the Japanese speaker became fluent in German, the more the conventional meanings of objects imposed themselves in everyday life. No doubt this was the case. But the fact that the now fluent speaker and writer of German is able to express subjective feelings such as those is because she has retained traces of the childlike imagination she had when she first started to learn German. Listening to language learners' interpretations of their experiences draws our attention to the possibility that for language learners and bilingual individuals language doesn't always mean what it seems to refer to. Learners can play with the two levels of meaning and express either one or the other. Their relation to the new language often has a subjective value that builds upon the conventional meaning and transforms it because desires, memories, and projections have become an essential component of its original meaning.

2 Perceptual similitude and analogical thinking

For newcomers to the language, words are not yet moored to their conventional meanings. They easily lend themselves to unconventional associations based on their shape, their music, and their similitude to other words. For native speakers, these associations might sound strange or untoward, but for non-native speakers, who imbue the new language with all the physical properties of their own bodies, they have personal and emotional meaning.

2.1 From word to thought

The first thing we notice is that for language learners (as for poets and advertising experts), meaning does not necessarily flow from thought to word, but from word to thought. In *Überseezungen* [*Overseas Tongues*] (2002), a title that captures in its pun (*Über* = super, *Seezunge* = flounder) the playful propensity of many non-native speakers, Tawada recounts how the German words, far from reflecting the conventional thoughts of a German speech community, trigger totally unconventional thoughts through their similitude with Japanese words.

> Excerpt 1.5
> I hear you are going to Heidelberg, says Mika.
>   Heidelberg, what a strange name, 'del' means in Japanese 'to emerge', so Heidelberg means the mountain [der Berg] where a shark [der Hai] emerges. What a name for a town.
> (ibid. 44 my translation)

> Excerpt 1.6
> How can you write German with ideograms?
>   Here I have the sign 蓮, pronounce it.
>   Has(u) [lotus]
>   Yes, 'der Haß' means in German hate, disgust, but you don't need to know that. You remember the sign for 'lotus' and you pronounce it in Japanese. You taste on your tongue the lotus flower, while the Haß [hate] goes into the ears of your listeners.
> (ibid. 49 my translation)

> Excerpt 1.7
> I like the fact that 'ich' [I] starts with an '*I*', a single stroke, like the stroke of an inkbrush that touches the paper and announces the beginning of a speech. 'Bin' [am] is also a beautiful word. Japanese also has the word 'bin', it sounds the same but means 'bottle'. When I start telling a story with the two words 'ich bin' [I am], a space opens up, the I is a brushstroke, and the bottle is empty.
> (ibid. 57 my translation)

Excerpt 1.5 offers a rather different take on the notion of interference than that usually found in SLA research. Here the learner is quite capable of using the word 'Heidelberg' properly, so strictly speaking there is no interference from the L1. But behind the native-like use, the non-native speaker gives this German city Japanese connotations that would sound odd to native speakers. In Excerpt 1.6 the negative dis-gust or dis-taste elicited on the tongue by the word *Haß* (as in *Ausländerhaß* or 'hatred of foreigners') is replaced by the pleasurable taste of the lotus flower *has(u)*, whose sound approximates that of the German word *Haß*. While she pronounces the word *Haß*, the Japanese learner of German thinks of the word *has(u)*, and the negative connotation of the German word is cancelled in her imagination by the positive counter-reality she has created. In Excerpt 1.7 the metaphorical imagination of the Japanese writer imbues the static Roman alphabetic shape with the movement of the Japanese ink brush and draws existential conclusions from the visual perception of the letters on the page. These examples reverse the usual assumption in SLA that learning a language is casting preexisting thoughts into L2 words. Here, we see thoughts emerge from the perception of new words. Even though these are sophisticated (re)constructions of meaning-making processes that might not have occurred to the narrator exactly in that way at the time, they are, nevertheless, potential scenarios of Japanese speakers learning to speak German, filtered through the particularly acute linguistic imagination of a literary writer.

2.2 Connotation as denotation

The fact that for language learners it is the words themselves that generate thoughts and feelings, not just the reality they refer to, is important if we want to understand why some learners cannot identify with the persona that the words create for them. The symbiotic relationship between a name and the person it denotes is well illustrated in Hoffman's language memoir *Lost in Translation* (1989). Hoffman describes her experience of being given a new name upon her immigration to Canada when she was 13 years old. For her, Ewa, and her sister Alina, the English names they are given, Eva and Elaine, lack the close relation that existed between them and their Polish names.

> Excerpt 1.8
> Nothing much has happened, except a small, seismic mental shift. The twist in our names takes them a tiny distance from us—but it's a gap into which the infinite hobgoblin of abstraction enters. *Our Polish names didn't refer to us: they were as surely us as our eyes or hands.* These new appellations, which we ourselves can't yet pronounce, are not us. They are identification tags, disembodied signs pointing to objects that happen to be my sister and myself. We walk to our seats, into a roomful of unknown faces, with names that make us strangers to ourselves.
> (Hoffman 1989: 105, emphasis added)

For Hoffman, her name is not just an arbitrary sign that refers to a 13-year-old Polish child, nor does it just represent who she is. Her name *is* her, just as surely as her eyes and hands *are* her. It is easy to dismiss such a statement as just a figure of speech; surely, a name is just a word, whereas eyes and hands are part of one's body. Yet this is precisely what Hoffman is trying to say. Objectively, of course, Ewa Hoffman is the same as Eva Hoffman, but subjectively they are two different persons, because the two signs *Ewa* and *Eva* refer to two different subjective realities. The journey into emigration has, she writes, 'cut a three-thousand mile rip through my life' (p. 100), but this rip is not just a geographical and historical distance. It has brought about a change in how she perceives herself to be.

The signifier 'E-w-a' is the objective reference for the signified 'a 13-year-old Polish girl'. In Cracow, the girl took that name for granted, a name that was shared by many children in Poland and that was part of her objective, social, and historical identity. Objectively, she could have been called differently at birth by her parents, and she will, upon immigration to Canada, be given another name. But in Vancouver, the sudden loss of her Polish name and the pain associated with it endow the name Ewa with secondary, subjective attributes. While on the referential level, the signifier *Ewa* retained its historical contingency and social objectivity, on the subjective level, the signifier *Ewa* points to a much larger, symbolic signified. It becomes the very essence of the narrator, not just what her name is, but an attribute of her innermost self, who she is. *Ewa* is the historical Ewa removed from its historical context. This subjective sign has now become recast as her 'real' self, to which she refers as 'I' and which she nostalgically endows with subjective feelings and memories, like she does for other Polish words 'lost in translation'.

In the following passage, her Polish 'I' feels the acute pain of the separation of the subjective and the objective in the English word 'river'.

Excerpt 1.9
[T]he problem is that the signifier has become severed from the signified. The words I learn now don't stand for things in the same unquestioned way they did in my native tongue. 'River' in Polish was a vital sound, energized with the essence of riverhood, of my rivers, of my being immersed in rivers. 'River' in English is cold—a word without an aura. It has no accumulated associations for me, and it does not give off the radiating haze of connotation. It does not evoke... The river before me remains a thing, absolutely other, absolutely unbending to the grasp of my mind.
(ibid. 106)

[T]his radical disjoining between word and thing is a dessicating alchemy, draining the world not only of significance but of its colors, striations, nuances—its very existence. It is the loss of a living connection.
(ibid. 107)

We should note that, for the Polish child living in Cracow, the Polish word *retz* ('river') might not have had the subjective resonances it acquired later in Canada, when it got supplanted by English 'river', nor did she have the awareness of its subjective potential before she became a mature literary writer in English. In fact, the subjective feelings of the Polish-speaking child would not have been given a public voice without the conventional resources of the English-speaking adult. What is worth noting here is that the now adult narrator uses the memory of these feelings to endow the English word 'river' and its simple denotational reference with the timeless aura of the Polish word and its subjective, nostalgic meaning (riverhood per se). It did this by using the iconic perceptions and sensations of touch (cold, immersion), vision (colors, striations, nuances), and sound (vital sound, aura, radiating haze), and linking them with concomitant feelings of self (*my* rivers, the essence of *my* being immersed in rivers, no associations for *me*). These perceptual links and the feelings they triggered enabled the narrator to transform the Polish sign *retz* into a natural, organic, subjective sign, and to reduce the English sign 'river' to a 'cold', 'dessicating alchemy'. She did this using the conventional resources of the English language and transforming them to express a quintessentially subjective view of what it means to learn another language.

2.3   The power of analogy

The language learners portrayed in language memoirs draw heavily on analogy to make sense of the world around them and the reality they construct, based on their perceptions of the foreign symbolic forms, is both imagined and real. In *Le Testament français* [*Dreams of my Russian Summers*] (1997), the Russian writer Makine recounts how he learnt French from his grandmother in Siberia. The images of a posh Parisian district mirror in his Russian imagination the characteristics of Russian villages. For him, the French word *village*, although it translates the Russian word *derevnya*, acquires an additional meaning through the subjective mapping of Neuilly-sur-Seine onto a Russian village.

Excerpt 1.10
Neuilly-sur-Seine was composed of a dozen log cabins. Real *izbas,* with roofs covered in slender laths, silvered by the rigors of winter, with windows set in prettily carved wooden frames and hedges with washing hung out to dry on them. Young women carried full pails on yokes that spilled a few drops on the dust of the main street. Men loaded heavy sacks of corn onto a wagon. A slow herd streamed idly toward the cowshed. We heard the heavy sound of their bells and the hoarse crowing of a cock. The agreeable smell of a wood fire—the smell of supper almost ready—hung in the air.

For our grandmother had indeed said to us one day, when speaking of her birthplace, 'Oh! At that time Neuilly was just a village...'

She had said it in French, but we only knew Russian villages. And a village in Russia is inevitably a ring of *izbas*; indeed the very word in Russian, *derevnya*, comes from *derevo*—a tree, wood. The confusion persisted, despite the clarification that Charlotte's stories would later bring. At the name 'Neuilly' we had immediate visions of the village with its wooden houses, its herd, and its cockerel. And when, the following summer, Charlotte spoke to us for the first time about a certain Marcel Proust—'By the way, we used to see him playing tennis at Neuilly, on the boulevard Bineau'—we pictured the dandy with big langorous eyes (she had shown us his photo) there among the *izbas*!
(Makine 1997: 23)

Someone hearing the young Makine speaking French and referring to Neuilly sur Seine would hardly know that the name Neuilly for him was more than a reference to a place on the map; but, in fact, it had acquired a far more personal, subjective meaning that was as real for him as the declarative statement of fact with which he opens this excerpt: 'Neuilly-sur-Seine was composed of a dozen log cabins'.

We find the same analogic imagination at work in the description by Esteban of his language-learning difficulties. Esteban, the autobiographical narrator in *Le Partage des mots* (1990), was raised by his Spanish father and French mother in France during World War II.[1] He was obliged in the French school to keep his two symbolic systems apart and to become in the classroom a monolingual speaker of French. But in his subjective apprehension of the two languages, French and Spanish are in tension with one another, both attracting and repelling each other in interesting ways.

Excerpt 1.11

Jaune (Fr. yellow) was subjected to the phonetic attraction of *jeune* (Fr. young). *Jaune* became a juvenile color, but as if weighted down, shriveled, darkened by the sound *au* in which I perceived a kind of weariness, melancholia, material heaviness. *Jaune* represented, if I may say, the sensory synonym, the chromatic equivalent of the contradictory, inacceptable notion of 'young old man'. Most of all it was eclipsed from my verbal horizon by the Spanish word *amarillo*, in which I recognized precisely all those characteristics that I connected with the color yellow—vivacious and frothy, unctuous and fragrant, appetizing and sweet—and that made in my mind the four syllables of the word *amarillo* into the quintessential yellow creamy dessert [that I loved]. This created all kinds of difficulty when I had to express myself in French. Since I was not allowed to use the word *amarillo* which immediately came to my mind—school had taught me to censor my desire—and since I could not longer retrieve this *jaune* that I had discarded, I was obliged, like certain aphasics, to resort to a circumlocution to express the presence of this color in my verbal schema—or, even more painfully, I had to forgo mentioning the color of the object altogether or use an equivalent color. These tiny defeats, of which my listeners knew nothing, were loaded with a moral sense of guilt that hurt me more than anything.

(Esteban 1990: 34, my translation)

This passage captures a young bilingual's subjective apprehension of language, where meaning is created not mainly through denotation, but through similitude and analogy, and an animistic view of inanimate objects. *Jaune* refers to the color yellow, but, by sympathy for the similarly sounding word *jeune*, it acquires the additional subjective meaning of 'juvenile color'. However, the sound *au* prevents *jaune* from being totally attracted to *jeune*, hence the tension the child experiences when speaking French. Moreover, French in his imagination is 'repelled' by Spanish for which he feels a much

greater attraction.[2] The word *amarillo*, with its iconic and emotional resonances, represents for him a perfect fit between sound, taste, appearance,
and meaning. Like the name *Ewa* for Eva Hoffman, the word *amarillo* offers
him the complete match between the objective and the subjective realms of
meaning. *Amarillo* reconciles him with himself.

3 Signs and their meanings in language learners' journals

The testimonies discussed above could be taken to be the literary fantasies of
particularly talented individuals, who interpret with a certain degree of poetic
license language-learning events that they experienced earlier. However, we
find quite similar testimonies given by ordinary language learners enrolled
in foreign language classes. Consider, for example, the following data, taken
from Belz (1997 and 2002a). Here is an excerpt from the multilingual journals that Belz had her students write in an intermediate German class and
the students' retrospective reflections on their writings. One student, whose
mother tongue is English, finds multiple and unusual meanings in the visual
form of the German double *ss*, written *ß*.

> Excerpt 1.12
> Nimm das Wort Streß. Genau wie auf Englisch. Stress. Auf Deutsch das
> Wort „Streß," mit diesem Eszett, takes on a whole new meaning. Schau
> mal, see how the two 'ss' in the English 'stress' zusammen verfilzen,wenn
> man 'Streß' auf Deutsch schreibt. Streß bekommt dadurch eine neue
> Bedeutung. Spaß. Fun, auf Englisch. Diese Wörter sehen vollkommen
> anders aus. Aber das Eszett in „Spaß" makes fun more fun, verruckt,
> ziellos, wild. Und fließend. Here it's in the middle. Fließend bedeutet
> moving, fluid, fluent. Hier gibt das Eszett Bewegung.
>
> [Take the word Streß. Just like English. Stress. In German the word 'Streß'
> with this ß takes on a whole new meaning. Look how the two ss of the
> English 'stress' get intertwined when you write Streß in German. Stress
> is thereby given a new meaning. Take the word 'Spaß'. Fun, in English.
> These words look totally different. But the ß in 'Spaß' makes fun more
> fun, crazy, gratuitous, wild. And take the word 'fließend' or flowing.
> Here ß is in the middle. Fließend means moving, fluid, fluent. The ß gives
> it movement.]
> (Belz 2002a: 69, my translation)

When interviewed on his journal, the student explained to Julie Belz in
English:

> Excerpt 1.13
> Streß in German means more to me than stress in English because of what
> the eszett looks like. With this tangle of ss at the end of the word you can
> see that stress really affects you. It's not just a word. It's your feelings and if

people could see the word coming out of your mouth, they would see that it's tangled up just like you are. I found out recently that in Germany they're changing the eszett into just two ss and I think that's unfortunate because they're losing an aspect of their language ... I just think it's too bad.
(ibid. 1997)

The student is fully aware of the denotational meaning of the word *Streß* in German, and what the sign refers to, namely a state of strain. He also sees this state of strain represented iconically in the tangled shape of the letter *ß*. The referential and the iconic activity would be expected of everyday and poetic uses of language respectively. But the student seems to give an additional, highly subjective meaning to the word that goes beyond iconic representation.

The physical 'tangle of ss' becomes a psychic entanglement ('it's tangled up just like you are'). For this student, *Streß* in German indexes a more acute stress than its English equivalent, a kind of hyperstress, because of the shape of *ß*. This new referential meaning not only enacts stress, but has a performative effect on the student who feels personally addressed by this word ('It's not just a word. It's your feelings'). By projecting his feelings of stress onto the German *ß* and by identifying with it, this learner of German feels validated in his feelings in a way he cannot experience with the equivalent English word. For him, *Streß* in German seems not only to represent stress but to perform it.

The iconic meaning of *ß* might be here quite arbitrary depending on its location; indeed, as the student admits in Excerpt 1. 12, the same *ß* sometimes means wildness, other times fluidity, yet other times entanglement. And yet, there is nothing arbitrary in the student's choice of iconicity for the particular word: he has projected onto the symbol *ß* his own subjective feelings and experiences and from now on the German word refers not just to 'stress', but to 'emotional entanglement'. The German word has acquired for him a new denotation.

Other learners of German reveal that they too, even though they have studied German for four or five semesters already, give a new denotational meaning to words based on what Jakobson and Waugh (1987) call their 'sound shapes'. Another student in Belz's class, of Spanish mother tongue, is thrilled at discovering that the verb-final position in the German subordinate clause and the physical change in just one vowel represent iconically the momentous change she has just experienced in her personal and social life. Here is what she wrote in her multilingual journal about her recent love affair and what explanations she subsequently gave her professor:

Excerpt 1.14
'La verdad es que no se ni como ni cuando, aber dieser Mann hat in meinem Herz einen Platz gefunden.'

[The truth is that I don't know how or when, but this man found a place in my heart.]

Some of the code-switching was either because it fit on the page or the structure. This part in German sounded better than in English or Spanish 'Dieser Mann hat in meinem Herz einen Platz gefunden'...um...it has this...you know...because of the verb at the end...it just has this beauty in it. Not just the words themselves but the structure the way it's set up...but in Spanish it would be so plain...well the part *corazon* would be romantic, but the rest?

'A year, only a year later, *waren wir* so much *verliebt* [in love], *daß* we were *verlobt* [engaged]' (italics in the original).

I love that part. It's so funny. I did that on purpose. I thought it was so cool because [*verliebt* and *verlobt* are] are like almost the same word...It has different meanings you know and it's just the vowel...at first I was going to write it...in English but 'engaged'...you know...engaged it just didn't go and so I looked for the word in German and I realized the match and I thought it was so cool that I just left it that way. I really love it. It's just the two vowels here and that one vowel there and that's the only change in the whole word.
(Belz 2002a: 71)

Like the student in Excerpt 1.12 and Excerpt 1.13, this student makes the German word order and the different sounds of the two past participles into icons of her inevitable destiny to fall in love with this man. One could argue that she is merely content to represent her love that way. However, the additional meanings with which she imbues these linguistic features and the emotional thrill she experiences suggest that there is more in her use of language than just the semantic and the iconic. They seem to engage a new level of symbolic meaning and emotional resonance. To understand the depth of these emotions, and to appreciate the full import of the testimonies above, we turn briefly to uses of language that have been called 'enchanted'. The use of enchantment is to express truths about language that cannot be captured by factual reports, only through what Germans call *Märchen*, or little myths.

4 Signifying practices in fairy tales

Fairy tales and fairytale-like narratives highlight the power of language to bring about events in a 'magical' way. Some of these narratives are featured in beginning language textbooks, precisely because they thematize language itself. For example, it is not uncommon, in beginning German texts, to find one or the other of the Grimms' fairy tales or one of the Swiss author Peter Bichsel's *Kindergeschichten* (children's stories) (1969) that deal with the magical uses of language. These stories are easy to read and they evoke in a fictional way the play with symbolic forms that language learners engage in.

In Grimms' *The Water Witch* (*Die Wassernixe*), a brother and a sister try to escape the evil witch who pursues them by throwing behind them a *Kamm* (a comb) that, combined with the name for mountain (*Berg*), becomes a *Kammberg* (high peaked mountain). Unfortunately, the witch manages to climb over the *Kammberg* and continue her pursuit. They then throw a *Spiegel* (mirror) that, combined with the word *Berg*, yields a new name, *Spiegelberg* (a mountain as smooth as a mirror). The witch hopelessly slides on the smooth surface, which stops her advance, and the children are saved.

In *Sweet Porridge* (*Der süße Brei*), a little girl forgets the magic formula to stop the porridge pot from boiling; the porridge flows out of the pot, fills the house, the street, and the whole town until at last the mother comes back and stops the flow of porridge by calling the pot by its name: '*Töpfchen steh!*' (little pot, stop!).

In *Rumpelstiltskin* (*Rumpelstilzchen*), the miller's daughter gets delivered from the evil dwarf who stole her child by correctly guessing his name— *Rumpelstilzchen* or Little Cripple. In his rage at having been named, that is, at having his identity discovered, Rumpelstiltskin stomps the ground with his foot so hard that he disappears half way into the earth, and splits himself in two.

In Bichsel's *A Table is a Table* (*Ein Tisch ist ein Tisch*), an old man decides to invent a new language by switching the names of everyday objects: bed becomes alarm clock, alarm clock becomes newspaper, newspaper becomes rug. The old man is thrilled at the idea of 'going to sleep in the alarm clock', 'reading the rug', and 'being woken up by the newspaper'. But when he tries to share his excitement with his neighbors, no one understands him. He ends his life isolated from his community, with no one to talk to but himself.

In each of these stories, language plays a role that is more complex than the referential, communicative exchanges of information taught in language textbooks. First, the protagonists are involved in serious life events, where knowing and using appropriately the names of persons and things are a matter of life and death. For example, knowing and pronouncing his name brings death to Rumpelstiltskin and saves the miller's daughter's child. The unconventional use of language in the Bichsel story cuts off the old man from his speech community and brings about his social death. Secondly, language is used resourcefully in quite creative and powerful ways but it is constrained by convention and ritual. For example, even though the daughter in *Sweet Porridge* has been granted by her mother the same magical authority over kitchen utensils, her authority depends on uttering the right formula. No substitute will do. And in the Bichsel story, the old man's cavalier treatment of conventional vocabulary and grammar is punished by ostracism. Thirdly, in these stories language is understandable because it conforms to standard grammar and vocabulary, but words always mean more, and seem less welded to things than in everyday life. For example, whereas a German-speaking child cannot imagine the sign *Kamm* as denoting anything else than a comb, a fairy tale child has the power to transfer the properties of a comb onto a mountain and, in a realm where 'wishing is having', can successfully wish the *Kamm* into a *Kammberg*. The reason, as Hoffman would say, that signifiers seem less welded to their signifieds is because in the realm of fairy tales words are not attached to their historical origins, but float freely as myths or ritualistic utterances. The phrase *Töpfchen steh!* does not refer to this particular pot, at this particular point in time. If it did, it would be a historical speech act that could be realized in many different ways, directly 'Stop boiling!' or indirectly 'That's enough!' Instead of a real speech act, we have here a ritualistic speech act that can be applied to any pot at any time, and that depends on the exact formulation of the utterance.

In fairy tales, the power of language to change the normal course of events by the sheer utterance of a name or a magic phrase comes from the fact that symbolic forms are seen to resemble or mirror the physical properties of the objects they denote. In *The Water Witch*, the sign *Kamm* becomes *Kammberg* through lexical adjacency. The conceptual linkage between the two words is enclosed in the German compound noun, which resignifies 'comb' from an object with teeth to the 'comb-like' shape of a mountain. It is the utterance of this compound noun in the course of the storytelling that impedes the advance of the witch. In *Rumpelstiltskin*, the elemental, dwarf-size creature that first saves the princess then refuses to return her child, gets his name from his physical attributes as someone who limps (*rumpeln* = to limp) and hobbles on a wooden leg (*Stelze* = wooden leg). As his limping gait defines who he is, it is in the logic of the fairy tale that upon the revelation of his name he self-destructs by stomping the ground with his foot. In the same manner as Hoffman thought that her name was one with who she was, the name Rumpelstiltskin didn't just denote a little evil spirit, it was welded to his very being. Once his name became revealed to others, it became the property of others and, having no more existence of his own, he vanished from the story.

Language learning in the real world is not usually a matter of life and death as it is in fairy tales. But this digression into the world of fairy tales has shown in magnified and enchanted ways how the use of symbolic forms is not just a nice way of expressing thoughts, naming things and people, and representing the world in poetic ways. Fairy tales reveal deeper truths about the nature and the power of symbolic forms to bring about social existence. We can draw on two theories of the self to illuminate what is going on in fairy tales and in learners' minds: semiotic theory and cognitive linguistics theory.

5 Semiotic theory: symbolic models of the self

Words not only have consequences for the way we know and define ourselves and how we act upon people and events, they also bring to life meanings that did not exist before. Beyond communicating information, they trigger emotions and shape feelings that exceed their informational value. In so doing, they shape the meaning we give to ourselves, as makers and users of signs.

5.1 The signifying self

The prevalent metaphor of language as a 'tool' for representing or acting upon the world has led to the widespread belief that, like any tool, it is independent of the tool user; like a pen, it can be taken up or put down without affecting the writer's identity. This view of language has been put into question by scholars in a postmodern, constructivist tradition (Latour 1999; see also Chapter 6). First, they say, an object is defined not by its structure but by its purpose and use. A pen-in-the-hand is not the same object as a pen-in-the-drawer, it has been given a meaning by the hand that has taken it out of the drawer and now puts it to paper (we shall return to this distinction in Chapter 6, when we look at the multilingual subject online). Second, our objects and the use we make of them define who we are. A pen used for writing makes its user into a writer, a pen used for stabbing makes its user into a criminal. Third, language as symbolic form is not an object that, except for the scientific purpose of linguistic analysis, can be separated from its user. Since it cannot be spoken or written without engaging the body of the speaker/writer, its use leaves cognitive and affective traces in the user's perceptual make-up and in his or her sense of self. These traces are different for insiders who have been socialized in a given speech community and for outsiders who are acquiring or using the language of a different speech community.

According to semiotic theory, both insiders and outsiders make meaning by choosing to interpret signs in three different ways (Peirce 1992/8):

1 They can interpret these signs as *symbols* of reality if they focus on the formal, agreed-upon conventions of their use, for example if they take *a table* to mean no more than its dictionary meaning.
2 They can see in linguistic signs *icons* of reality if they focus on their similarity or analogy with their immediate objects of reference or with other symbols. Thus Belz's student sees in the *ß* an icon of a river, or of fun.
3 They can also interpret linguistic signs as *indices* of reality if they focus on the correlation or association between signs and more distant and diffuse entities, for example, when for Makine the Russian word *derevnya* indexes cows, forests, and izbas.

These three ways of mediating, that is, giving meaning to, reality are not mutually exclusive. As Terrence Deacon notes in *The Symbolic Species* (1997):

> the differences between iconic, indexical, and symbolic relationships derive from regarding things either with respect to their form, their correlations with other things, or their involvement in systems of conventional relationships.
> (ibid. 71)

> Being capable of iconic or indexical interpretation in no way diminishes these signs' capacity of being interpreted symbolically as well...the same

signs can be icons, indices, and symbols *depending on the interpretive process*.
(ibid. 72, emphasis added)

For example, for a native speaker of German the sign *Streß*, like the word 'stress' in English, is a linguistic symbol that denotes pressure or strain. It applies metaphorically to the human body a term that comes from the physical sciences. A person is 'under stress' or 'stressed out' when she is working too hard or is under pressure to meet deadlines. For Belz's learner of German (Excerpt 1.12), the conventional German symbol becomes the starting point for an analogic use of the word that integrates into its denotational value the subjective connotations of 'psychic entanglement' based on the iconic shape of the *ß*.

> Objective denotation: s-t-r-e-s-s = pressure
> Subjective connotation: *Streß* = psychic entanglement

This iconic use of speech is creative as it allows the learner to imbue the foreign sign with personal, sometimes highly idiosyncratic meaning, but it is also risky, as the unconventional meaning might not be sanctioned by the dictionary or accepted by German native speakers. This is not to say that native speakers of German don't add metaphoric meaning to the word *Streß*, but it is of a different kind. German native speakers, who have borrowed the word from its use in American English, have added to the referential English meaning of 'pressure' (German *Druck*) the indexical meaning of 'American-style fatigue', that is, a kind of fatigue associated with the hectic pace of work-obsessed, competitive life in America. For both non-native and native speakers, the metaphoric meanings of the word are based on analogy: the iconic analogy between the perceived shape of the *ß* and a tangled self in the first case, and the indexical analogy between the lexical item of the English code and the perceived way of life of American speakers of English in the second case. In both cases, the meaning of the word has been enriched, from its standard dictionary definition of 'physical pressure or strain', by a new subjective coloring that now becomes part of the original meaning. *Streß* has acquired a layer of metaphoric meaning, based on an iconic or an indexical relationship to reality. If the American student spends some time in Germany, his use of the word might begin to acquire the connotation of 'American-style fatigue' given by German native speakers, and might end up with the following new denotation:

> S-t-r-e-*ß* = psychic entanglement associated with American-style pressure

or, as the student gets more proficient in German, the word might lose its original iconic and indexical meanings and become just another German symbol that denotes pressure or strain. The semiotic life of the word will no doubt be further enriched and transformed by other experiences the student will have, both in the classroom and abroad, but, as we shall see in the next chapter, it remains inscribed in his body as an early affective contact with the language that can continue to color his relationship to both the L2 and his L1.

5.2 Serious life of the self

As discussed in the Introduction, symbolic uses of language are not just flights of the imagination that can be dismissed as 'not serious'. According to language memoirs and learners' testimonies, the language-learning experience is likely to engage learners cognitively, emotionally, morally, and aesthetically. Thus it has characteristics of what Durkheim (1912) called 'the serious life'—referring to any aspect of an activity that is given a deeper ritualistic, symbolic meaning than everyday activities usually have. Unlike conventional uses of language, the subjective use of symbolic forms expresses a world of larger symbolic significance than the one we usually express in our day-to-day transactions—an exotic and mysterious world of desire, escape, empowerment, and transformation.

Both Kaplan and Watson imbued their language-learning experiences with the subjective meanings we ascribe to serious life-changing events. The non-conventional meanings they attributed to symbolic forms enabled them to make sense of the foreign and resolve some of the uncertainty in meaning that they encountered. Kaplan was not quite sure a word was the proper one before she had tried it out on someone and seen its effect. One of her uncertainties was that words in one context might not mean the same in another context, or that they might not mean in context what the dictionary says they should. For Watson, merely uttering the French words put him in a perilous social and cultural position where his identity might be at risk. The very symbolic forms that these learners applied to the world in order to grasp it were a source of uncertainty. Kaplan used the conventional referents to solve this uncertainty through rational dialogue with others. Watson (1995: 56) used a more resourceful approach. According to him, he uttered French words and arranged the French words into English sentences—a tactic often reported by non-native speakers who, in order to (subjectively) compensate for their lack of proficiency in the L2, speak L2 but pretend for themselves that they are speaking in their L1.[3]

Watson's tactics are those used by tricksters in fairytales or *bricoleurs* who make do with the resources at hand to solve problems.[4] They are characteristic of those who find themselves in what Turner (1969: 95) has called 'liminal' situations, because they occupy a space that lies at the threshold (from Latin *limes*) of the old and the new. Apprentices, lonely old men, adolescents at puberty, and, arguably, language learners, are in this sense liminal people. Subjective use of language removes individuals from their here-and-now responsibilities, allowing for play, irony, distance, and the integration of language use into a freer realm of subjective perceptions and meanings—the realm of the trickster. However, speech communities are quick to stigmatize and to keep under control non-conventional meanings, accents, and ways of talking, as well as incorrect or non-standard grammars and vocabularies.

5.3 Symbolic self as real self

As we enter the world of symbolic forms and the affective impact they have on those who use them, we have to reexamine the traditional distrust of words, images, and other symbolic forms that are captured in such folk sayings as: 'Sticks and stones can break my bones, but words will never kill me', or 'Actions speak louder than words', or 'Talk is cheap'. Linguistic structures are seen as separate from psychic states, words as distinct from thoughts, form as quite different from emotion. These and other ways of scorning 'mere' words and of minimizing their effects have led to a misunderstanding of the relation of language and thought.[5] They have led to a misrecognition of the symbolic nature of a person's identity. In *The Symbolic Species*, the biological anthropologist Deacon helps us understand the reality of the symbolic self. He argues that not only is the way we think channeled by the symbolic forms we use, but the self we are conscious of being is of a symbolic nature. For we can apprehend ourselves and others only through the symbolic forms we have created.

> Consciousness of self implicitly includes consciousness of other selves, and other consciousnesses can only be represented through the virtual reference created by symbols. The self that is the source of one's experience of intentionality, the self that is judged by itself as well as by others for its moral choices, the self that worries about its impending departure from the world, this self is a symbolic self. It is a final irony that it is the virtual, not actual, reference that symbols provide, which gives rise to this experience of self. This most undeniably real experience is a *virtual* reality.
> (Deacon 1997: 452)

The virtual reality Deacon refers to here is the world of the symbolic. We shall discuss in Chapter 6 what becomes of the symbolic self when it goes online in the virtual world of the computer.

In sum, semiotic theory suggests that the acquisition of a new language includes a tension between conventional and non-conventional interpretation of signs. More than in their native language, language learners experience that tension as a struggle for meaning: between their obligation to use conventional symbols, icons, and indexicalities and their desire to make meaning on their own terms; between objective meaning, based on shared social and historical conventions, and subjective meaning, based on individual imagination and creativity. Both the historical and the imagined are real, as they get inscribed in the flesh-and-blood reality of the language users' embodied minds. Moreover, as we shall see in Chapter 3, both are necessary to understand the full symbolic dimensions of self and other. Language as symbolic signifying practice partakes of both, and while it brings about this tension, it also has a role to play in resolving it, as a cognitive linguistic approach can show.[6]

6 Cognitive linguistics theory: idealized cognitive models of the self

Semiotic theory is not sufficient to explain why Watson came to hate what the French language represented, whereas Kaplan loved it. For this we need to draw on a theory that explains what or whom the two learners identified with, namely prototypes or idealized cognitive models of self. Let us consider a more extended excerpt from Watson's testimony:

Excerpt 1.15
These new French [spoken] forms threatened to destroy what little progress I had made so far. Not only did I use English forms in speaking French, I was appalled to find myself using French forms when I was writing English. French was undermining my very being! My personality was in danger of disintegrating!... what made me realize how much I dislike the sound of French was the continual, unctuous, caressing repetition of 'l'oiseau' ('the bird'). It is a word the French believe to be one of the most beautiful in their language. It is a word that cannot be pronounced without simpering, a word whose use should be restricted to children under five... American men don't like to simper.
(Watson: 1997: 57 cited in Schumann 1997: 147)

What prototypical American man could such a statement be based on? The folk notion of what it means to 'be an American' seems clear enough: if a French person is someone who speaks French, then *an American is a person who speaks American English*. And that is generally what is taught in language classes. But it doesn't explain why men who speak American English don't like to purse their lips, whereas men who speak French seem to find it all right to do so. It's because this definition does not cover the full range of cases. *To be an American* is a concept that is based on a complex model in which a number of individual cognitive models combine. Some of these models might be:
- The nationality model: to be an American means to have a US passport.
- The ideological model: to be an American means to be a free citizen of a free country, i.e. to be free to speak any way one likes.
- The belief model: it means to believe in the American democratic values of individualism, autonomy, ruggedness, and simplicity, free from tyranny and censorship.
- The social class model: it means to be a member of the down-to-earth working class or middle class.
- The ethnic model: it means to be Anglo-American.
Many people around the world also use a racial model ('American' means white American), and even a gender model ('American' means 'male American') to categorize 'Americans'.[7]

There are divergences from these prototypical models. For example, Asian-Americans or African-Americans have, of course, American passports and speak American English, but only white European-Americans have been able to remain, until recently, unhyphenated, that is, unmarked, 'Americans'. Dissident Americans are also American, but they do not fit the prototype, and are, in fact, sometimes considered to be 'un-American'. Female Americans are less likely to be associated with the rugged brashness indexed by the stereotype 'American'. And the sophisticated, upper-class Boston gentry don't fit the prototype either.[8] So when Watson's narrator claims that 'American men don't like to simper', he is relying on the reader's familiarity with some of the prototypes listed above, upon which a complex cognitive model is built. This idealized cognitive model contains:

- Propositional models characterizing our knowledge about 'American men'; these models would include, for Watson, directness, generosity, virility, and forthrightness.
- Image-schematic models that specify schematic images, for example, the CONTAINER schema, that originates in the physical, bodily experience of being inside or outside, of having one's mouth open or closed, empty or full, etc.
- Metaphors that map a propositional or image-schematic model from one domain onto a corresponding structure in another domain, for instance, the BODY AS CONTAINER metaphor, where 'open' indexes frankness and generosity, as in 'to hold an open house', 'to have an open mind', while 'closed' indexes pettiness, avarice, and effeminateness as in 'to be tight-mouthed' or 'tight-fisted', or 'to simper'.
- Metonymic models, that represent a part–whole structure, where the mouth stands for the whole person.

It is because of this complex cluster of propositional models, image-schemas, and metaphors that we immediately understand the term 'American' here to mean more than just someone speaking American English or holding an American passport. We also understand that 'simpering', like whining, is, in Watson's idealized cognitive model, not something that an American man just happens not to like, but, rather, that this dislike is constitutive of himself as an American male. In the same manner as 'not being a housewife mother' is constitutive of 'the working mother', 'not simpering' is the very definition of who Watson perceives himself to be.[9]

In sum, idealized cognitive model theory can explain how the metaphors we live by in our own language can impede or, on the contrary, facilitate our production of a language that is foreign to our body. These metaphors are grounded in our bodily experience of big versus small, up versus down, inside versus outside, etc. We imbue these bodily characteristics with moral values that are expressed both in Watson's testimony and in the fairy tales discussed above: bigmouthed is good, tightmouthed is bad; walking upright is good, walking crooked like Rumpelstiltskin is bad; porridge inside a container is good, porridge outside the container can flood and destroy a whole city. Watson's metaphors are particularly dramatic as they suggest that the foreign language, like porridge on the loose, is attacking his bodily integrity and his ability to stand upright: 'French was *undermining* my very being! My personality was in danger of *disintegrating!*'

How can Watson reconcile speaking French while retaining his idealized cognitive model of what it means to be 'American'? How does our body accommodate to the new sounds while retaining an embodied memory of the old? In other words, how does one become a speaker of a foreign language while one's body retains the memory and the value attached to one's own native tongue? The way out of this dilemma has been theorized in cognitive linguistics by Fauconnier and Turner's notion of conceptual or metaphorical blend, that characterizes, they argue, the very 'way we think'.

7 Blended space theory

In *The Way We Think*: *Conceptual Blending and the Mind's Hidden Complexities* (2002), Fauconnier and Turner argue that the mind is metaphorical in nature. It understands events by bringing two mental spaces together such as, in the example above, the concrete space of rugged outdoor activities and the more abstract entity of the American male. In this case, they would say that Watson understands himself by bringing the mental space of speology and rock formations on the one hand and the space of the self on the other, and by blending these two spaces together under one metaphor of the kind: THE SELF IS A ROCK. This is the metaphor he lives by as we can see from his description of being 'undermined' or 'disintegrated' by the foreign language—two metaphors that are entailments of the first as they are usually applied to solid objects destroyed by external or internal hostile forces. These terms are not just figures of speech, but ways of thinking and making sense of events. Watson can feel as threatened as he does because the metaphor that gives him a sense of self is precisely: THE SELF IS A ROCK. We have seen how the authors of language memoirs and language learners make ample use of similar metaphors to describe their experience. Kaplan's dominant metaphor in Excerpt 1.1 is LANGUAGE LEARNING IS A DANGEROUS GAME. For Belz's student in Excerpt 1.14, her dominant metaphor at the time was LOVE IS A TWO-PRONGED GERMAN VERB. Fairy tales also construct their plots by blending two cognitive spaces, for example in *The Water Witch*, the realm of such domestic articles as combs, mirrors, and hairbrushes and the realm of nature such as mountains and water witches. Fairy-tale heroes get saved in the blend, where new metaphors are created, such as comb-peaks or mirror-mountains. We have seen in Excerpt 1.6 how Tawada blends the sound of the German word *Haβ* with the Japanese word *hasu* to make a new blend she can live with.

Another passage from Tawada makes this blending process particularly vivid. The Japanese-German author writes in German about her stay at the Massachusetts Institute of Technology in 2001. She has just tried to reach a German colleague, Kurt.

Excerpt 1.16
Kurt was not in his office. I spoke into his answering machine.
Technological progress has made human voices more and more
independent [*unabhängig*] of human bodies. One can leave voices, copy
them, record them, duplicate them, color them, estrange, accelerate or
reverse them. But can a voice really exist independently [*unabhängig*]
from a body? I noticed that the word 'unabhängig' does not sound as
euphoric as the word 'independent'. How do the Americans manage to
serve this word with such conviction? Are you given a secret recipe on
Independence Day?
(2002: 100, my translation)

The fact that this native speaker of Japanese writes in German about an
experience she lived in an English-speaking environment gives her the distance
necessary to reflect on her attitude toward both the German and the English
word for 'independence' and to give us glimpses of her multilingual imagination at work. She maps German *unabhängig* onto technological prowess in
the age of mechanical reproduction (Benjamin 1968), and American English
independent onto the euphoria of the American Revolution. For the non-
native speaker of either German or English these two terms seem strangely
non-equivalent, although the dictionary gives one as the faithful translation
of the other. From *Unabhängigkeit* as mechanical event, to *independence* as
revolutionary euphoria, the multilingual imagination jumps to *independence*
as a major American democratic value and *Independence Day* as *the* national
holiday, featured here, slightly tongue-in-cheek, as a culinary dish, that is,
as food that has to pass through the mouth, like words. Not every foreigner
would be able to put these imaginary constructions into words as elegantly as
Tawada does, but her narrative gives us a glimpse of the metaphoric mappings
that can happen under the surface of seemingly straightforward vocabulary
acquisition.

Let us examine more closely Tawada's question: 'How do the Americans
manage to serve this word with such conviction?' To understand the meaning
of *Independence Day* for an American, she suggests, one has to understand
the emotional resonances it has in American culture. One could represent the
two mental spaces occupied by German *unabhängig* and American-English
independent as in Fig. 1.1.

The dictionary definitions of the two words focus on two different aspects of
the concept 'independence'. American dictionaries stress the freedom from
any external constraint and control, they focus on self-governance and the
liberation of man from any subjugation by others. The connotation of the
English word is decidedly political. It is a *freedom from*. By contrast, German
dictionaries stress the development of the individual from the 'dependent' child to the mature grown-up, the access to *Volljährigkeit* (full age) or
Mündigkeit (etymology: *-mund* as in *Vormund*, 'he who has the power to

American-English *independent*	**German** *unabhängig*
Not subject to control by others	Financially autonomous
Self-governing	Socially emancipated
Free from subjection	Of age, mature (syn. *mündig*)
Exempt from external control or support	Etym. *–mund*: who has the power to protect others

Blend

Personal and social self-sufficiency

Emancipation as moral, legal, and
political categories

Irony

Figure 1 German–English conceptual blending

protect others'). The German synonym *'mündig'* echoes Kant's definition of Enlightenment as 'Die Befreiung des Menschen aus seiner selbstverschuldeten Unmündigkeit' (the liberation of man from his self-inflicted dependency). It underscores the natural process of personal growth into a state of increasing maturity and rationality. From financial independence to social power and responsibility, the connotations of the German word *Unabhängigkeit* are distinctly moral, not so much a *freedom from,* as a *freedom to.* In the blend, the German and American voices mesh uneasily, dependent as they are on the bodies in which each has been socialized and acculturated ('can a voice really exist independently from a body?' Tawada asks). As Tawada learns English, she tries to imbue the German moral (rational, mature) notion of independence with American political/ideological euphoria and conviction, but as a Japanese, she keeps clear of both through a distanced irony conveyed through gastronomical metaphors ('How do the Americans manage to serve this word...? Are you given a secret recipe on Independence Day?').

This blend is, as Fauconnier and Turner (2002: 17) point out, only 'the tip of the iceberg'. Emergent structures arise in the blend that are not copied directly from any input space. For example, blending might provide new *compositional* relations, such as the relation of the moral and the political, or of evolution and revolution. It might be *completed* by elements that were not explicitly in the original spaces, such as eighteenth-century German Enlightenment and the 1776 American Declaration of Independence. We can also, as Fauconnier and Turner say, 'run the blend' so that it provides *elaboration* of one or the other of its aspects, such as a discussion of the third place of the Japanese learner of German and English, the current tensions between the European and the American concepts of democracy, cosmopolitanism, and globalization, and the uneasy blend of *freedom from* and *responsibility to* in capitalistic democracies. Composition, completion, and elaboration lead to emergent structures in the blend, thus forging 'integration networks' and blended spaces with which foreign language learners try to make sense of a foreign reality as expressed through its language.[10]

In sum, blended space theory offers a fruitful way of conceptualizing the way language learners deal with the relation of language and thought in their various languages and how differently they might think in that respect from monolingual native speakers. Many of their blends are idiosyncratic, based on past and present life events, but they are no less worthy of attention for SLA researchers intent on understanding the meaning of their language-learning experience.

8 Symbolic activity in SLA research

As a social science well known for its rigorous positivistic methods of inquiry and its ability to describe and predict the conditions of language learning, SLA research has not dealt with the full range of a learner's symbolic activity. It has focused more on the communicative and informational value of utterances than on their symbolic aspects and their emotional effects. It is not that SLA research has neglected issues of subjectivity and identity in language learning but it has studied them separately without tying them to the use of symbolic forms *as a symbolic activity*. For example, it has explored affective factors in SLA with a psychological and neurobiological framework (Schumann 1997) or emotions in multilinguals with a lexical and cognitive approach (Pavlenko 2005), or identity development in bilinguals within a feminist perspective (Norton 2000), but it has not explicitly associated affect, emotions, and identity to language learners' experience of symbolic form. By remaining on the level of symbolic [1], it has not taken the full measure of the symbolic [2] activity that learners engage in and that constitutes them as multilingual subjects (see Introduction).

The data we have examined in this chapter are all the product of symbolic activity. They all mediate a multilingual experience that was lived in a much more amorphous or indistinct way before it was put into words. Some readers will disagree with my interpretation of the data (see Block's (2007: Chapter 5) misgivings). They will see in their metaphoric style nothing but the product of overheated imaginations or literary sensibilities. Surely the experiences recounted have to be taken with a grain of salt, they cannot be taken seriously as scientific data! But, as testimonies of language learners remind us, the power to arouse emotions and to create subjective effects in both speakers and listeners comes less from the content of what is said than from the form in which it is said. Indeed, the power to act comes more often than we think from words, i.e. from symbolic forms, spoken or written, heard or remembered, parroted or recounted, thus making our actions part of a larger symbolic reality.[11]

In order to understand this symbolic reality, we have to look at the way multilingual speakers and writers make use of linguistic symbols to refer to, represent, or index subjective truths that cannot be conveyed by simply 'telling it like it is'. That is true not only of literary texts. For everyday speakers and writers, but especially for those who speak and write in more than one language, everyday verbal practices are saturated with symbolic activity of various kinds. Awareness of the symbolic power of language can make a bilingual seminar participant overwhelmed with emotion, as she is reminded of her other Persian self when she speaks Persian. She can then engage in physical action, but the meaning of that action will be found in the symbolic self she was in touch with at that moment. It will have meaning for others only if they see beyond the physical and pay attention to the symbolic value of words and actions.

Notes

1 The title *Le Partage des mots* contains a play on the word *partage*. It can mean both *the separation of words* (as in the language of the father and the language of the mother), and *the inheritance of words* (as in the words the child inherited from his parents).

2 It might be, of course, that this rejection of French comes from the child's rejection of the French-speaking parent or of the French school and not from the nature of the language itself. In multilinguals, language becomes the target of a host of subjective experiences and feelings that express themselves differently for monolinguals.

3 This make-believe can also be the stuff that multilingual dreams are made of. One such dream was recounted by Dan Slobin (personal communication) who was about to go to China but was terrified that he didn't know Chinese. Trying to fall asleep that night and in a dreamlike state, he managed to share his anxiety with his alter ego, who suggested: 'Well, since you know Russian, why don't you speak Russian and pretend it's Chinese?' The next morning his body woke up with the exhilarating feeling that he had spoken Chinese all night, even though in fact it was Russian.

4 See Basso (1990), Hyde (1998), Kramsch (2002a). For *bricolage*, i.e. the ability to make do with available resources, see Lévi-Strauss (1962).

5 For a review of work on linguistic relativity, in addition to Lucy's important monograph (1992), three edited volumes give the state of current research on the relation of language, thought, and culture: Duranti and Goodwin (1992), Gumperz and Levinson (1996), and Niemeier and Dirven (2000). For a survey of language relativity and its importance for applied linguistics, see Kramsch (2004).

6 The traditional dichotomies: cognition/emotion, language/thought, form/meaning have been put into question by recent work in neurobiology and cognitive linguistics. The close relation of cognition and emotion in the brain (Damasio 1994; Tomasello 1999), the relationality of symbolic form and thought, also called linguistic relativity (Lakoff 1987; Slobin 1996), the metaphoric nature of the mind (Lakoff 1987; Fauconnier and Turner 2002) have been studied by cognitive linguists and neurobiologists alike. They have revolutionized the way we conceive of language and the self.

7   Categorization is one of the major sources of cross-cultural misunderstanding and prejudice even though we cannot think without categorizing (Rosch and Lloyd 1978). Lakoff begins his discussion of idealized cognitive models (ICM) with a passage from Borges (1964: 103), 'The Analytical Language of John Wilkins'. In this story, Borges discusses the possibility of a human language that could organize and contain the whole of human thought. He examines several ways in which such a language would categorize reality. One, in particular, catches his (mythical) fancy, namely that attributed by a Dr Franz Kuhn to a certain Chinese encyclopedia entitled *Celestial Emporium of Benevolent Knowledge*. 'On those remote pages', writes Borges, 'it is written that animals are divided into (a) those that belong to the Emperor, (b) embalmed ones, (c) those that are trained, (d) suckling pigs, (e) mermaids, (f) fabulous ones, (g) stray dogs, (h) those that are included in this classification, (i) those that tremble as if they were mad, (j) innumerable ones, (k) those drawn with a very fine camel's hair brush, (l) others, (m) those that have just broken a flower vase, (n) those that from a long way off look like flies.' This passage has been used by language-learning researchers to show the difficulty of understanding someone from another culture—not because of the foreign words themselves but because of the foreign system of classification.

8   The debate as to whether the 'real' American is a monolingual English speaker or not is a recurring theme in the American press. During the 2008 election campaign, the Republican candidate for vice-president, Sarah Palin, used it forcefully against the democratic nominee, Barack Obama, who in turn ruffled quite a few feathers by stating publicly: 'You know, it's embarrassing when Europeans come over here, they all speak English, they speak French, they speak German. And then we go over to Europe and all we can say is "merci beaucoup".' He was accused in some media of snobbery and lack of patriotism (Powell 2008).

9   This analysis draws heavily on Lakoff's (1987: 80 ff.) analysis of the ICM of a 'working mother'.

10 This analysis draws on Fauconnier and Turner's (2002: Part I) analyses of various blends.

11 For example, one could argue that the informants in Norton's well-known study of women immigrants in Canada developed through their written journals the symbolic selves that empowered them to stand up to their landlord and improve their working conditions. Martina, for instance, who wrote: 'I knew I could not give up', did not simply muster the psychological courage to stand up to her landlord by drawing on her identity as a mother. Rather, she had internalized a newly learned English idiomatic phrase: 'don't give up', with its catchy rhythm and its seductive intonation, had made it her own by writing it in her journal, and had thereby constructed in writing a symbolic self that was able to interpret and recount her altercation with the landlord in a way that matched her desire to be taken seriously.

2

The embodied self

We have seen that language learners make meaning in ways that are sometimes different from the way most native speakers make meaning in their daily lives. They make analogical relations between words and things, where ordinary speakers would just see through the words to the things they refer to. They imagine letters and sounds indexing unexpected attributes, they resonate to dictionary definitions and grammatical rules with heightened awareness of signs and their possible meanings. As they use symbolic forms to give meaning to their environment, even the environment of the classroom, they rely not only on cool reason, but on the embodied aspects of a cognitive and socialized self: emotions, feelings, memories. It is to these embodied aspects that we now turn.

1 Testimonies from language memoirs

Let us revisit Watson's testimony, discussed in the previous chapter, but focusing this time on the physical, bodily way he describes his language experience.[1] Motivated to specialize in the history of Cartesian philosophy, he decided to take French in college.

> Excerpt 2.1
> I loved learning to read this new language. It was all in the mind. The instructor devoted, at most, fifteen minutes of the first class period to French pronunciation, but we were never required to speak or write the language, only to read it. I read it very well, earning an A for the yearlong, ten-hour course. Moreover, some years later when I took the Ph.D. reading exam in reading French, I scored 100 percent.
> (Watson 1995: 1)

Watson's encounter with French reinforced a sense of himself as an intelligent, rational human being, endowed with superior intellectual faculties and in control of his life. Learning to read French did not disturb his unconscious feeling of self, which is why Watson's body seemed to be so self-evident to him as to be not even worth mentioning. '[French] was all in the mind', he writes. Reading French confirmed his brain's representation of his primary happy sense of self. His body responded to the task at hand with pleasure and positive evaluation. He 'loved' learning to read this new language, and he read it 'very well'. As we saw in the last chapter, Watson's self was used to constructing a stable, invariant image of himself as an intelligent mind, and a manly, competitive, and quintessentially American body.

As he takes a course with a French native speaker at Washington University in St Louis he is shocked at his inability to speak the language:

> Excerpt 2.2
> It was like diving naked and alone into ice water. I was frozen with panic. I found to my horror that I was not an able student, as I always had been before.
> (ibid. 8)

His body records strong emotions (*panic, horror*) associated with physical pain (*diving naked into ice water*) and emotional duress (*alone*), which his brain immediately represents as feelings of inadequacy (*I was not an able student, as I had always been before*), disappointment, and fear. For the first time, the representation that his mind is giving of his body is in dissonance with his former sense of harmony. These negative representations of himself are exacerbated when he studies French at the Alliance Française—'a terrifying experience', as he recalls.

> Excerpt 2.3
> I was more tense than I have ever been in my life or ever want to be again...The first time I ever climbed a mountain wall with hundreds of feet of exposure below me, that time we arrived back at the entrance of a cave to find a wall of water roaring in and had to crawl down stream as fast as we could for a long distance to clamber up into passages above water level, my Ph.D. oral exam—none of those times could begin to compete with the state of tension I was enduring now.
>
>   And how am I to characterize or express adequately my sensations when with every indication of justified anger and disgust, The Professor called me an idiot and an imbecile? To be sure, she called others in the class the same as the days went on, but I was the first. I, who had been a professor in charge of my own classes for twenty-five years...
>
>   It was not the first time in my life that I had been called an imbecile in class. But imbecility is in America, so to speak, a relative thing. In France, it is exactly defined, and certified.
> (ibid. 39, 40)

In this passage, written by a Cartesian philosopher who is also an amateur speleologist, the narrator first constructs perceptual images of physical sensations (*climbing a mountain wall with hundreds of feet of exposure below, wall of water roaring in, crawling downstream as fast as we could...*) that get represented as feelings of *tension*. In fact, the feelings associated with the emotions of 'anger and disgust' attributed to his teacher in the second paragraph and characterized as 'justified', seem to apply to his own feelings of self-directed anger and disgust when she called him an idiot and an imbecile. All this immediately triggers memories of the Ph.D. oral exam and unaccept-able anticipated futures (*more tense than I … ever want to be again*) that the narrator brings into the picture. To add insult to injury, the words *idiot* and *imbecile* used by 'The Professor' are applied by a female teacher to an intelli-gent male university professor with twenty-five years of teaching experience. The unusual capitalization of these two words are the narrator's way of rep-resenting both the event and his sarcastic evaluation.

Indeed, as we saw in the last chapter, his disgust at the French language is triggered not just by the behavior of his teacher, but by the sounds the French language forces his body to produce, in particular by the sound 'wa/zo' in Jacques Prévert's 'cute' and 'detestable' poem 'Pour faire le portrait d'un oiseau' ['How to Make the Portrait of a Bird'], that Watson associ-ates with 'simpering'. What kind of image did Watson's brain produce upon hearing or pronouncing the seemingly innocuous French noun? In order to produce this sound, you have to first open your mouth wide lengthwise /lwa/, then make it small again and purse your lips /zo/ as if sucking on a lollipop or sipping tea /lwazo/. Such a movement of the mouth is perceived as childish or effeminate by men such as Watson who prize the masculinity that goes with having a 'loud mouth' or a 'big mouth'.[2] The verb 'to simper' used by Watson means 'to don an affected, silly, self-conscious smile'. The narrator catches his body reacting to the sound /lwazo/ and finds this sound incompatible with the image it has been socialized in over the years and that is consonant with that of a sturdy, straightforward American male. Interestingly, this self might not have come to his consciousness had it not been for the sudden obligation to pronounce the foreign word.

Excerpt 2.4
So how does one handle such an irrational response? I wondered if it was just the contrast with the English 'bird', which is a strong hard word … American men don't like to simper. And as I said, they get their notion of Frenchmen from the movies. Certainly no American boy of my generation ever wanted to grow up to be Charles Boyer.
(ibid. 53)

Adolescent memories of erotic French films and of Charles Boyer's sexy behav-ior invade the present, as do (unwanted) anticipated futures, for example 'growing up to be Charles Boyer'. They flood the perceptions and emotions of the body, and their representations by the brain, and in turn, they cause the body to feel disgust at the very representations the brain has produced. This is because these representations are not just objective images that refer to a par-ticular sound or sound-image. They involve good and bad memories, judgments of self-worth, ritualized behaviors—the stuff that myths are made of. They are neural representations of symbolic forms not just in the brain but in the body. The 'alarm bells' set off by all these representations transform what was only a triggering occasion, namely the word 'oiseau', into a type (one could say, a stereotype) regarding the French, the Americans, French and American men, and the very survival of his identity as a scholar, as a man, as an American. For the narrator, pursing one's lips indexes constraint and restraint, smallness of body and pettiness (from the French *petit*, small) of spirit, and the opposite of the valor and hardiness that a healthy intellectual and cave explorer would ascribe to himself.[3] The teacher had probably no clue as to what was going on in her student's mind, nor would the student have been able to verbalize it at the time.

The discordance between French sounds and Watson's perception of himself as a scholar and as an American is radically different from the experience recounted by Kaplan, she too an American learner of French, later to become a scholar of French at Duke University. Shortly after the excerpt we discussed in Chapter 1, Kaplan describes her experience in her French class in Geneva, as she had to recite aloud her lines for the day. She too first focuses on the state of her body:

> Excerpt 2.5
> I speak my lines with muscles quavering... The Mouth [has to be] in the right position to make the vowel sounds: lip muscles forward and tighter than in English, the mouth poised and round. Americans speaking French tend to chomp down hard on their consonants and swallow their vowels all together.
> (Kaplan 1993: 54)

In the following extract, she translates the perceptual images of her body (quavering muscles, lips forward and tight, mouth poised and round) into representations, but these representations are different from Watson's.

> Excerpt 2.6
> In September my 'r' is clunky, the one I've brought with me from Minnesota. It is like cement overshoes, like wearing wooden clogs in a cathedral. It is like any number of large objects in the world—all of them heavy, all of them out of place, all of them obstacles. *Je le heurte*—I come up against it like a wall.
> (ibid. 54)

The narrator represents the movements of her mouth, not with images of affected smiles and effeminate poses, but with objects that remind her of the rural, rough-hewn Minnesota town she comes from. She brings back the memories of all she wanted to escape: sacks of cement, rubber overshoes, wooden clogs, wooden structures, cinder block walls, and juxtaposes them in her imagination with the elegance and refinery of French cathedrals and the 'smooth', 'plush' and 'suave' French *r*. Note how she personalizes this 'r': 'my "r"', underscoring how much she perceives the language to be a part of her body. Kaplan's bodily experiences of French are different from Watson's because she has other memories, desires, and representations of who she is. These representations trigger emotions in her body that she describes as *heavy* and *out of place*.

Kaplan then goes on to describe in detail the feelings triggered by these emotions:

Excerpt 2.7
So that feeling of coming onto the 'r' like a wall was part of feeling the essence of my American speech patterns in French, feeling them as foreign and awkward. I didn't know at the time how important it was to feel that American 'r' like a big lump in my throat and to be dissatisfied about it. Feeling the lump was the first step, the prerequisite to getting rid of it
(ibid. 54)

It happened over months but it felt like it happened in one class. I opened my mouth and I opened up: it slid, out, smooth and plush, a French 'r.'...It felt—relaxed. It felt normal!
(ibid. 55)

What Kaplan, like Watson, discovers by speaking French is the essence of her Americanness. We can see how quickly sounds and mouth and body postures take on symbolic meanings. The capitalization of *The Mouth* in Excerpt 2.5 was already a sign that the position of the mouth is not just a muscular affair, but a metonymy for her whole personality. In the same manner as Rumpelstilt-skin's or Hoffman's name represented the very essence of who they were, we have in Watson and Kaplan two learners who map the position of their mouths onto who they are, namely, Americans. But Kaplan represents that bodily posture not with feelings of pride, indignation, and anger, like Watson, but with feelings of shame (*feeling them as foreign and awkward*) and embarrass-ment (*big lump, out of place, obstacle*), coupled with memories of unhappiness (*dissatisfied*) and anticipations of liberation (*getting rid of it*). The words *feeling* and *feel* repeated eight times in Excerpt 2.7 are the self-conscious way in which the narrator tries to convey the embodied dimensions of the language-learning experience.

This experience is not reserved for middle-aged scholars reminiscing about their travails in language learning. It is echoed by that of undergraduate language learners learning a variety of languages at the college level as part of their general education.

2 Metaphors by which we learn languages

At the University of California at Berkeley, where some sixty different lan-guages are taught on a regular basis, many undergraduate students between the ages of 18 and 22 take one or two semesters of a foreign language, despite the lack of a foreign language requirement. Between 60 and 85 per cent of these students already have some knowledge of another language besides

English, for example 88 per cent of those studying Portuguese also have some knowledge of Spanish, 82 per cent of those studying Korean already know some French or Chinese. Thus we are dealing with a multilingual student population that is more sensitive to language than is usual in the US. Because UC Berkeley is a large public university, many students come from modest, recent immigrant backgrounds and are often the first in their family to go to college. In order to explore how foreign language students construct their learning experience across the first two or three years of instruction, I conducted in spring 1998 a survey of 953 students learning fourteen different languages. The languages were: Arabic, Chinese, Danish, Finnish, French, German, Hebrew, Italian, Japanese, Korean, Norwegian, Portuguese, Spanish, and Swedish. The survey was conducted in English and was phrased thus:

> How would you describe your experience learning this language? Choose a phrase, an expression, or a metaphor that best captures your experience learning to speak and write in this language.

1 Learning a language is like ...
2 Speaking this language is like ...
3 Writing in this language is like ...

The purpose was to find out the students' range of experiences of learning a foreign language, the variations in metaphor patterns within individual language groups, and the differences between language groups. The questionnaire was distributed to the instructors who gave it to their students to fill out anonymously in class. Between them, the students generated 1,496 different metaphors in response to all three questions (for more on the methodology, see Kramsch 2003a). As contrasted with the input–output information-processing metaphors that dominate second language acquisition research (Ellis 1997: 61), this survey yielded a wealth of statements that all attempt to give meaning to a very personal and physical encounter with the language, a resonance to persons and things evoked by words, and the identifications these words elicit in the students.

2.1 General observations

The choice of descriptors used by the students varied according to the medium. While the spoken forms of the language were heavily linked to the desire to identify with native speakers ('Learning Portuguese is like feeling a little bit Brazilian'), role-playing, physical and emotional experiences, and flights or romance and exoticism associated with the foreign sounds, writing seemed to be the mode in which the terms 'beauty', 'creativity', 'elegance', and 'self-expression' recurred most frequently. The written medium made students aware of the double presence of language: as a means for the private expression of self, and as a mode of public communication exposed to formal and cultural scrutiny. Echoing the tension we noted in the last chapter between subjective and conventional speech, one student wrote: 'Language learning is a constant struggle between an internal speaking voice which can try out many different approaches in order to state something, and a public voice which is very aware of its inadequacies.'

The choice of descriptors varied also according to the level of instruction. In several languages (French, Italian, Hebrew, Japanese, Spanish), the metaphors used in the first two years clustered around the physical duress and the skill-learning aspects of language acquisition, as well as around a return to childhood and the acquisition of new ways of thinking, whereas the metaphors used at the advanced levels tended to cluster around changing identity, acquiring a new social and emotional self, traveling through new worlds, engaging in an artistic, creative process, acquiring a secret code. In other languages, the level didn't seem to influence the choice of metaphors used. For example, the students of first-year Arabic in this sample had many metaphors related to beauty and aesthetics (perhaps due to the Arabic script), and the small number of advanced students of German represented in this survey favored overwhelmingly metaphors of physical duress and struggle.[4]

The choice of metaphors was also inspired by what the students knew or imagined about the country, the people, and the culture. Their associations were for the most part taken from traditional or stereotypical cultural discourses. They were not always based on the direct experience of learning the language but, rather, on myths and dreams, that served as potent incentives for learning the language in the first place. For example, Chinese, Korean, or Japanese characters were typically called 'pretty', and their 'simplicity' was praised, whereas Arabic script or French sounds were invariably perceived as 'beautiful', 'elegant', or 'distinguished'. Such adjectives were less an objective observation on the part of the students than a subjective way of characterizing a whole culture. Some students of Arabic showed a predilection for secret doors, keys, and treasures to be discovered—no doubt inspired by fantasies of *Arabian Nights*. One student of Swedish compared learning Swedish to 'eating a smorgasbord'; one learner of Hebrew compared learning the language to 'expressing truth from the crevasses of words'. Learning Japanese was often compared to a 'battle' in which 'strategies' have to be deployed; in learning, there is, writes one student, 'so much to conquer'; for another, learning German was perceived as 'mastering the language' and 'gaining control'. Such metaphors, by contrast, are rarely used for French, which seems to inspire students less through the battles of Napoleon than through the splendors of the court at Versailles. French was perceived by many as having the mythic power to make learners feel 'more intelligent', 'more educated'.

We can get a glimpse of how such phrases came to be used when we look at how students responded to one additional trigger: 'When I hear someone speak the language, it makes me think of...'. Arabic made learners think of 'deserts, the sea, waves rolling and retreating, music, beautiful arabesque architecture, Arabian nights...'. Japanese made learners think of 'rain falling on a metal roof; the meditative qualities of its brush writing, samurai, neat green hedges and housewives with aprons on'. When learning French, students acknowledged thinking of 'springtime in Paris, elegance, beautiful literature, good food, great wine on a warm Sunday afternoon, romance, love, culture, intelligence'. And when learning German, students thought of *Vorsprung durch Technik,* cars, *Lederhosen,* beer and sausages, prison guards, and pastry chefs. These subjective representations of the language got mapped onto the language-learning experience and its metaphors, which we now examine more closely.

2.2 Learning a language is like …

The metaphors used by the students display an inordinately diverse range of embodiments of the self. Far from being perceived as primarily a tool for communication and exchange of information, the foreign language is first and foremost experienced physically, linguistically, emotionally, artistically. Very often for beginning students it is a painful experience: 'Learning a language is like having a molar extraction', 'passing a kidney stone', or 'pulling my hair out'. It is an intimate encounter between learners and their bodies, between the body and its new mode of meaning-making. As one student of Arabic wrote: 'Learning Arabic is like walking across a desert with a camel. Sometimes you meet other nomads, or an oasis here or there, but most of the time it is just you and your camel.' For advanced students, the experience can be an aesthetic one: 'Learning a foreign language is like an artist adapting to a new medium', or 'conducting a symphony'. For heritage learners the experience is different, since for them the language represents a 'homecoming' of sorts. 'Learning Korean is like my grandmother's canary in the window waiting to sing a song I do not recognize, but with time it will be part of the scene.' In the following, I have clustered the descriptors used by all categories of students under various aspects of their embodied experience.

Challenging the body's physical limitations

The first cluster compares language learning to experiencing one's body in new physical spaces.

Excerpt 2.8
Learning a language is like:

1 scaling a barbed-wire fence
2 getting a rush from free-falling
3 skydiving without a parachute
4 riding a roller coaster—sometimes I go up (I know what I'm saying), sometimes I go down (when I don't know what I'm saying). Overall a thrilling experience

5 a battle where you have to strategically place your tongue for the right sounds and you have to understand what's going on to win

6 fighting a battle—with strategy, it can be done!

7 learning to write with my right hand (I am left-handed)

8 surfing a wave—sometimes I catch it and sometimes I don't

9 struggling to pick up tabouli with a small piece of bread

10 learning how to cook a new meal ... with your feet

11 trying to untangle the necklaces that have become jumbled together at the bottom of my jewelry box.

This group of metaphors expresses language learning as a spatial, physical challenge: avoiding physical dismemberment by barbed wire, defying the laws of gravity, surviving the highs and lows of a roller coaster, conquering strategic terrain against an enemy, overcoming congenital left-handedness, confronting the risks of unpredictable ocean waves, reconfiguring your body's natural functions (cooking with your feet), reordering pearls in the bounded space of a jewelry box. These spatial metaphors are suited to capture the grammatical and lexical constraints that language learners have to maneuver in order to find their way around the new language. Their vocabulary is often taken from the familiar outdoor activities experienced by adolescents in California.

Escaping the limits of one's skin

The next set of metaphors focuses on the experience of maneuvering constraints, from the perspective not of the obstacles, but of the explorations of new dimensions of the body.

Excerpt 2.9
Learning a language is like:

12 kissing a new girlfriend

13 trying oysters for the first time

14 learning a whole new way of thinking

15 breaking a hole in a wall and installing a window

16 entering a new world, with new rhythms and colors

17 assuming a new identity, a new persona

18 acting out a role

19 wearing a new dress

20 learning to fly, a breathtaking, wonderful experience

21 taking a break from the world I live in.

Here the common theme is one of newness, first-time sexual experiences, breaking out, escaping the limits of one's familiar world, physical space, social role and identity, activities. They have to do with a new dimension of the body's perceptions: the mouth (12, 13), the brain (14), the eyes and ears (15, 16), social appearance (17, 18), physical appearance (19), general bodily feeling (20), and a shedding of the body's constraints (21).

The experience of biological time

The next group of metaphors deals with the time of anticipation, projection, and imagination.

Excerpt 2.10
Learning a language is like:

22 eating popcorn—once you've had one kernel you reach for another
23 geometry: logical, reliable
24 learning science: either you get it or you don't
25 growing a plant; if you do not feed and care for it daily, it dies
26 mowing the lawn; you can't stop learning and practicing or else it will grow out of control
27 standing in front of a door and having a huge ring of keys and trying to find the right one to open it and thinking the whole time about the great treasures that lie beyond that door!

Metaphors 22–6 see language learning as a food addiction or an organic growth that has to be fed and kept under control. It is a predictable, logical process like the growth of plants and grass, and the appetite for popcorn. Metaphor 27 arguably fits into that group because it thematizes anticipation and imagination and the belief that, once the door is opened, great treasures will be revealed. The metaphors stress the logical continuity from one stage of learning to the other and the anticipated benefits. Pleasure comes here from the ability to imagine the future.

Pain at not being able to anticipate the future

The following cluster, by contrast, highlights the frustration at not being able to anticipate events and being caught in a repetitive present.

Excerpt 2.11
Learning a language is like:

28 walking on a frozen lake without being able to see where the ice is thin
29 being transferred into a somewhat frustrating world in which reference is not always stable, since the word does not always come to mind, and the word that does come to mind might be incorrect
30 getting hit by a truck over and over again
31 having a six-inch nail pounded into my head every morning at nine
32 waking up daily at 9:30 and carrying 200 lbs of bricks back and forth across the Bay Bridge.

In these metaphors, the frustration and physical pain is expressed in spatial terms through passive verbs, expressing physical duress (*being transferred, getting hit, having…pounded*) and, in number 32, a verb of action (*carrying*) without movement, since the bricks are merely displaced from one end of the bridge to the other and back again. Here, language learning is viewed as an experience of space without movement in any particular direction, and without the sense of sight that would allow the subject to orient him or herself—a kind of circular, mythical time that does not seem to include progress in any direction.

Physical experience of embodied change

The next metaphors are built around two clauses representing a change in condition from frustration to pleasure.

Excerpt 2.12
Learning a language is like:

33 putting on a brand new pair of shoes; it's uncomfortable at first, but you break them in
34 having cement poured into your mouth and EBMUD [East Bay Municipal Utility District] coming to jackhammer it out
35 a dove held captive since birth and finally let go free; or my eyesight blurred most of my life and finally receiving glasses
36 learning to ice skate; at first the process is technical and mechanical, and only after much practice does one attain fluidity and grace
37 at first...pulling teeth, and now...putting finishing touches on a beautiful painting
38 a fine wine, better with age
39 a sense of satisfaction/accomplishment when I have crafted a perfect phrase
40 finding a friend in a crowd.

The first five metaphors are built around the same double syntactic movement: 'At first...but then/and then/and now/and finally...'; the last one collapses the two clauses into one: '[At first you feel lost in a crowd, but you end up] finding a friend.' They all express the joy that comes from relief of pain or anxiety. Note that the joy is not in the state of painlessness itself, but in the relief, the transition, the relation of one to the other. It is almost as if one can appreciate the achievement only if one appreciates the trajectory in time and the emotional and physical tension that accompanies it. This tension between frustration and pleasure gets resolved now in the metaphor that can hold both in the same embrace or in a retrospective glance on the past in light of the present.

Enhancing the self

To these self-conscious metaphors, another group of metaphors adds the self-centeredness of the language-learning experience and the feeling of self-enhancement it brings about.

Excerpt 2.13
Learning a language:

41 is like learning how Ford cars work instead of just Chevy
42 makes me sound more educated, like an intelligent person, accomplished, like native Japanese

43 makes me feel educated, cultured, and urbane all at once, distinguished
44 [is like] becoming one of them, and participating in their fascinating conversations
45 makes me like myself. I become a little more introspective as a result.

While number 41 was written by a student of German, numbers. 42–5 are representative of the kind of metaphors generated by students of French or Japanese, and by writers of French, Arabic, or Chinese. They are rarely encountered in my data among students of Spanish or German. As I mentioned above, desire is heavily conditioned by the cultural stereotypes and fantasies prevalent among students.

Becoming a trickster of language

The desire for renewal and self-enhancement is closely related to the pleasure of dissimulation, and the power that comes from seeing without being seen, that we find expressed explicitly in this set of metaphors.

Excerpt 2.14
Learning a language is:

46 like having a secret, especially when you can talk about someone and the others don't understand what you're saying
47 neat...no one knows what I'm writing: they don't even have the slightest clue
48 like getting away with murder (grammatically)
49 another secret code between friends.

Much has been made of the desire of language learners to gain access to a community of native speakers. What we find in metaphors 46–9 is, by contrast, the pleasure caused by forming a secret community, that draws special privilege and distinction from the use of a foreign code, because it excludes others.

Breaking spatial boundaries

This special distinction is seen as enabling the members of this community to explore undiscovered terrain and to satisfy learners' natural inquisitiveness, as we can see from the next cluster.

Excerpt 2.15
Learning a language is like:

50 entering a dark strange terrain
51 exploring new places
52 spelunking in a cave with challenges of unknown passages and total darkness
53 a long winding road, with each turn you are a step closer, but there is always another unforeseen twist ahead
54 adventuring into uncharted waters

55 standing at the edge of a cliff, when the wind is blowing me back, away
    from the sea—but I want to be on the edge and capable both of falling
    and of seeing clearly what is below
56 opening secret doors or Christmas packages.

Metaphors 50–6 display some of the themes we have encountered already:
challenges, risks, a gambling spirit, and the ability or inability to anticipate
events and conquer space. But here the accent is put less on physical endurance
and prowess than on curiosity, adventure, and exploration: strange terrains,
new places, caves and unknown passages, winding roads, unforeseen twists
in the road, uncharted waters, cliff edges, and secret doors. The vocabulary is
taken from the adventure and mystery stories that nourish the imagination of
adolescents and young adults.

The reflexive self

Two metaphors touch on an aspect of language learning that we have not seen
up to now and that highlights the reflective nature of learning a new symbolic
system.

Excerpt 2.16
Learning a language is like:

57 swimming in mud and *watching it* turn into water
58 going to the candy store but instead of buying candies to eat, it's more
    like tasting them and *forcing myself to try to remember exactly how
    they tasted.* (emphases added)

We notice here the objectification of the language-learning process that
requires both production and performance and an objectified account of the
performance—a highly conscious process in adolescent and adult learners in
instructional settings.

The final cluster of metaphors was generated by more advanced learners
mostly in response to the trigger: 'Writing in this language is like…:'

Excerpt 2.17

59 Writing in a foreign language is like painting on a blank canvas; I can
    use any of the tools I have to create a living work of art
60 Fluidity of the strokes; elegance
61 drawing with all the beautiful accent marks, like recreating an ancient
    language
62 all the cool tildas [*sic*] and ç that make the normally dull vowels look
    so pretty and alive. Personally, I think that the –ão is really sexy, but
    the –é has a kind of aggressive look. My mom warned me about those
    types of letters.

Not only are the foreign characters seen as aesthetically—and erotically—
pleasing, and writing perceived as creating an elegant, beautiful 'work of

art', but in no. 59 the learner seems to include himself in his writing to form a 'living' work of art, that symbolically transforms him through the foreign signs.

What all these statements have in common is their self-centeredness and physicality. Learning a foreign language makes these students more conscious of their bodies (emotions, feelings, appearance, memories, fantasies) and of the language's body (its sounds, tastes, shapes, and forms). In the case of adolescent and young adult learners, the physicality of the experience adds to an already exacerbated consciousness of their corporeal presence in the world. The metaphors they generated reflect the world of young Northern Californians who, over the weekend, may surf the waves, or drive cars across the Bay Bridge into San Francisco or along the cliffs overlooking the ocean, where they may windsurf or handglide. Like all metaphors, these map a concrete source onto the abstract target of maneuvering around grammatical difficulties, navigating treacherous lexical waters and dealing with the unpredictabilities of human cross-cultural communication. The genres from which the students draw their metaphors are familiar to teenagers: tales of quest and conquest, mystery novels, adventure stories, exploration reports, *Arabian Nights*, and others. In trying to express their personal experience, they draw on a common stock of intertextual references that might have been different in a different cultural context. We shall return to these narrative dimensions of the multilingual subject in Chapter 5.

The embodied self that comes across in language memoirs and learners' statements has been conceptualized by somatic theories and ecological theories of the self.

3 Somatic theories of the self

This section draws on the work of brain neuroscientist Antonio Damasio (1994, 1999, 2003) who has explored emotions and the somatic relation (from Greek: *soma*, body) of body and mind, and on the work of John Schumann (1997) and others who have studied the role of neurological mechanisms and affect in language learning from the perspective of somatic theory. They all consider the self as the relation of body and mind. What can we learn from somatic theory about the kind of embodied self that gets developed when one learns a foreign language?

3.1 Body and mind

Brain neurologists such as Damasio show that the strict dichotomy Watson made between the body and the mind does not hold. In *Descartes' Error* (1994), he demonstrates, through various case studies of people with brain damage, that cognition is embodied, and that the body and the mind are inseparable. The mind is not in the brain but is the combination of body and brain. In fact, rational cognition, judgment, agency, and moral value, that are usually associated with the brain, could not exist without emotions, usually associated with the body, for it is emotions that guide us in our decision on what to select from the onslaught of information we receive, and which direction we should take to ensure the physical and social survival of our organism.[5]

3.2 Images and representations

We saw in the last chapter that learning a language was primarily a matter of perception—our bodies hear spoken sounds and see shapes on a page—and a matter of processing and representing the acoustic and visual input through various symbolic means. But the body is not a passive recipient of perception of the outside world. The brain, according to Damasio, is constantly and actively producing images of the body, or bodymaps, that in turn affect the way the body reacts to the outside world. The body/mind never ceases to listen to itself, as it is listening to others.[6] While our mind is actively representing the words and their grammatical and lexical meanings, it is also busy representing itself in the process. In an effort to ensure its biological and emotional continuity, the body reaches into the timeless representation and construction of an idealized, ahistorical self.[7]

Damasio distinguishes three basic kinds of images or representations produced by the mind:

1 *Perceptual images* are formed of various sensory modalities: the shape of German letters, the sound of foreign voices. The students above have captured them through such metaphors as 'having cement poured into your mouth', or 'pulling teeth', or tasting 'a fine wine', or 'finally receiving [eye]glasses'.

2 *Constructed images* are constructions of the mind based on past perceptual images or on projected events that might or might not happen in the future. For example, the image-sound that Kaplan recognizes as the morning greeting on the Swiss news (Excerpt 1.1), or the alarm bells set off by the alien forms of the French language in Watson's perception (Excerpt 1.2) constitute the construction not just of present perception, but of a past that was and of a possible future. We can see this construction at work in the learners' metaphors (Excerpt 2.10) that represent the recall of a past experience to anticipate the future ('eating popcorn—once you've had one kernel you reach for another', or 'learning science—either you get it or you don't'; or 'putting on a brand new pair of shoes—it's uncomfortable at first, but you break them in' (Excerpt 2.12). The inability to recall images of the past to predict the future is a characteristic of language learners such as Hoffman for whom the language was reduced to its referential meanings, without the symbolic aura that gave it subjective meaning and relevance. The students' statements above express this absence of a linguistic past through metaphors of pain in Excerpt 2.11.

3 *Dispositional representations* are images stored not as facsimile pictures of things, words, or sentences, but rather as patterns along which memory does not replicate but reconstructs the past. Dispositional representations are potential patterns of neural activity, traces of past firing patterns, rather than images themselves. Precisely because, unlike images, they are not organized in any particular topographical pattern, they can, once activated, reconstruct old images as new ones. Thus, for example, the young Makine's mythical construction of Neuilly-sur-Seine as a Russian village (Excerpt 1.10) remains in the memory of the adult as a dispositional representation that he reactivates upon telling the story. The students above experienced this reconstruction in the mythical representation of themselves as, for example, 'more educated', 'accomplished' when learning Japanese, or 'cultured', 'urbane', 'distinguished' when learning French (Excerpt 2.13).

The images and representations analyzed by Damasio converge with the image-schemas of cognitive linguistics discussed in the previous chapter. We categorize people and events according to idealized cognitive models that have an immediate, incontrovertible, physical reality in our neural pathways. What somatic theory offers is a biological correlate to a semiotic theory of symbolic forms that uses symbolic representation, memory, and projection to shield the body from the contingencies and unpredictabilities of historical time and the random diversity of social experience.

3.3 Emotions and feelings

Whereas we tend to use the terms *emotion* and *feeling* interchangeably, Damasio makes a distinction between the two. Emotions are movements of the organism (Latin *ex*, out of; *motio*, movement), unconscious neural patterns that come before (and sometimes independently of) any feeling. Feelings emerge from these neural patterns or bodymaps generated by the brain. They are image-representations of the state of our body relative to itself and to external objects. They are always linked with bodily states of pleasure or pain, that is, of internal stability (or homeostasis) or instability, and of the body being in harmony or disharmony with its environment. We have seen how, in certain situations, a false bodymap is created to block pain or fear, as in Excerpt 1.6, when Tawada decided to pronounce an unpleasant-sounding German word while thinking of a pleasant Japanese word that has a similar sound.

Damasio distinguishes two different kinds of emotion that correspond to two kinds of feeling.

1 *Primary emotions* are the result of neural activity in the limbic circuitry, the amygdala, and other early sensory cortices of the brain. They constitute someone's emotional state-of-being and are visible through a combination of tone of voice, body posture, pitch, etc. When these effects extend over a certain length of time, they can constitute someone's 'mood'. For example, in Excerpt 1.3, Tawada describes how, in her first months of living in Germany,

her body was in a constant mood of frustration. The feelings that correspond to these universal, primary emotions—happiness, surprise, sadness, anger, fear, or disgust—are unconscious representations of the body, not related to any particular object in the external world. They can be triggered by general states of the body, such as when one feels happy just because one's body is healthy and at peace with itself or, on the contrary, ashamed and dissatisfied. Makine describes basic happiness growing up in a small village in Siberia (Excerpt 1.10). Hoffman associates Polish rivers with primary feelings of vitality, warmth, and immersion (Excerpt 1.9). Their feelings of well-being are not necessarily linked to any particular village or river, but to the timeless, mythical 'villageness' of Russian villages and the 'riverhood' of Polish rivers. By contrast, Kaplan felt dissatisfied with what she perceived as the intrinsic dreariness of rural Minnesota. Primary feelings correspond to the prevailing state of our body when it is not 'moved' by secondary emotions.

2 *Secondary emotions*, that originate in the prefrontal areas of the brain, are changes in the body state: racing heart, tense muscles, sweaty palms, hair on end, visceral sensations, etc. caused by some external object or by remembered or imagined objects. Emotions, being unconscious neural processes in the body, are given biological names such as 'neural activity' or 'flushed skin'. For example, in Excerpt 1.3, Tawada reports how certain German idioms gave her 'goose pimples'. The feelings associated with specific secondary emotions are differentiations of the basic primary ones, for example, excitement or euphoria as variations of happiness; depression or boredom as forms of sadness; irritation or frustration as expressions of anger; panic or shyness as aspects of fear; lack of interest or indifference as indicators of disgust. They include also social emotions: sympathy, embarrassment, shame, guilt, pride, jealousy, envy, gratitude, admiration, indignation, and contempt. These secondary emotions and feelings are linked to specific objects that the organism is solicited to respond to, for example the German sounds *ö* and *r* for Tawada (Excerpt 1.3), the Spanish sound 'amarillo' for Esteban (Excerpt 1.11), the 'cool tildas' [*sic*] and 'ão' diphtongs for the learner of Portuguese (Excerpt 2.17). S*omatic markers* are a special instance of feelings generated from secondary emotions. These somatic markers act as automated signals to warn of future dangers or future gratifications. Somatic markers, or 'gut feelings' that 'mark' the representation of emotions, are shortcuts that increase or decrease the accuracy and efficiency of the body's reaction to external events. One somatic marker, is as we saw above, was Watson's bodily revulsion and feelings of disgust when having to pronounce the sound /lwazo/ in French.

The sense of continuity of the self comes from being firmly grounded in the body and its neurological processes. It is precisely this continuity that foreign language learners lack. Tawada, in Excerpt 1.3, has no narrative of her bodily processes in German ('There was no word in my mother tongue either that expressed what I was feeling'). Hoffman, in Excerpt 1.9, feels no continuity, no 'living connection' between words and things in English.

To summarize: in somatic theory emotions are body states, feelings are bodymaps or representations of emotions. Primary emotions and their corresponding feelings are neither conscious nor tied to specific objects, they form over time the body's memory, its 'dispositional representations', patterns of neural activity that can be activated when the body encounters stimuli it has encountered before. Secondary emotions, that arise in response to specific objects, can trigger somatic markers, that is, feelings generated over time from specific experiences. In both cases, what the body remembers are not facts, persons, and events, but neural patterns associated with these phenomena. These neural patterns form the basis of meaning-making practices that are symbolic in the objective and the subjective sense: they respond both to the fragmented time of objective reference and to the holistic time of subjective memory and imagination.[8]

4 Ecological theories of the self

While recent somatic theory helps us give a biological account of what goes on in the body/mind of language learners, an ecologically oriented psychological theory can illuminate how they get to know who they are in their relation to others. In the last twenty years, the psychologist Ulrich Neisser and his associates (Neisser 1988, 1993; Neisser and Fivush 1994; Neisser and Jopling 1997) have theorized that the way we know ourselves is related to the way we know, that is, perceive, construct, and make sense of others in our environment. There are different ways in which a language learner does this.

The learner's ecological self emerges from direct perceptual experience and from the responses of the body to external and internal stimuli (be they persons, sounds, objects, or events). As we have seen in the last section, it consists of emotions and representations of body-states in the mind. It is often non-verbal, but is accompanied by a 'definite—and often powerful—kind of awareness' (Neisser 1988: 41). This is the self of Kaplan who is woken every morning by the sounds of French and becomes aware of herself hearing foreign sounds (Excerpt 1.1). This is the self of learners who become aware of the physical limitations of their bodies (Excerpt 2.8), or of the opportunities provided by the new language (Excerpt 2.9).

The learner's interpersonal self is also directly perceived, and is based on mostly kinetic information. But while the ecological self is based on the response of the organism to itself and to external objects, the interpersonal self comes into existence when the body responds *to the response* of another body engaged in personal interaction. This is the case of Kaplan trying out her new words on people around her and reacting with pleasure to their positive response (Excerpt 1.1) and of those learners who want to 'become one of the [native speakers] and participate in their fascinating conversations' (Excerpt 2.13) or share 'a secret code between friends' (Excerpt 2.14). In language learning the self develops a sense of intersubjectivity through its response to other selves. It understands others by understanding itself in tune with others.

The learner's extended self is based on memory and anticipation. Memory is both an episodic memory—the memory of specific events that happened in the past and that can be easily verbalized—and a general representation of events or scripts. It is both the things I remember having done, and the things I think of myself doing regularly. As discussed above, language learners often lack an extended self in the foreign language. This lack is described by Hoffman as 'the dessicating alchemy' of learning new names for things without being able to link them to memories and lived experiences (Excerpt 1.9). Watson compensates for this lack by applying his English-speaking extended self to his French-speaking self and finds comfort in negative, but predictable, stereotypes of the French. In language learning, a large part of what constitutes the language learner's self has to be conceived as extended in time through memories, projections, and fantasies, encoded both in the mother tongue and in the foreign language. As we have seen in the case of Molloy, mentioned in the Introduction, the extended self of a bilingual speaker might voice a word in one language, but attribute to it subjective feelings and memories associated with a similarly sounding word from another language (Molloy 2003: 73–4).

The learner's reflexive self: Neisser considered it useful to have a fourth self that is conscious of the other three—conscious not only of the outside world, but also of its own experience of the outside world. He describes this self thus: 'In addition to seeing a pencil and picking it up, one can attend to the *experience* of seeing it and picking it up' (1988: 51)—an important metaprocess that echoes the process of the brain that reflexively, albeit unconsciously, maps the body-state in the form of images that, in turn, affect the body. This is the self highlighted in learners' statements such as 'learning a language is like swimming in mud and watching it turn into water' (Excerpt 2.16). In the case of Hoffman that we saw in Excerpt 1.8, it is her private self that notices the gap between her name and the person she is. In language learning, the self is constantly engaged in reflecting upon itself, aware of its state of well-being and of its relation to others.

If learning the language of others is to lead to a better understanding of others, the reflexive self envisaged by Neisser is important for conceptualizing the way we know and understand others, that is, put ourselves in other people's shoes. It is by reflecting on our experience and seeing ourselves from this meta-place, so to speak, that our reflexive self can start remembering who we were and who we could have been and might still become, and that we can imagine the real and the potential other. Neisser calls this kind of knowledge 'a knowing founded on memory and imagination'.

> In other words, it is not a form of 'knowing that'. Nor is it like knowing how to ride a bicycle or win a battle or what to do in case of fire... that is to say, it is not a form of 'knowing how'. What then is it like? It is a species of its own. It is a knowing founded on memory and imagination [Berlin 1969: 375–6].
> (Neisser 1988: 52)

Like the interpersonal self, the extended and the reflexive self both apprehend the world in relation to others, that is, other persons in their environment and the self as observable other. But while the interpersonal self relates to others in a symbolic [1] way (based on natural and historical facts and the symbols that represent them), the extended self and the reflexive self relate to real or imagined others in a symbolic [2] way through the subjective filter of memory and the imagination. (See Introduction.)

The learner's conceptual self is the self that uses concepts, categories, and symbolic systems to make sense of reality. The way we relate to people in the social world is shaped not only by our direct perceptions and our memories and projections, but also by our theories of how we relate, or ought to relate, to others. In language learning, the conceptual self has grown out of the stories learners have been told about themselves and others, the stories they have heard told or written to others, in the family, the media, at school. Like other concepts, these theories tend to govern what learners notice and what they find relevant, as we have seen with Watson's 'theory' of what it means to be a white male American. These theories are not necessarily correct or true and they don't always match the way learners behave, but they hold on to them, for they enable them to anticipate events and deal with the inconsistencies and paradoxes of the language-learning experience.

A passage from Hoffman's memoir (1989: 218) illustrates well the multiple kinds of self we have just discussed. After several years in the New World and in her second year of graduate studies at Harvard, the Polish narrator is sitting with an American friend, Tom, in a Cambridge coffeehouse. She listens to one of his stories, what she calls 'one of his solos, his riff—that all-American form, the shape that language takes when it's not held down by codes of class, or rules of mannerliness, or a common repertory of inherited phrases'. 'A riff' she explains, 'is a story that spins itself out of itself, propelled by nothing but the imagination' (ibid.). She writes:

Excerpt 2.18
I listen breathlessly as Tom talks, catching his every syncopation, every stress, every maverick rush over a mental hurdle. Then, as I try to respond with equal spontaneity, I reach frantically for the requisite tone, the requisite accent. A Texas drawl crosses a New England clip, a groovy half-sentence competes with an elegantly satirical comment. I want to speak some kind of American, but which kind to hit? 'Gee,' I say, 'what a trip, in every sense of the word.'

Tom is perfectly satisfied with this response. I sound natural enough, I sound like anybody else. But I can't bear the artifice, and for a moment, I clutch. My throat tightens. Paralysis threatens. Speechlessness used to be one of the common symptoms of classic hysteria. I feel as though in me, hysteria is brought on by tongue-tied speechlessness.
(ibid. 219)

In this passage, Hoffman's *ecological* self has all her senses attuned to the syncopations, the different stresses and speeds of Tom's voice, but also to her body's feelings of shame and guilt. The *interpersonal* self tries to match the tune of her voice with Tom's tune. The *extended* self remembers a former Texas lover we were told about earlier (p.187), and tries to mix his drawl with her own Harvard clip, ending up with the groovy 'Gee, what a trip' of a young Texan male, followed by the satirical 'in every sense of the word' spoken by the sophisticated New England female she feels she has become. The *reflexive* self watches herself do and think all these things... and stalls ('clutches'), horrified and ashamed at her own ability to usurp so perfectly the language of the native speaker. The *conceptual* self makes sense of the whole event by attributing it to a hysteria induced by speechlessness—a metaphoric way of explaining a phenomenon that is familiar to non-native speakers using someone else's language.

To summarize: an ecological theory of the self complements somatic theory by relating the self to various ways of knowing—perceptual, interpersonal, based on memory and the imagination, reflexive, conceptual—that use symbolic forms to make that knowledge meaningful.

5 The missing link: the narratorial self

But there is one aspect of published language memoirs that keeps nagging the reader. How do we know that this is how these writers really experienced things? After all, these are talented writers, who have carefully put together a narrative of language learning that borders on the literary. These narratives fit into conventional genres of autobiographical writing (Pavlenko 2001a) that can be recognized by a larger readership and published by reputable publishing houses. These stories are undoubtedly true, but this truth might be of a different kind from the truth found in social science data.

Hoffman's memoir is neither the transcript of a psychoanalytic session, nor data collected by a psycholinguist. It is a literary creation, produced by the *narratorial self* of a Polish speaker writing in English for an anglophone audience. Somatic and ecological theories fall short of this crucial dimension of the multilingual self. This self has exquisite control over the cadence of her sentences, masters the art of epigram, and shows the reader that she has read Freud on hysteria, thus anticipating the time when she will inform her reader that she has undergone psychoanalysis (Hoffman 1989: 261). It is a self who is highly conscious of her art and of her ability to combine narrated events (Texas lover, Tom's friendship, psychoanalysis) to evoke in the reader the very same emotions of pleasure and distress that she, as an author, experienced at the time. We get to know the author's multiple selves only through the discourse of this narratorial self. But we don't get to know them only in their transient truths. The narrative, framed here as a memoir in three parts 'I Paradise', 'II Exile', 'III The New World', yields transcendental truths of mythic proportions. It echoes other myths of paradises lost and regained, promised lands, betrayals, and new beginnings. Hoffman's memoir would never have gained the success it had if it did not resonate deeply with the mythic uncon-scious of immigrants and language learners who identify with her adventures and are ultimately buoyed up by them.

So let us return to the narrator's description of the scene. Here is the auto-biographical Eva, in perfect command of English, giving her friend Tom a perfectly appropriate response—what more does she want? She has shown perfect communicative competence, but *she knows* that she is putting on an act and she feels ashamed and, possibly, guilty. As a conceptual self, Hoffman might have followed the usual view that the physical symptoms of taut throat muscles, paralysis, and speechlessness are brought on by the psychosomatic illness called hysteria. But as a narratorial self, who depends on speech for her well-being and her sense of self, she constructs speechlessness itself as the cause for the feelings of hysteria she experiences. This hysteria is to do precisely with the feelings of transgression, usurpation, and betrayal that sometimes accompany the use of someone else's language and 'passing' for a native speaker (Piller 2002). By constructing these feelings in writing, the narratorial self can be said to exorcise the hysteria.

The notion of narrative construction of self enables us to draw from Damasio and Neisser's theories without taking on their rather static meta-phors of the self. We are no longer dealing with *images, maps, representations*, and various *aspects* of self, but with *constructions, relations, simulations, synchronicities*. It is narrative that allows Hoffman to construct herself both as a native speaker and as a freak, and to make it possible for her readers to suspend their disbelief.

SLA theory has focused mainly on two kinds of knowledge in language acquisition: *knowing that* (facts about the language) and *knowing how to* (language performance). The narratorial self brings into focus the indis-pensable role of private memory and imagination in language learning: *remembering how* (past experiences and emotions) and *imagining what if* (future scenarios for action). Many aspects of the narratorial self overlap with those of Neisser's conceptual self, but the narratives we consider in this book do not represent only the conceptual self of their authors. They are also artistic constructions of narrators who abide by the conventions of accept-able genres, albeit with their own style and voice. The conceptual self has to be seen as the voice of reason, logic, and symbolic mediation. The narratorial self gives a voice to poetic verisimilitude, myth, and aesthetic practice.

6 Understanding the embodied self in language

Language memoirs and learners' statements capture some important aspects of the relation of body and mind in language learning. The symbolic nature of language discussed in the last chapter plays itself out in the body of language users in the form of representations that are at once objective as emotions and subjective as feelings. As emotions and feelings, they are associated with the serious life of the self: desire, fear, and survival. The body does not respond directly to input or impulses from outside, but to idealized representations that it has constructed within itself over time. The impulse to learn a foreign language, and when learning it, to actually acquire it well or not, might have less to do with the objective demands to get a job, become integrated into a native speaker community, identify with native speakers or with a particular ideology, and more to do with the fulfillment of the self, that is, the drive of the learner for physical, emotional, and social equilibrium. I deliberately use terms such as *impulse* and *drive*, and not *appraisal* or *evaluation* (see Schumann 1997) to suggest the urgency and the intensity of the desire or repulsion that can accompany the learning of another language. We return to this desire in the next chapter.

Emotions and feelings are part of the larger category called *affect* in SLA research, but the distinction Damasio makes between emotion and feeling is useful to understand such phenomena as empathy, identification, and alienation in language learning. Emotions or body states are generated through experienced, remembered, or imagined events, before any feeling appears, but they always entail the possibility of generating the corresponding feelings. The separation of emotion and feeling enables us to empathize with others by imagining their pain via a reactivation in our body of dispositional representations, that is, patterns of neural activity associated with pain. When this happens, it enables a learner of German, for example, to empathize with Goethe's Werther by identifying with his sorrows, even if he has not had the exact same experience, because his neural circuits may 'remember' similar experiences even if his conscious mind does not. As we shall see in Chapter 5, literature appeals to emotions through the evocation or description of the emotions and feelings of others, that in turn trigger in the reader's mind a representation of physical states that his or her body has experienced in the past or could experience in the future.

The separation of emotion and feeling further enables us to understand how actors can, through memories or body conditioning, activate the necessary neural patterns that will put their body in the state necessary to enact a given emotion. In turn, the emotion may generate the corresponding feeling. Many language learners, like actors and the authors of language memoirs, have mastered the art of loosening the link between emotion and feeling, in order to establish some distance between themselves and the new language they are trying to gain control over. In the beginning, they might, like Hoffman, deplore this distance (Excerpt 1.8), but as they become more proficient they can gain pleasure from it and even a sense of power.

Finally, as discussed in the Introduction, intersubjectivity is not just a matter of interacting with an Other. It is, rather, an appropriateness or coordination of bodies with themselves and their environment, language learners with themselves and the foreign language, non-native speakers with other non-native and with native speakers, teachers with their students. Appropriateness here is not just an adherence to pragmatic or social norms, but a deep coordination of body and mind, self and other. A better term might be relationality or synchronicity, in which the organism feels in sync with itself, its language, its environment and others (see Note 5). In the next chapter, we explore in greater detail this relation of Self to Other necessary for the construction of the subject—a subject that is at once real and symbolic, embodied and imagined.

Notes

1   The passages below are also cited in Schumann (1997).

2   As the French sociologist Pierre Bourdieu (1991: 86) pointed out, the mouth is a major component of a person's articulatory style. It is part of his or her bodily hexis, i.e. 'a certain durable way of standing, speaking, walking and thereby of feeling and thinking' (ibid. 69–70). Bourdieu describes how, in France, popular usage condenses the opposition between the bourgeois relation and the popular relation to language in the sexually overdetermined opposition between two words for 'the mouth': *la bouche* [the mouth] and *la gueule* [dog's muzzle]. Both the French and the American popular imaginations map the size of the mouth onto sexual potency, but the French, in addition, map it onto social class. Bourgeois and petit-bourgeois dispositions, as they are envisaged in the popular mind, are associated with being petty, tight-lipped, and fussy (*faire la petite bouche* = to have a small mouth, to be fussy, difficult to please, and therefore feminine), whereas *la gueule* as in *casser la gueule* = to smash your face in, or *gueuler* 'to bawl' connotes the calm certainty of strength and the capacity for physical violence associated with the working class.

3   Watson's resistance to French is linked to an idealized cognitive model of manliness that Bourdieu would interpret as mapped onto the perceived ruggedness of the working class versus the perceived effeminate mores of the dominant bourgeois class. 'It is not surprising that...the adoption of the dominant style is seen as a denial of social and sexual identity, a repudiation of the virile values which constitute class membership. "Opening one's big mouth" means refusing to submit, refusing to "shut up" and to manifest the signs of docility that are the precondition of mobility. That is why women can identify with the dominant culture without cutting themselves off from their class as radically as men [because they have been socialized into greater docility than men...but] this docility leads one towards dispositions that are themselves perceived as effeminate' (Bourdieu 1991: 88). The revival of French-bashing in the American press during the war in Iraq was linked only marginally to the French government's opposition to the war. It awakened age-old stereotypes about French effeminacy and Anglo-American virility that we see replicated in Watson's (tongue-in-cheek) discourse. It is worth noting that the French stereotypes of Anglo-Saxons run along similar lines.

4   The students' choice of descriptors had only minimally to do with the actual teaching methodology used in class. It was more likely determined by a host of factors: family heritage, films and TV, national stereotypes, prior travel, dreams of escape, romantic aspirations, perceptions of self. The representations of the language and of the target culture seemed to be a strong motivating factor for the immense effort they had to put into learning the language, even if these were very often of the stereotypical kind. These findings, however, might be an artifact of the limited sample of students in each group.

deeper nature of my German; *it was a belated mother tongue, implanted in true pain (es war eine spät und unter wahrhaftigen Schmerzen eingepflanzte Muttersprache)*. The pain was not all, it was promptly followed by a period of happiness, and that tied me indissolubly to that language. It must have fed my propensity for writing at an early moment. (Canetti 1977/9: 70, emphasis added)

Canetti's striking oxymoron of an 'implanted mother tongue' is able to capture the paradox of learning a language that is both foreign and familiar and that was learned with all the emotions associated with the child's loss of his father and love for his mother. The drastic condensation of the metaphor MOTHER TONGUE AS IMPLANT expresses with poetic clarity his ambivalent feelings vis-à-vis his 'mother' tongue—a tongue 'set free' as he chose to title his memoirs, and yet not his own. Canetti's metaphor of an implanted mother tongue blends the cultural space of grafts, implants, and artificial inseminations with the natural realm of mother tongues and other native inheritances.

But the narrator goes one step further. In his account, all the events he experienced in his childhood in various languages got stored in his memory as 'German' events. The fairy tales told in Bulgarian by the maids, the songs sung in Armenian by the woodcutter, the Ladino Spanish spoken to him by his parents and his family were all overwritten, he says, by the German symbolic system that was his parents' language and that his mother 'implanted' in him when he was eight. It is in this language that he now writes.

Excerpt 3.2

Of the fairy tales I heard, only the ones about werewolves and vampires have lodged in my memory. Perhaps no other kinds were told... Every detail of them is present to my mind, but not in the language I heard them in. I heard them *in Bulgarian [auf Bulgarisch]*, but *I know them as German [ich kenne sie deutsch]*; this mysterious transposition is perhaps the oddest thing that I have to tell about my youth... All events of those early years were in Spanish or Bulgarian. It wasn't until much later that most of them *were translated into German within me [haben sich mir ins Deutsche übersetzt]*. Only especially dramatic events, murder and manslaughter so to speak, and the worst terrors *have been retained in me [sind mir geblieben]* in their Spanish wording, and very precisely and indestructibly at that. Everything else, that is most things, and especially anything Bulgarian, like the fairy tales, *I carry around as German [trage ich deutsch im Kopf.]*
(Canetti 1977: 15; my translation, emphases added)

The switch from 'in Bulgarian' (*auf Bulgarisch*) in line 4 to 'into German' (*ins Deutsche*) in line 5 to 'as German' (*deutsch*) in the last line indexes a progressive germanification of the narrator as subject. But it also signifies a switch from a code of speech (*auf Deutsch*/in German, *ins Deutsche*/into German) to a mode of being, expressed by an attribute (*deutsch*/German in the last line) that one could translate as 'german-ly'. The narrator represents this switch as occurring without his doing, as we can see from the abundance of reflexive passives and static verbs in this passage (*haben sich mir ins Deutsche übersetzt, ich kenne sie deutsch, sind mir geblieben, trage ich deutsch*), as if his body was unconsciously switching symbolic worlds.

Canetti the writer was literally reborn in/into/as German and so was his embodied self. This rebirth was a total reunification, on the symbolic plane, with a Germanness that was itself symbolic of the love between his two parents (his Spanish mother and Bulgarian father had courted each other in German when they met in Vienna). Canetti attributes his commitment to German to his deep desire to link up with his father, and his subsequent return to his mother, who was a lover of literature. His passion for German literature becomes easily understandable as his deep desire to recapture the subjective beneath the social use of language of his mother's audiolingual and translation drills. In fact, his obsessive return to a mythical Other becomes a source of distress for his mother when she visits him in Zurich in 1921. She finds him immersed in his beloved German literature and oblivious to the world around him. She calls him arrogant and a parasite, and urges him to go to Germany, 'a country marked by the war'. Her stern admonition makes a profound impression on him:

> Excerpt 3.3
> 'You think it's enough to *read* about something in order to know what it's like. But it's not enough. Reality is something else. Reality is everything. Anybody who tries to avoid reality doesn't deserve to live.' ... Each of her words lashed me like a whip, I sensed that she was being unjust to me and I sensed how right she was ...
> (Canetti 1979: 264–5)

> I was smitten with letters and words [*ich war den Buchstaben und den Worten verfallen*], and if that was arrogance, then she had stubbornly raised me in that way. Now she was suddenly carrying on about 'reality', by which she meant everything that I hadn't as yet experienced and couldn't know anything about ...
> (ibid. 266)

> The only perfectly happy years, the paradise in Zurich, were over. Perhaps I would have remained happy if she hadn't torn me away. But it is true that I experienced different things from the ones I knew in Paradise. It is true that I, like the earliest man, came into being only by an expulsion from Paradise [*Es ist wahr, daß ich, wie der früheste Mensch, durch die Vertreibung aus dem Paradies erst entstand*].
> (ibid. 268)

Even though this narrative is written so as to fit the larger myth of the fall and the expulsion from Paradise, it illustrates the dangers of myth that we discussed in the Introduction. The mother feared that Elias's desire to escape into literature would enclose him in a narcissistic world of the imagination and would prevent him from interrogating his living relationship with real others in everyday life.

Many language memoirs single out a decisive moment of emotional separation or alienation that accompanies a death in the family, the emigration to a foreign country, a parents' divorce, or allegiances to two nations at war. While the events themselves are different, the losses and separations are all mapped subjectively onto the languages experienced by the child. After the death of his father, the eight-year-old Canetti is taken by his mother to Vienna, where he is exposed to German. After the death of her father, the 13-year-old Kaplan is taken by her mother to Montpellier, where she is exposed to French. Both authors describe the world of the father as weighing heavily on their desire to learn the foreign language—for Alice, because her father had been involved in pursuing war crimes in Europe; for Elias because his father had first taught him how to read and discuss history books. Similarly, in *Hunger of Memory* (1982), the Mexican-American narrator Rodriguez recounts how his awareness of and shame concerning his Mexican parents' lack of English (a shame fueled by the school), spur his efforts to learn English. His identification with the English-speaking Other and the impossibility of identifying with the Spanish-speaking world of his parents serve to color his language-learning experience.

In other memoirs, it is the parents' divorce that is translated into linguistic alienation. In *Enfance*, the French writer Nathalie Sarraute, of Russian origin, recounts the traumatic and endless train rides she used to make between her family in Russia and her family in France and her feelings of being torn between the two. Sarraute describes how the child in her distress clings to language as a lifebuoy, mapping the objective distance between Russia and France onto the subjective distance between *solntze* and *soleil*:

Excerpt 3.4
Now and then my distress abates, I fall asleep. Or else, I amuse myself
by chanting the same two words in time with the sound of the wheels ...
always the same two words which came, no doubt, from the sunlit
plains I could see out of the window ... the French word *soleil* and the
same word in Russian, *solntze*, in which the 'l' is hardly pronounced,
sometimes I say sol-ntze, pulling back and pushing out my lips, with
the tip of my curled up tongue pressing against my front teeth, and
sometimes, so-leil, stretching my lips, my tongue barely touching
my teeth. And then again, sol-ntze. And then again, so-leil. A mind-
destroying game [*un jeu abrutissant*] which I can't stop. It stops of its
own accord, and the tears flow. I knew we were at the border.
(1984: 94–5)

Separation may also be identification with a divided Other. The language learner is portrayed as striving to bring together what has been separated by history. For instance both Sartre, the French writer of Alsatian origin, and

Dorfman, the English writer of Chilean origin, map their respective countries' linguistic and cultural histories onto their own. In *The Words* (1981), Sartre recounts in French how, by studying French literature, he wanted to reunite the two identities of a province that had changed hands so often between France and Germany.

Excerpt 3.5
In most of the lycées, the teachers of German were Alsatians who had chosen France and who had been given their posts in reward for their patriotism. Caught between two nations, between two languages, their studies had been somewhat irregular, and there were gaps in their culture...I would be their avenger: I would avenge my grandfather. Grandson of an Alsatian, I was at the same time a Frenchman of France...in my person, martyred Alsace would enter the École Normale Supérieure, would pass the teaching examination with flying colors, and would become that prince, a teacher of letters [en ma personne l'Alsace martyre entrerait à l'École Normale Supérieure, passerait brillamment le concours d'agrégation, deviendrait ce prince: un professeur de lettres.] (ibid. 1981: 156)

Dorfman explains how, after having lived in the US the first twelve years, then in Chile the next twelve years of his life, he comes back to the US at age 24, only to discover two years later why he really identifies with South America, not with North America. He writes, in English:

Excerpt 3.6
Quite soon I began to understand that this was probably what I needed, a continent as mixed up as I was, itself a combination of the foreign and the local, unable to distinguish at times where one started and the other ended. Before I knew what had hit me, I was entranced by a Latin America that called out to my own deeply divided, hybrid condition. I located in that culture my secret image, the mirror of who I really was, this mixture, this child who dreamed like so many Latin Americans of escape to the modern world and had found himself back here, in the South, *en el sur,* forced to define his confused destiny as if he were a character in a story by Borges.
(1999: 162)

Of course, not every language learner nor every bilingual associates learning another language with separation and alienation, even though in a great number of language memoirs the experience of learning another language is linked to the trauma of emigration. If language memoirs and other published testimonies tend to highlight alienation, it is because separation and loss form the quintessential impetus for a narrative that gives coherence to a story lived across two or more languages. It serves to legitimate a personal quest for the Other that will take various forms. We have seen already how German literature had become, for Canetti, an object of desire (Excerpt 3.3). We saw how

Hoffman fell in love with Tom's American riff—the quintessential Other for a Polish sensibility (Excerpt 2.18). One of the most dramatic renditions of such objects of desire is the adult narrator's obsession with André in Kaplan's *French Lessons*.

1.2 The Other as object of desire

The narrator Kaplan meets André at the beginning of her junior year abroad in Bordeaux, and falls in love with his physical beauty. The French language between them seems pregnant with potential meaning. She sends him a love letter that clearly blends André and the French language in their common physicality and attractiveness.

> Excerpt 3.7
> 'When I lose my words in French,' I wrote, 'a radical transformation
> occurs. My thoughts are no longer thoughts, they are images,
> visions. More important—the feeling of power in not being able to
> communicate, the feeling of being stripped down to the most fundamental
> communication. I am with you, I see black and then flashes: a leg, a sex, a
> nose. Seen, felt, tasted. The taste of your body pursues me,' I wrote. 'Like
> an essence.'
> (1993: 86)

André returns the letter with spelling and grammatical corrections (!), which, she says, makes her all the more attached to him. In hindsight, she realizes that what she really wants from André is language.

> Excerpt 3.8
> What I wanted more than anything, more than André even, was to make
> those sounds, which were the true sounds of being French, and so even as
> he was insulting me and discounting my passion with a vocabulary lesson,
> I was listening and studying and recording his response.
> (ibid.)

When André leaves her for a French girl, Maité, it is, again, Maité's language that she is most envious of.

> Excerpt 3.9
> It was the two of them against me. Two people who had the words
> and shared the world and were busy communicating in their authentic
> language, and me, all alone in my room. Maité had something I couldn't
> have, her blood and her tongue and a name with accents in it. I was
> burning with race envy.
> (ibid. 89)

Clearly her desire for André goes beyond the actual French young man. It is a symbolic Other, an ahistorical, mythic Frenchman that is the object of her desire.

Excerpt 3.10
He was in all my daydreams now. I wanted to crawl into his skin, live in his body, be him. The words he used to talk to me, I wanted to use back. I wanted them to be my words.
(ibid. 88)

I spent a lot of time reading and sitting in cafes... and writing in my diary about André and what he meant. He wanted me to be natural, and I wanted him to make me French. When I thought back on the way the right side of me had swelled up, my neck and my ear and my eye, it was as if half of my face had been at war with that project. Half of me, at least, was allergic to André.
(ibid. 89)

But desire can easily turn into disgust and revulsion, and that seems to be precisely what Kaplan's body was telling her with that mysterious swelling (which turned out to be a herpes she contracted from André). She finally understands what is happening to her:

Excerpt 3.11
It hadn't been spelling that I wanted from [André]. I wanted to breathe in French with André, I wanted to sweat French sweat. It was the rhythm and pulse of his French I wanted, the body of it, and he refused me, he told me I could never get that. I had to get it another way.
(ibid. 94)

Her own diagnosis of this adventure sounds like a textbook case of a language learner who in the end realizes that her yearning for the Other can be fulfilled only in the symbolic realm—by becoming a French scholar.

Kaplan's love affair with André has been read as a classic love affair between a non-native and a native speaker during a sojourn abroad, and has been used to bolster the argument that non-native speakers strive to emulate native speakers (Siskin 2003). This might be so, but it seems that the desire for the Other can often go far deeper than the passion for any given individual. The foreign language, in its symbolic dimensions, can be as intoxicating as Tristan's magic philter. But reality often falls short of desire. Kaplan had fallen in love with French long before she met André. Indeed, as I discuss in section 3 below, psychoanalytic theory would say that André was merely the incarnation of a fascination with language that was forever linked, in her body's memory, with the father she had lost. The exact nature of this link will become clear to her when she encounters the French novelist Céline's thoroughly seductive, but virulently anti-Semitic use of the French language, and she discovers that her father was an American officer at the Nuremberg trials.

We have examined published testimonies of well-known authors, who look back as adults on their childhood or adolescent experiences with a foreign language. As I pointed out in the Introduction, these are literary constructs, which invite their readers less to check the facts than to listen to themselves as readers and examine how well the experiences described in these testimonies relate to their own. Whether the narrators are foreign language learners like Kaplan, second language learners like Hoffman and Rodriguez, heritage learners like Canetti, or bilingual youngsters like Sarraute and Dorfman, their story is one of dealing with someone else's language and of trying to bond with a mythical Other through this language. This is precisely what 18- and 19-year-old college students did after reading some of these language memoirs when they were asked, as part of a class assignment, to write their own 'linguistic autobiographies'.

2 Testimonies from linguistic autobiographies

The American undergraduates whose testimonies appear below were enrolled in either of two courses. One was an 'American Cultures' course that is given every year and that yielded about 250 'linguistic autobiographies' of Asian-American students, some native, some non-native speakers of English, between 1995 and 1999 (Hinton 2001). The other was a Freshman Seminar on 'Language and Identity' that I give every year and that between 2001 and 2003 yielded about 50 linguistic autobiographies of native and non-native speakers of English learning or speaking foreign languages (see Chapter 5). The assignment in the first course was:

> Write a 2–5 page essay about your own linguistic experiences and heritage. You might want to write about your home language(s), other languages you learned as a child, foreign languages, ancestral language(s), dialects of English, family trees, linguistic adventures and misadventures.

The assignment in the second course was:

> Write a one-page essay on what it means to be multilingual and multicultural. Choose the genre, the style, the code or mix of codes you prefer. Remember that being multilingual does not necessarily mean that one uses several languages as fluently as do monolingual speakers of each language. There are various degrees of multilingualism, as there are various degrees of identification with multiple cultures.

I have chosen a cluster of testimonies from the first group (3.12–13) and three focal students from the second (3.14–15) to illustrate various aspects of the multilingual subject discussed in this chapter.

2.1 Alienation/separation

Here are some excerpts from four different Korean-American autobiographies in Hinton's corpus. The first three students are American-born of Korean ancestry, the fourth came to the US at age 12.

Excerpt 3.12

1 I am *Korean-American*. Not American or even American-Korean, but simply Korean-American. I have black hair, brown eyes, and a yellowish complexion. No matter what I did to my outside appearance, my inherent outer characteristics did not allow me to be purely American like Caucasians. I tried to hide some of the differences in my appearance and culture and tried to be American-Korean, but as I got older, I realized I could not ignore *my heritage*.
(ibid. 243, emphases added)

2 An important question popped in my mind, 'Do I want to live the rest of my life feeling unattached from my first spoken language? to *the culture that passed down in my family for generations*? Do I actually belong in any culture?' True, I guess to the last question, I feel that I do belong to a culture, one that consists of individuals who feel most identified with America… I might consider myself an American, but will they? This is not a sign of insecurity, but instead a reality faced by an Asian-American in *a white, male-dominated society*.
(ibid. 244, emphases added)

3 In my junior year, I began to realize the importance of my culture. Being Korean is part of *my identity*. I saw the folly of anglicizing my name and at that point I made a mental note to change my name back to [Korean name] in college. Now, thinking of my parents who had immigrated to find a better life in America, I find my parents' decision to cross over to be tragic… I feel a need to return to Korea… I know that I can study hard and soon become equally fluent in both languages, and by then, I will return and live in Korea.
(ibid. 245, emphases added)

4 I don't have the blond hair nor the white skin; I had lived three fifths of my life in Korea, not in the U.S.A.; and also, I definitely speak better Korean than English. All of these *segregate* me from being a white American. However, who are *the true Americans*? Isn't the U.S.A. a country for everyone? *I truly believe* that being a white American is not the only reason that makes a person a *true American*.
(ibid, emphases added)

What is striking in these young adults' testimonies is the identification with the way Anglo-Americans see them. Unlike the other authors we have considered, here are youngsters who have to various degrees mastered English, the dominant language, and yet feel rejected from the start because of their 'other' features. Their object of desire was first the blond hair, the white skin and the Anglo name, but because the Other they were supposed to emulate is a physical impossibility, alienation was built into their sense of self. Course assignments such as these allow them to reflect critically on this alienation and their relation to their English-speaking self.[2]

This relationship is ambiguous. For example, in testimony 4 above, it is not clear how the writer is positioning herself within the discourse conventions of American-English. *Who are the true Americans?* sounds like a response to the accusation that Korean-Americans are not *true Americans*, which is in itself a prejudicial statement by an Anglo-American Other. *I truly believe* is a quintessentially mainstream American phrase, borrowed here by a writer who claims not to belong to the mainstream. And in the statement: *being a white American is not the only reason that makes a person a true American*, the phrase *true American* seems to want to resignify the myth of purity claimed by the Anglo term *true*. The writer seems to be a self in search of a subject position.

In addition to a search for a subject position, we can see in these testimonies a tension between the students at once becoming English-speakers in their own right and having to prove their legitimacy as English-speakers. Words such as *Caucasian* and *Korean-American*, that are census classifications imposed by the Federal government, are interrogated: *Am I (pure) (true) American? American-Korean? Korean-American? Korean?* But references to *my heritage, my identity, the culture that passed down in my family for generations* are part of a recognizable minority discourse that has become pretty mainstream on some American campuses and is used here without being problematized. Instead the statements problematize a state of affairs that is captured in a politically correct liberal discourse with such phrases as *white male-dominated society* and the reference to *segregation*. It is as if these 'minority' students must narrate themselves in the words of the Other even though they now wish to distance themselves from the Other. On the other hand, in a society that prides itself on being democratic but is dominated by Anglo-American discourse, they have to belong to an identifiable ethnic group if they want to be listened to and respected.

All the more striking as a contrast is a Vietnamese student's composition in Hinton's corpus, in which the narrator tries to use the English language both to express his alienation and to go beyond it.

Excerpt 3.13
As for English, I do speak the language but I don't think I'll ever talk it. English is the language that flows from the mind to the tongue and then to the pages of books. It is like a box of Plato blocks which allows you to make anything. But a Plato house cannot shelter human lives and a Plato robot cannot feel! I only talk Vietnamese. I talk it with all my senses. Vietnamese does not stop on my tongue, but it flows with the warm, soothing lotus tea down my throat like a river, giving life to the landscape in her path. It rises to my mind along with the vivid images of my grandmother's house and of my grandmother. It enters my ears in the poetry of *The Tale of Kieu*, singing in the voice of my Northern Vietnamese grandmother. It appears before my eyes in the faces of my aunt and cousins as they smile with such palpable joy. And it saturates

my every nerve with healing warmth like effect of a piece of sugared
ginger in a cold night. And that is how I only talk Vietnamese.
(Hinton 2001: 243)

In this testimony, the subject reflects on his experience and on the language
that he is now using to express it. He interrogates his English-speaking self and
his Vietnamese-speaking self (putting them 'on trial' so to speak), and makes
a clever distinction between 'speaking English' and 'talking Vietnamese'. We
have here an English text with Vietnamese intertextualities. In a sense, one
could say that this student, like many non-native writers, from Chinua Achebe
to Hoffman, uses the English language to express feelings that only non-native
speakers have experienced. In other words, he seems to be using the referential
system of the Other, but permeates it with the subjective resources offered by
his non-native experience. Of course, it might be that this student has taken a
course in creative writing and has thus acquired a particularly effective writing
technique. At issue, however, is not *how* the student acquired the necessary
distance from the language of the Other, but *that* indeed he did. I discuss in
Chapter 5 how giving students the opportunity to construct themselves nar-
ratively is one way for them to understand what it means to be multilingual.

2.2 Desire

We have seen that in language memoirs alienation and separation are often
indissociable from the desire for an absent Other. Here is an excerpt from the
linguistic autobiography of a 19-year-old Anglo-American, Nathalie, who
took Spanish in high school, and is now taking German in college.

> Excerpt 3.14
> The teacher tells us to open our books. I rush to the page at the disdain
> of my classmates and raise my hand. 'Yes, Nathalie, you may read' (not
> in Spanish). So I read. The words roll off my tongue with increasing
> confidence and speed. *I don't even know what I'm saying, but I
> concentrate on making it perfect.* After finishing the paragraph I become
> instantly jealous, as the native speaker reads the next paragraph. What's
> the difference between her and me? Why does she look at me with such
> disgust? *Why aren't I worthy of the language the same way she is?*
>   Everyday I wait patiently for an opportunity to read aloud. At brunch
> I hardly say a word. In my English class I expound dryly on theme and
> tone. At lunch I eat quietly and chat with a few friends, then in Spanish
> *I long to hear my own voice again,* transformed into this *romantic
> spillage* of simple constructions, the Spanish 'r's falling from my tongue
> with ease. I'm not saying anything deep or meaningful—*it's not the
> meaning that matters. I feel Spanish. I feel new.*
>   College. *I feel the need for something else.* The classroom is an efficient
> machine, turning out kids afraid to ask German-related questions in any
> language other than German. Class is the only place *where I am allowed*

to speak, to hear the sounds that I have now become addicted to. I am given this outlet, to *say things (silly meaningless things) that I would never say in English.* My roommate is German. Why not? Then we can speak to each other and it will be fun, right? *I become engulfed in the idea of German,* constantly bugging my roommate: 'Wie sagt man...auf Deutsch?' (she rolls her eyes). Then she says: 'If you speak in German one more time I'm going to hit you!' I feel hurt. My heart is torn between wanting to speak in a language not my own or not speaking at all, *and remaining the shy withdrawn person I've grown up with.* My roommate looks at me with *that same disdain, that same irritation I remember from the native Spanish speakers in high school.* It kills me...

My bias toward music may very well be traced back to my lack of confidence in speech. In music I take on a *confidence* unparalleled in speech. Music *liberates me from my silence...* In jazz, I dare express pure ideas through improvisation and the use of my tool, the trombone. In class, I can play so passionately I could cry, *enveloped by the sounds of oneness. Never could I express such raw emotion, never could I speak so freely using a conventional language.*
(emphases added)

Nathalie's various language-learning events form a rich blend of linguistic, emotional, and aesthetic experiences that echo those of the published authors we have encountered. For her, as for the young Kaplan, meaning is not primarily in the objective reference but in the subjective experience of words (*it's not the meaning that matters*). Perfection is not necessarily approximation to the L2 rules of phonology, but has to do with the fit between her body as a mediating instrument and the forms, the sounds it produces (*I don't know what I'm saying, but I concentrate on making it perfect*). The pleasure Nathalie describes does not come from having brought her message across but from being in subjective harmony with herself, one with her words. It is a sense of plenitude and joy that comes across in many of these learners' testimonies. Hearing herself speak in Spanish enables Nathalie to monitor her speech in ways that have become blunted in her native English, it 'liberates her from [her] silence', validates her existence (*I am allowed to speak, to hear the sounds...to say things I would never say in English*). Given this overwhelming pleasure of a unified self, she expects her feeling of self-worth to come from the embodied experience itself and feels disappointed that it must measure up to a social, native speaker, norm (*Why aren't I worthy of the language the same way [the native speaker] is?*).

For Nathalie, acquiring another language is, like playing music, a highly emotional experience (*I feel Spanish. I feel new...addicted...engulfed...it kills me...my heart is torn*). It is linked to painful personal memories (*that disdain...I remember from the native Spanish speakers in high school*) and longing (*I long to hear my voice again*). The foreign language is, like music, a way for her to access a wholeness (*sounds of oneness*) that she feels she has lost in the English world of everyday life. The social rebukes she experiences along the way do not still her longing but, like Kaplan, only make it more acute. One can imagine that, like Kaplan, Nathalie will 'get by other means' what she cannot get from Spanish peers or German roommates. Finding refuge in music is one way. Another could be constructing an intersubjective and intertextual subject position in language itself, as Nathalie does in this written autobiographical narrative. I return to the construction of this narratorial self in section 3 below.

2.3 In-process/on trial

Finally, let us examine the essay that Valerie, a US-born 19-year-old Korean-American college student, wrote in the form of a poem. Valerie's first language is Korean. She started learning English when she was five, learned Spanish in high school, and is now learning Chinese in college. Her experience of multilingualism is somewhat different, but it bears some analogy to Nathalie's (I have retained Valerie's sometimes unconventional spelling).

> Excerpt 3.15
>   To belong
> *In what category do I fit?*
> Name. Valerie.
> DOB. 11/05/83
> Korean American
> Am I Korean and American?
>
> South Korea. Thecrowdedstreetsfilledwithbustlingpeople.
> They all pass by...
> An elderly *halmuni* from the local *yakgook* with medication for her ailing back
> An *ahghushi* in business garb stepping off a hurried bus
> A girl clothed in a *che-ik bok* with her *mulrhi dae-ed*
> ...and I remain unnoticed
>
> I am a cactus. Water. Need water
> *Q: Mool jool soo ees suhyo?*
> Here is fertile ground—the homeland
> *A: It can make me whole*
> *Soak in the culture*
> *Immerse yourself with Koreans*, with the language, the environment
> But I begin to drown...
> Drown...
> Drown...
> At the bottom of the pool awaits a woman.
> 'Ah you prum Ah-meh-rhi-ca?'
> *I am caught. Discovered.*
>
> California. The streets are wide. Maybe here I will feel like *I belong.*
> They all saunter by...

A woman so involved in putting on her eyeliner that she runs into me
An angry teen on the phone screaming in Spanish
A black boy running, dribbling a basketball gracefully
...am I at home here?

Yes, I was born in the U.S.
Yes, I speak the language without an accent.
So why do you stare? What more do you want?
Do you want me to dye my hair, bleach my skin, forget my history...
merely to 'assimilate'?

You're Korean?
Yep.
Jin jah? I thought you were Chinese...or Japanese.
Nope. I'm Korean. American. Korean American. Actually...
My name is Val.
I am Val. Valerie. *Hyunna.*
A daughter, sister, granddaughter, and friend
A *keun ddal, unni, sohn nyuh saekki,* and *chin goo*
A girl who loves and is loved
Sarang eul joogo battgo
No category necessary

Glosses for the Konglish (mixture of Korean and English):
Halmuni: a grandmother
Yakgook: a pharmacy
Ahghushi: middle-aged man
Che-yook bok: a school uniform
Mulrhi dae-ed: braided hair
Mool jool soo ees suhyo: Can you give me some water?
Jin jah: chin chah—gasp (oh my goodness!)
Hyunna: term of endearment used by her grandmother
Keun ddal, unni, sohn nyuh saekki, chin goo: eldest daughter, sister, grand-
daughter, friend
Sarang eul joogo battgo: You give your love and then your receive love.

Like Hinton's students, Valerie's motivation to identify with the people in South
Korea stems from the social dichotomy she feels is forced upon her in the US:
In what category do you fit? Korean or American? This very question, repeated
across census questionnaires, governmental statistics, college admissions, and
examination forms, constantly puts the subject on trial and forces her to reflect
on who she is. The question is ventriloquated on the page as a question that
she has internalized and reproduces here in the first person: *In what category
do I fit?* As Valerie herself admitted in a subsequent interview, learning Chinese
rather than, say, an advanced language or literature course in Korean, has been
her way of escaping the social categories imposed by her environment.

The theme of subjective wholeness comes back here with a cultural twist
in a dialogue Valerie entertains with herself (the same split subject we shall

see in Estella in Chapter 5). In this dialogue between Korean-speaking Valerie and English-speaking Valerie, the question is asked in Korean (*Mool jool soo ees suhyo* [Can you give me some water?]). As she noted in her subsequent interview with the researcher, the question has no addressee ('I don't know who I'm asking I'm just kinda asking'), it is the pure question mark of a body in search of a subject position. The answers are given in English (*It can make me whole, soak in the culture, immerse yourself, I begin to drown*). Like Hinton's Vietnamese student, Valerie uses the resources of the English language to express an experience that can be rendered only metaphorically.

While Nathalie desired to sound other to herself, Valerie fears being caught in disguise by 'the woman at the bottom of the pool' who finds her out. The feelings of shame, betrayal, illicit transgression, and the concomitant physical sensation of drowning echo those of Hoffman (Excerpt 2.18), Esteban (Excerpt 1.11), Chang-Rae Lee (see below) and many others, who feel they have transgressed the limits of referentiality by introducing subjective elements into their use of language. In this case, the American particularities of Valerie's Korean into the standard forms of peninsular Korean prompted the woman to recognize her immediately as coming from America. The native speaker acts as a gatekeeper against non-standard, non-legitimate uses of the language. Here, Valerie, a heritage language speaker, is made aware of the social shame that awaits anyone trying to 'pass for' a native Korean when she is, in fact, American. Conversely, the Korean-American narrator in Lee's *Native Speaker* is accused of being a 'surreptitious/B+ student of life/... illegal alien/emotional alien/... stranger/follower/traitor/spy' (1995: 5), when he speaks English like the native English speaker that he is.[3]

For foreign language speakers, who are in quite a different position of social power from immigrant English speakers, 'passing for a native' can be coupled with singular pride and pleasure. Piller's multilingual subjects describe the pleasure that non-native speakers derive from eluding classification, being taken for someone else.[4] One of them, Allan, a 33-year-old English speaker who first went to Germany at age 23 and now lives there, says: ' "I know I can't avoid that I'm a foreigner, but I enjoy it that some people don't know where from, they think...sometimes Italy or—they don't have a clue, and I quite enjoy that...I'd never hide it completely, no" ' (Piller 2002: 195). What is at first a necessity becomes the pleasure of seeing without being seen, of making yourself invisible, so to speak. Here is the testimony of a German woman studying abroad in Britain:

What is your fondest memory of England?
Ever since my first visit I have made an enormous effort to get rid of a German accent. When I first arrived at York everybody noticed something foreign in my pronunciation and took me for an American. After a few months people thought I was Scottish, which I saw as a big step towards my target accent. Just before the end of the year I ended up having a chat with an elderly couple from York and they were actually convinced that

I was from Durham, which is not far from York. Can you imagine how
proud I was?
(ibid. 191)

A Chinese-American traveler recently returned from China recounts the
change in people's perceptions of foreigners and his thrill at being taken for a
Chinese from a nearby town:

> The last time I was in China, I recalled feeling quite strongly that not
> being automatically taken for an American was a big time honor, because
> it connoted near-fluency in the language and the culture. Japan? Fine.
> Singapore? Better. Taiwan or Hong Kong? About as good as it could get.
> So imagine how I felt when I traveled to Guizhou Province, a stunningly
> beautiful and achingly poor region in China's interior... 'You're from
> America?' the man said. 'We thought you were from Machangping.'
> (Chen 2003)

But the thrill is sometimes matched by the *Schadenfreude* of those on the
other side, the native speakers, who are eager to detect the slightest trace of
an accent, real or imagined. Huston, the French-English bilingual Canadian,
living and writing in Paris, describes this game in *Nord perdu*:

> The foreigner, then, imitates. He practices, improves, learns to master
> better and better the adoptive language. There remains nevertheless,
> almost always, despite his relentless efforts, something. The small trace
> of an accent. A suspicion of an accent. Or else... an atypical melody or
> phrasing... an error of genre, an imperceptible awkwardness in the verb
> agreement... And that is enough. The French are on the look out... it is
> as if the mask slid down... and you are discovered! They have a glimpse
> of the *true you* and they pounce on it... You said 'une peignoire?' 'un
> baignoire'?... Ah, that's because you are an alien! You come from another
> country and you are trying to hide it from us, to disguise yourself as
> French, as francophone. But we are shrewd, we have guessed that you are
> not from here... Are you originally German? English? Swedish?
> (Huston 1999: 33, my translation)

Ultimately, through writing, multilingual subjects such as Valerie, Lee, and
Huston manage to define a third, symbolic place between two incompatible linguistic and cultural worlds, despite the fact that they are rejected by
both.[5] We will examine such a 'place' in Chapter 7, but for now, let us note
that Valerie found a way out of her dilemma not by sidestepping, but by
resignifying the dilemma itself, that is, by reformulating the question. What
she does, namely, is rephrase the question: '*Where* do I belong?' into '*How*
do I belong?' What does it mean to be situated in particular places, what
does it mean to belong, and what different ways (or modalities) of belonging are possible in the contemporary milieu? As the post-modern social
historian Grossberg (1997) notes: 'It is no longer a question of globality (as

homelessness) versus place (as the identification of the local territory and national or regional identity), but of the various ways people are attached and attach themselves (affectively) to the world.' Such a way of viewing identification and belonging transforms the notion of identity into that of subjectivity—from a static, spatial, territorial concept to a dynamic, spatio-temporal, symbolic concept.

> Belonging is a matter less of identity than of identification, of involvement and investment, of the line connecting and binding different events together. The question of our present and our future is a matter of the different possibilities or modalities of belonging. It is a question of the ways people are attached to, and the ways people attach themselves to—what? A complexly structured set of practices and events, a milieu. But belonging is also a production. To belong—in a different mode and in a specific temporality—or a specific piece of time-space—is also to belong to a different time-space.
> (Grossberg 2000: 154)

3 Psychoanalytic/semiotic theories of self and Other in language

The testimonies we have just discussed would no doubt provide fertile ground for psychoanalysts, but literary critics too would find in them grist to their poetic mills. We turn therefore to Julia Kristeva to theorize what is going on in these testimonies. Kristeva, who is both a Lacanian psychoanalyst and a Bakhtinian literary critic, has theorized how language, as a symbolic system, constitutes the very core of a person's Self. Her work can help us understand the subjects that learners of a second language are in the process of becoming.

3.1 The language of the other

To understand the intensity of the yearning we encountered in these testimonies, we have to take a slight detour into the world of children learning their native language. Non-native speakers are in a similar position as that described by Jacques Lacan in his famous essay 'The Mirror Stage as Formative of the Function of the I'. Lacan (1977: 1–7) showed that around the age of nine months, a child discovers that the image in the mirror is both herself and not herself. She reaches out to grasp 'herself'. But, even though the mother exclaims: 'Yes, baby, that's you!' the child realizes that this 'you' remains forever unreachable to her grasp, and experiences herself as split. This other in the mirror is, in fact, a part of the child that remains alien to her. Lacan used this mirror stage as a metaphor to explain how, like Narcissus in love with his own image and with the sound of his voice echoed by the nymph, the child will forever strive to recapture the unity of being both his own and his mother's body in the mother's womb. The realization of the split between self and other at the mirror stage occurs roughly at the same time as language emerges in the child. Language, Lacan argues, is as deceptive as the image in the mirror. It reflects reality but is not reality. It is predicated on a fundamental absence or alienation that is constitutive of the subject. Language belongs to the child who acquires it, and yet it never was hers to start with: we are all born into a world of discourse that preceded our birth and will live on after our death. Our mother tongue, says Lacan, is the language of the Other. Not only the language, but the consciousness that goes with it, are given to us from others. As the child learns to talk, the very fact of having to put feelings, desires, statements about the world into the words of others already restricts his or her range of sayable things and experiences.

To become a subject, Lacan explains, the child must abandon the pre-linguistic realm, a rhythmic space that apprehends and semioticizes, that is, gives meaning to, experience in its totality, like Hoffman and Kaplan who, as children, wanted to 'say the whole world at once' (Hoffman 1989: 11). It must embrace linguistic reality, a space of symbolic reference and denotation, that is, a world that can be designated and discussed only through the grammatical and lexical structures provided by a society's language, and experienced with the emotions indexed by these structures. For this process to take place, both absence and separation are necessary. The child cannot grow into its own without becoming aware that the words that surround him and are used to address him are not the exclusive property of his mother but are shared with a multitude of absent Others. The child must separate itself from the realm of the mother and, as Lacan says, enter the realm of the father, the social and the cultural. Without separating itself from its childlike fantasies and embracing the rules of the speech community, the subject can never come into its own nor survive. We saw an example of this in the sad story of the old man who thought he could single-handedly rename his universe and share it with his neighbors (see Chapter 1).

The child's desire is to identify so fully with mother or father that she strives to have what they have, be who they are, and become, in return, their exclusive and unconditional object of love and desire. Because this desire for total love and unity can never be fulfilled, says Lacan, it remains throughout life. It can cause a primordial, overwhelming experience of well-being that Lacan calls *jouissance* and that manifests itself in the form of intense emotional involvement, in particular with language, as we saw with Kaplan and Hoffman as children, and later, in Kaplan's infatuation with André's language. In a similar manner, the testimonies of non-native speakers show evidence of a passionate desire to become native speakers and be accepted and loved as one of them. We have seen some of this in Canetti's account of his love for German and in Kaplan's account of her interest for French to fill the void left by their respective fathers' deaths. Both Canetti and Kaplan were later forced by circumstances to confront reality.

3.2 Subject-in-process

How does the child become a subject? This is where Lacan and Kristeva diverge. For Lacan, a subject is the subject of enunciation or speaking subject, that is, the entity that emerges from positioning itself in the world through symbolic reference to an 'I'. The subject is a Self that has separated itself from its narcissistic desires, recognized and accepted its separation from the Other, and gained autonomy and agency by embracing the 'symbolic order', that is, the social world of linguistic and discourse conventions. Here the term 'symbolic' is taken in the first meaning we encountered in the Introduction as the realm of reference and denotation, or symbolic [1]. A child who has learned to speak becomes a full member of a speech community and an autonomous subject by virtue of having mastered its symbolic [1] system, according to Lacan.

But Kristeva—and our data—tell another story. Many language learners have indeed mastered another symbolic system only to feel divided in their allegiances, conflicted in their identity, or rejected from both their native and the target speech communities, as we have seen with Nathalie and Valerie, who chafed under the constraints of convention and yearned for 'wholeness'. Other language learners seem to have retained the subjective meanings associated with a more holistic apprehension of reality, or symbolic [2]. As children, Kaplan and Hoffman enjoyed making up words and using the language of adults in quite unconventional ways. Piller's multilingual subjects seem to enjoy playing at being someone else and being both in and out of distinct speech communities. Huston feels both accepted and rejected among French native speakers, even though she has become proficient enough in French to write best-sellers in the French language. The realm of the symbolic seems to be much less homogeneous and stable and the subject seems to be much less finished than Lacan would have it.

In *Revolution in Poetic Language* (1986: 99–100) Kristeva transforms Lacan's notion of subject into that of a subject-in-process. According to her, the subject emerges at the intersection of a world without words (but not without signification) and the world of words. The first she calls the realm of the semiotic, the second, following Lacan, the realm of the symbolic. The subject is born as it positions itself not within the symbolic, but at the border between the semiotic and the symbolic. This positioning process, that she calls *thetic* (from Greek *thesis* or positioning) is ongoing; the subject, always hovering on that thetic border, is never finished, it is always in construction. Because of the unstable nature of the symbolic at the border with the semiotic, the subject is not only constantly made and remade, that is, a work in progress, but it constantly interrogates and problematizes itself, because in this symbolic order, the Other is in the Self. We are, in Kristeva's famous phrase (that Hoffman picked up in Excerpt 1.8) 'strangers to ourselves' (Kristeva 1991).

Hence the French phrase *sujet en procès*, that can mean both *in process* and *on trial*. We saw examples of this double meaning in Excerpt 1.11, where the French-Spanish child Esteban struggles to define himself. Not only is he caught between two incompatible ways of experiencing the color yellow: *jaune* and *amarillo*, and struggles in the process of becoming a bilingual subject, but he also puts his French and his Spanish self alternately 'on trial' with all the concomitant feelings of shame, guilt, and defeat. We find a similarly ambivalent subject-in-process in the 13-year-old Hoffman in Excerpt 1.9, where she problematizes the English word *river* she has just acquired, realizing how unstable it is, in fact, for her and how 'unbending to the grasp of [her] mind'.

In Kristeva's words, every use of language partakes at the same time of the semiotic and the symbolic. The semiotic modality represents a pre-verbal, ahistorical, psychosomatic realm of signification, to which Kristeva (1986: 94) gives the name *chora*. In the semiotic chora, that Kristeva associates with the maternal (as distinguished from the symbolic, which Lacan sees as the domain of the father), signification is produced through a variety of material supports: voice, gesture, colors, kinetic or chromatic units and differences, resemblances and oppositions. This is the subjective domain of emotions, feelings, and beliefs. It represents many of the semiotic processes that occur in dreams, fairy tales, and children's fantasies. One of the characteristics of the semiotic modality is *rhythm*, a main component of ritual and the core of intersubjectivity. It is also the main feature of poetic discourse, that is, of creative literary and non-literary language, since, as Kristeva (ibid. 97) writes pointedly, 'literature is a rhythm made intelligible by syntax'. The symbolic modality, by contrast, represents a denotative/connotative, historical, highly structured realm of signification.[6]

Kristeva defines the semiotic as a precondition of the symbolic, and the symbolic, in turn, as allowing the subject to reflect upon itself as it makes linguistic and stylistic choices. She echoes in that sense the somatic models of the self discussed in Chapter 2, in which the body listens as much to itself as it does to others and its environment. This is the realm of the semiotic, where the subject strives for identification, replication, and homogenization and tends to see others as a mere image of itself, replicating the voices of others in its discourse. But ecological models of the self include also the symbolic, that is, the reflexive and the conceptual self that through symbolic reference can detach itself from the original semiotic chora, talk to itself as Other, and put itself in others' shoes, so to speak. Because it can do this only through the mediation of available symbolic forms, it is more accurate to say that the semiotic in Kristeva is the source of what I have called symbolic [2]—the subjective and affective meanings given to symbolic forms, their creative and performative use. By recognizing symbolic [2] in symbolic [1], and the Other in the Self, the subject can put itself on trial and show empathy and understanding.

This fundamental insight is clearly illustrated in Excerpt 2.18 where we encounter Hoffman in love with Tom's riff and searching for an appropriate response. She positions herself as a subject-in-process through three different 'I's. Here is, once again, the relevant passage with the 'I's numbered for ease of reference.

> 'Gee,' I (1) say, 'what a trip, in every sense of the word.' Tom is perfectly satisfied with this response. I sound natural enough, I sound like anybody else. But I (2) can't bear the artifice, and for a moment, I clutch. My throat tightens. Paralysis threatens. Speechlessness used to be one of the common symptoms of classic hysteria. I (3) feel as though in me, hysteria is brought on by tongue-tied speechlessness.

I (1) is Eva's 'experience of intentionality', her desire to sound like a native speaker of English by imitating the speech of her American friend Tom. I (2) is the self that judges the first I 'for its moral choices' and accuses it of artificiality. I (3) is the self that worries about its social survival as a bilingual between two worlds, and finds itself struck by speechlessness and hysteria. All three selves are symbolic selves, the first one showing some semiotic identification with its object of desire (for a discussion of personal deictics in the construction of the subject, see Benveniste 1966). But I (3) is the 40-year-old Hoffman's narratorial self, who keeps symbolic control over the story and gives a voice to I (1) and I (2).

3.3 Remodeling the symbolic order

Because Kristeva is keen on defining creativity in language and the potential of literature for bringing about 'social revolution' (ibid. 61), she goes beyond Lacan and explores the relation between the semiotic and the symbolic. She argues that the thetic phase is not as unidirectional as the emergence of language in children might suggest. In fact, the semiotic continues to irrupt into the symbolic every time subjects articulate language in ways that are different from conventional use—from the creativity displayed in everyday conversations, to language play, to the disruption and resignifying of myths and fetishistic language, to the rhythms and parallelisms of poetry, to the multilingual games we see in students' writings.[7] All these instances of language use, which Kristeva would associate with the workings of the semiotic, 'remodel' the symbolic order of speech communities.

One way of remodeling the symbolic order is to capitalize on the polysemy of words and on the diversity of systems of reference (iconic, indexical, symbolic). This means capitalizing on the diversity of what Kristeva calls 'sign systems' or genres, that is, text types. Newness comes into the symbolic order through *intertextuality,* that is, 'the transposition of one (or several) sign systems into another' (ibid. 60), such as the transformation of a *Märchen* into an anti-*Märchen* as in Bichsel's story (see Chapter 1), or an experience lived in one language and recounted in another (see Canetti in Excerpt 3.2).[8]

Foreign language learners who are able to manipulate the foreign symbolic system in such a way as to express their personal experience are often found not surprisingly to resort to metaphoric, poetic language. There are various reasons for this. The acquisition of a symbolic system that belongs to an Other can evoke deep childhood resonances and memories of one's first encounter with the Other; these memories are heavily indebted to the preverbal realm of the semiotic and are thus best expressed indirectly through parables and metaphors, as we saw in Nathalie's and Valerie's essays. While these essays are not literary masterpieces, they nevertheless are constructions of a narratorial self that is to be found not only in the ideas expressed but in the style in which they are expressed.

Furthermore, a multilingual subject position can draw on more modalities of signification than one single symbolic system, as we saw in Belz's students' multilingual journals (Chapter 1) and in Valerie's Korean and English poem. Finally, part of the privilege of using a foreign language is the ability to transform it, or, as the Italian German author Gino Chiellino says, 'dislocate it' through intertextual practices. I cite Chiellino (1995: 28) in the English translation: 'It is only by maintaining his or her difference that the foreign author writing in German can contribute to dislocating the German language. (Comment by my German editor: according to the dictionary, to dislocate is to radically disrupt. Surely that is not a desirable goal. I suggest "contribute to extending the boundaries of national goals"!)'

Chiellino's parenthetical remark about his German editor's comment reads like a gloss to Kristeva's notion of the (disruptive) semiotic. His response to the editor is enough tongue-in-cheek as to retain the flavor of the mythic discourse of a trickster who retains the upper hand in the bilingual language game, all the while that he abides by the symbolic order of the German language in his letter to his editor. An example of such a dislocation can be found in one of his poems (Chiellino 1992: 53, no title):

Wenn das Schweigen	When the silence
Gegen uns sich weiß färbt	becomes white against us
Me spagnu	I am afraid
Ja, ich deutsche mich sehr	Yes, I turn very German

In the third line, the poet first codeswitches to his Calabrian dialect (*me spagnu* = *ich fürchte mich* = I am afraid), then dislocates the German lexicon to coin a new verb *ich deutsche mich* (on the model of *ich fürchte mich*), that would mean 'I turn very German' while the reader expects the German translation of *me spagnu*, that is, 'I am very afraid'. Thus we read *ich deutsche mich* as *ich fürchte mich* with a bitter aftertaste of Germanness. Linguistic dislocation is not far from political dislocation as the following multilingual poem also shows (ibid. 77, no title):

Come together	Come together
nel mondo dei colori di Benetton	to the world of colors of Benetton
and learn to live as friends	and learn to live as friends

im Lande der Nichtraucher	in the land of non-smokers
wo die Fremde	where the foreign
wie Farben von Benetton	is smoked like colors from
geraucht wird.	Benetton.

It is left to the reader to interpret this poem as a criticism of the world of consumerism and its euphemisms (we are all 'friends' because we all buy Benetton), or of environmental correctness (a world of non-smokers) that conceals xenophobia and discrimination against people 'of color'.

3.4 The political promise of the symbolic

Throughout the last three chapters, we have heard many learners relate experiences of dislocation or transformation as they attempt to gain access to the symbolic order of the Other: the shape of foreign sounds and shapes dislocates Tawada's sense of her own body (Excerpt 1.3), Hoffman feels suddenly estranged upon hearing herself speak perfect English (Excerpt 2.18), Canetti's childhood memories undergo a linguistic metamorphosis (Excerpt 3.2), Kaplan's body shows sudden symptoms of an allergic reaction to French (Excerpt 3.10), and Nathalie not only feels rejected by her German roommate, but 'her heart is torn' between speaking the language of the Other and remaining silent (Excerpt 3.14). In each case, the dislocation is due to a sudden irruption of the semiotic, that is, the affective, embodied, idiosyncratic experience of language, into the symbolic, that is, the rational, socially sanctioned domain of language use.

This discussion of the semiotic in Kristeva brings us back to the discussion we had about myth in the Introduction to this book. A contemporary of Kristeva, Michel Foucault sees in the creative force of the semiotic a kind of myth-making, or mytho-poiesis, that can serve to counteract the overly positivistic/scientific discourse of our times. In his posthumously published lectures at the Collège de France 1975–6, Foucault (2003) argued that the problem is not myth itself, as Barthes suggested, but the political uses that have been made of myth, that is, its naturalization in the service of power or what he calls 'biopolitics'—a way of governing people that emphasizes the biological integrity of a nation, its God-given mission, and its 'manifest destiny'. In fact, he argues, myth, critique, and revolt work together, 'because myth fosters an opening, a polyvalent strategy that refuses to be discursively or intellectually contained' (Murray 2003: 217). Myth is endowed with 'insurrectionary and emancipatory power' (ibid.), it is the 'counterdiscourse to sovereignty' (ibid. 208). Myth, then, has to be seen as the indispensable ingredient for the emergence of the multilingual subject who, by appealing to the semiotic, strives to liberate itself from the dominance of a monolingual symbolic order. But if it turns into ahistorical slogans and ready-made formulas, myth can threaten the autonomy of the multilingual subject and reduce multilingualism to just a polyglot exercise or a fashionable trend.

In this chapter, we have encountered two major concepts for understanding the multilingual subject: the *thetic space*, located at the shifting boundary between the symbolic and the semiotic, enables the language user to establish a subject position both in conformity with and in opposition to the dominant symbolic order; and the *subject-in-process* that is constantly engaged in interrogating and problematizing itself and the discourses that shape it. From the insights offered by Lacanian psychoanalysis and Kristeva's semiotics, and from the testimonies of learners themselves, we can say that language learners experience a fundamental paradox. On the one hand, they experience the pain of using a symbolic [1] system that irremediably belongs to others, whose use is to a large extent dictated by others, and that enables them to measure the distance that separates the Self from the Other. On the other hand, by gaining access to that symbolic order they become subjects who can choose to reproduce or subvert the symbolic [1] order by letting the symbolic [2] operate its silent poetic and social revolution. Such a revolution can be the source of immense pleasure and intense joy. Language can never express all that its users want it to express, yet it expresses much more than they ever intended. In all cases, myth and metaphor serve to open up the domain of the sayable, beyond the constraints of the speech community. They help to remodel the symbolic order in which the subject has to play a role as social actor. It is to this social actor that we turn in the next chapter.

Notes

1   In the US, it is not usual to talk about speakers of languages other than English as 'foreign', because these languages are very often spoken in the homes of immigrants to the US and are strictly speaking their heritage language. For languages spoken outside the US, euphemisms such as 'world languages', or 'international languages' are used. I have retained the term 'foreign' to characterize someone who is subjectively perceived as being different from oneself because of the different language he or she speaks. This language may be the national language of another country, or the language of another ethnic community within one's own country. In all cases, the otherness of the language is subjectively apprehended as an irreducible difference that is theorized in this chapter as 'the language of the Other'. The capitalization of the word Other indicates that, in Lacan's psychoanalytic theory in which this word is used, human beings other than oneself are characterized by their difference from the Self. In Lacanian terms, the Self constitutes itself against an Other that it both strives to embrace and must separate itself from. This tension is expressed through language.

2   This sense of alienation is not the exclusive experience of minorities learning English. Here, for example, the testimony of an Anglo-American learner of Chinese: 'Most of my difficulties arose out of my mistaken assumption that literacy in English and Chinese was differentiated only by the shape of the squiggles on the paper...Had I realized I was attempting to develop a new way of thinking, learning a new way to present myself to the world, and developing a new set of values, I might have been more prepared for the impact this would have on my self or identity' (Bell 1995: 701).

3 The veiled racism involved in such prejudice is obvious and is of great concern to teachers of English around the world.

4 However, there are also risks involved in being taken for a native speaker or in being too closely associated with native speakers. One recent case in point is the number of Iraqis, who, currently under US occupation, have been found to speak either broken English or perfect American English depending on the circumstances and the interlocutor. Similarly, it is said that George Papandreou, the son of the late Greek politician, who spoke perfect English and was sometimes accused of being too US-friendly, put on a Greek accent when featured speaking English on Greek television. Which foreign dignitary speaks English, which deliberately chooses to speak through a translator when visiting Washington, and the symbolic statement that each choice of language makes, would be an interesting study in itself.

5 The social and cultural identities of these three writers are, of course, quite different. Valerie was a US-born 19-year-old Korean-American. The 30-year-old Lee was born in Korea and emigrated to the US at age three. The 37-year-old Huston is an English Canadian writer who lives in France; she writes and publishes in French. The social value of English, French, and Korean are different and so is the social status of these three multilinguals. In this book, I use testimonies from both 'minority' multilinguals speaking English and 'mainstream' multilinguals speaking or writing in a foreign language. This is contrary to usual practice that is to keep these two groups separate because of the quite distinct conditions under which they have learned the other language. If I draw them together in this chapter it is because I believe that their subjective experiences have some features in common, even if their social and cultural identities are different (for the distinction I make between subjectivity and identity, see Introduction Note 9).

6 The notion that the symbolic can always be overtaken or subverted by the semiotic is somewhat analogous to the following idea, proposed by Ortega y Gasset and referred to by Becker (2000: 5): 'Two apparently contradictory laws are involved in all uttering. One says, 'Every utterance is deficient'—it says less than it wishes to say. The other law, the opposite, declares, 'Every utterance is exuberant'—it conveys more than it plans and includes not a few things we would wish left silent.' In other words, because signs are polysemous and the signifier is not one with the signified, the symbolic always leaves a semiotic residue that has to be accounted for in the interpretation of utterances. We could say that, since the 13-year-old Hoffman had learned but not yet experienced the English word 'river', it did not yet have the deficiencies and exuberances of a living language. Lacan (1977: 86) writes: 'The function of language is not to inform but to evoke.' For the 13-year-old learner of English, the word 'river' didn't evoke anything, even though she knew what it referred to.

7 After recounting her adventure with André, Kaplan devotes an entire section of *French Lessons* to her fascination with the seductive prose of the French writer Céline. In *Desire in Language*, Kristeva (1980:141 ff.) attributes the seductive quality of Céline's style to the irruption of the semiotic in the symbolic: its rhythmic drive, its polyphony, gesturality, and kinesthesia.

8 Kristeva (1986: 113) makes very clear that this remodeling is an ongoing process: 'Though absolutely necessary, the thetic is not exclusive: the semiotic, which also precedes it, constantly tears it open, and this transgression brings about all the various transformations of the signifying practice that are called "creation" ... What remodels the symbolic order is always the influx of the semiotic.'

4

The multilingual social actor

Throughout the last three chapters, and following various theories of the self, we have seen how the language learner gets constructed through language as a multilingual subject, in a constant tension between language's conventional and subjective ways of making meaning, between its symbolic [1] and its symbolic [2] dimensions. As we have seen, the language-learning Self cannot become a subject without acknowledging in itself the presence of the Other whose language he or she is appropriating. But up to now, we have considered the Other in the more abstract or imagined incarnations offered by language memoirs or learners' journals. We turn now to encounters with concrete, living others in sociolinguistic data.

1 From experiencing language to doing language with others

For each of the following sets of data, I discuss how current SLA theory might go about explaining the phenomena under scrutiny and what it leaves unexplained. In section 2, I then suggest ways of reframing the problem.

Case 1: 'This is just not something I can do' in French

Here is the unsolicited account of a young Australian student, whom we shall call John, who has just returned from study abroad in France. John is describing to his Australian professor of French his reluctance, while in France, to 'barge into' the secretary's office the way he saw French students do, without getting official permission or at least a glance from the secretary that it is OK to do so. He speaks with passion, his face flustered, his tone of voice quite emotional:

> This was a very hard thing to do. I hated it. It felt like I was violating someone else's space, that I was an invader. I know that's not the way they see it, but that doesn't matter. It still feels the same. This is just not

something I can do. I mean I really feel that there's this really important barrier there and I just can't get through that without permission. That's an invasion. I can't go into another person's space, well I know it's not really their space, it's an open space, but I can't—it's just not—it really is their space for me. I can't change that and I can't be an invader like that. It's too traumatic. It doesn't even matter that no-one seems to mind. I mind.
(Liddicoat 2003)

A cursory reading of this statement tells us that John experienced a culture shock at the differing social practices in the two countries. Schema theory (for a review, see Cook 1994) would explain such a conflict in terms of the clash between differing mental structures of expectation, or schemata. John had just been brought up with a schema of politeness that didn't fit the new circumstances. Activity theory (Leontiev 1978; Engestrom, Miettinen, and Punamaki 1999; Lantolf 2000) would focus on the (in)ability of the language learner to regulate his own mental and physical activity in the context of a foreign culture. His contact with the secretary is mediated by his conception of polite behavior, by the French language, by the door frame in which he is standing, and, in his culture, by the eye contact he expects to have with the secretary as a sign that he is welcome to come in. He is conscious that the rules of behavior shared by the members of the French-speaking community are not made explicit, for example, through a sign on the door that would say: 'Please wait before entering'. According to activity theory, the task of crossing the threshold to the main office was, for John as for the French students, the same task, but because it had another social value, it was a different 'activity'. Cross-cultural pragmatic theory (Müller-Jacquier 1981; Blum-Kulka, House, and Kasper 1989) would explain that in France, offices usually keep their doors closed and one is expected to knock before entering. Secretaries are part of a bureaucracy that serves the state or the institution in an official, that is, anonymous, way. Thus for these French students, an office whose door was, by exception, permanently open might have been perceived as an invitation to freely enter a public space in which an anonymous 'civil servant' is at the 'service' of the public. Hence the lack of politeness niceties and the perceived freedom to 'barge in'. By contrast in Australia, office doors traditionally remain open and secretaries often display their names on their desks. Thus, entering an office is a personal encounter with an 'administrative assistant' whose job is to 'assist' you meet your 'needs'. John was using Australian pragmatics in a French setting.

According to these theories, John's behavior had meaning within its own functional system. Through conversations with his professor or through classroom instruction on French culture, John might transform his views on the comparative value of open and closed doors, offices and secretaries, and the use of verbal versus non-verbal behavior in French and Australian cultures, and learn to develop strategies for dealing with such situations in French settings. However, we are still left with some questions that current theory cannot account for. In particular, what is the nature of the taboo that prevented John from behaving like the other French students? What role did the English language play in this taboo, and in the way John understands himself as an Australian required to speak and act 'French'? And anyway, in now multicultural France, what does it mean to act French?

Case 2: 'Hanif: Schnell, schnell—Mr N.: Schnell, schnell exactly. Vite, vite!'

The British high-school learners of German studied by Rampton (1995, 1999, 2002) attempt to resignify the boring ritual of the classroom for their own purposes. In the German class he observed, Mrs Wilson, the German teacher, makes ample use of the conventionalized pedagogic practice of choral responses, pattern drills, and verbal rituals. These routines, Rampton argues, serve the purpose of minimizing the threat to face, creating a sense of rhythm or flow, and bonding the class into a rite-like initiation. However, it is emotionally one of the most constraining forms of pedagogy, because it requires total allegiance and unquestioned participation, and can mean the abandonment of individual autonomy and creativity. Here, we have Mrs Wilson drilling 'having breakfast' with her class.

1	MRS W.	right
2		if everybody can ( ) now (.)
3		**ICH ESSE FRÜHSTÜCK**
		((*translation: I eat breakfast*))
4	SINGLE PUPIL	**ich esse Frühstück**
5	MRS W.	**ICH ESSE FRÜHSTÜCK**
6		**bitte alle zusammen**
		((*translation: all together please*))
7	SEVERAL VOICES, but not HANIF	
		((*ragged chorus:*)) **ich esse Frühstück**
8	MRS W.	**ich e:sse Frühstück**
9	OTHER VOICES	((*still ragged*))
		ich esse Frühstück
10	HANIF ((*quite quietly*))	**ich e::sse Frühstück**
11	MRS W.	**ich esse Frühstück**
12	SEVERAL	**ich esse Frühstück**
13	HANIF	**esse Frühstück**
14	BOY ((*loud*))	(QUIET)
15	MRS W.	**BITTE**
		((*translation: PLEASE!*))
16		((*shouting very loud*))
		ALLE ZUSAMMEN
		((*translation: ALL TOGETHER*))
17		**ICH ESSE FRÜHSTÜCK**
18	OTHERS	**ich esse Frühstück**
19	HANIF	((*sounding less than whole-hearted:*))
		ich esse Frühstück:
20	ANON	( )

21 GUY	it's breakfast time
22 BOY	what / is it
23 MRS W.	**(was das) auf Englisch** *((translation: what ( ) that in English))*
24 GUY	breakfast
25 MRS W.	breakfast
26	I eat breakfast.

It is clear that the students are bored and resent the exercise. However, in an intriguing development, as soon as they have left the class some of them reuse the German they have learned there with other teachers in other classes and in the hallways with one another. Here for example, in Mr N.'s class. The pupils have just entered the English classroom:

1 MR N.	erm (.) take your seat everybody take your coats off please (.)
2 HANIF	**schnell schnell** *((German: Quick quick))*
3 MR N.	**schnell schnell** exactly **Vite vite** *((French: Quick quick))*

The same lesson, a little later on:

1 MR N.	as I've said before
2	I get a bit fed up with saying
3 HANIF	*((addressed to Mr. N?))* LOU/DER
4 MR N.	you're doing your SATs *((tests))* now
5 HANIF	**VIEL LAUTER SPRECHEN** *((translation: speak much louder))*
6	**VIEL LAUTER SPRECHEN**
7 JOHN	*((smile-voice))* **lauter spricken** whatever that is.

(Rampton 2002: 497–8)

As Hanif, a 12-year-old Banglade shi, and others recycle selected samples from the institutional ritual of the German classroom in another interactional ritual outside the classroom, addressed both to teachers and to fellow students within earshot of teachers, something more is at stake than just the random production of German linguistic structures. As Rampton (2002) points out, what the students are creating is a ritualized *Deutsch* persona that positions itself in opposition to institutional authority and paradoxically distances itself from high-school ritualized German through the use of a no less ritualized *Deutsch*. *Deutsch* seems to serve as a release from the emotional intensity experienced in Mrs Wilson's German class and as a way of resignifying the (hated) ritual of the classroom for subversive purposes.

Both traditional and sociocultural theories of language acquisition account for the ability of learners to produce correct and appropriate utterances in the foreign language. They attach referential meanings to the forms taught in class: *schnell* in German 'means' quick, as does *vite* in French. SLA researchers look to see if the learner is using these forms correctly in appropriate contexts of use. This, here, is clearly the case. But it is equally obvious that the meaning of these two words in this context goes beyond the referential. For example, what is the significance of repetition and parody as a form of social action and transgression? How do Hanif, John, and others position themselves as multilingual social actors in these various contexts?

Case 3: 'An eating disorder *is a psychological illness'*

An adult ESL class I observed in 1990 illustrates the clash between different social positionings, again within the power dynamics of a language classroom. The lesson was based on Chapter 7 in Beckerman's *Heartworks* (1989), 'The Secret of Good Health'. The students have been shown a video clip taken from a 1980 commercial film, *Fatso*, chosen by the teacher, that features the plight of a male overeater, hounded by his family and his own guilt feelings and growing ever more desperate as he tries to fight the social pressures around him through eating. The teacher has distributed a handout that gives the students relevant vocabulary and questions to focus the discussion. The following classroom dialogue has been reconstituted from field notes.

T	What problem does the video show?
Ss	(silence)
T	what are fatness and overweight due to?
S1 (Ivory Coast)	the environment doesn't help
S2 (Mexico)	he is addicted
S3 (Venezuela)	milk and fried food are fattening...eggs
T	have you gotten fat since you came to America
S3 (Venezuela)	I don't feel like in Venezuela
T	why did the man in the film binge? (writes *to binge/to be on a binge* on the blackboard)
S1 (Ivory Coast)	many reasons...excessive behavior...former deprivation...something is missing in his life
S2 (Mexico)	too many ads on TV ...they create the desire to binge
S4 (Japan)	he is not wise...the environment is bad but it's a psychological illness
S1 (Ivory Coast)	yes but TV makes it worse
T	'eating disorders' is an illness (writes *eating disorder* on the blackboard)...anorexia is seen as psychological illness...bulimics too (writes *anorexia* and *bulimia* on the board) but there are support groups (writes *support group* on the board). What are support groups for?
S4 (Japan)	for vices

Ss	for alcoholics
	cross-dressers
	drugs
T	there are support groups for everything—unmarried mothers with children, divorced people...

It seems that the American teacher, following the textbook, considers overweight to be an 'eating disorder', that is, a psychological illness, to be cured by support groups and, possibly, psychotherapy. By teaching them the phrase 'eating disorder' and 'psychological illness', the teacher is not only teaching them English vocabulary but a specific, historically marked, American discourse of individual responsibility and personal initiative in a pluralistic society. An SLA researcher focusing on the task at hand—namely, the brainstorming of possible causes for eating disorders—would view the students' responses as appropriate realizations of the speech function 'expressing opinions', an important function in communicative language teaching and one that is facilitated by the vocabulary preview and discussion questions in the textbook. These discussion questions move the theme of the lesson from overeating as an illness to overeating as an individual problem: 'What problem did this man have with his diet?' 'Why do you think he binged?' 'Why do people overeat or starve themselves?' 'What is your attitude toward food? Do you live to eat or eat to live?' This theme is further reinforced by the dialogue in the textbook titled 'The Best Medicine' in which a teenage son teaches his mother that 'we have to take responsibility for our own health' and 'doctors don't really make you get better. You have to do that yourself.'

But what has become of the dissenting voices in the classroom? The ESL textbook resists putting the blame on food corporations and corporate advertisements and places it instead squarely in the lap of the consumer. This discourse is dutifully echoed by the Japanese student (*he is not wise...it's a psychological illness*), but is resisted by the Mexican student (*too many ads on TV...they create the desire to binge*), the student from Venezuela (*milk and fried foods are fattening...eggs*) and repeatedly refuted by the student from Ivory Coast (*the environment doesn't help, former deprivation, something is missing in his life, TV*). How does the classroom discourse position the various students for whom overeating is not an individual challenge but a societal ill or the result of TV advertising? How do they oppose the ideological content of the very pedagogy through which they are learning English?

Case 4: '¡ay no! que tú sabes el inglés'

Camila, a 34-year-old Salvadoran who emigrated to California with her husband Marcos in 1989, and now lives in Kingston, California with her two children, Marquitos (12) and Adela (8), had studied English at the Community English Center for two and a half years when she was interviewed by the Anglo-American researcher, Julia Menard-Warwick (2004a, 2005) as part of a larger study on female immigrant English learners. Julia asks Camila why she didn't want to learn English at first, but then decided to learn it by watching English-language television. Camila begins by explaining that when she first came to California she did not take English classes at the college near their previous home in San Francisco because they would have cost her $70 per semester, plus books. She wasn't working, and her husband was saving as much money as he could from his job as an electrician toward his dream of buying a house. The event she recounts took place some eight years prior to the telling of the story, which was related in Spanish. I give the English translation in the right hand column. [Excerpts below provided by Julia Menard-Warwick 2009.]

Entonces yo pensaba, ese dinero es dinero menos para su sueño de él o para el estudio de mi hijo. Entonces por eso yo nunca no exigí ir al Ocean College, y siempre me conformé con la televisión, siempre me conformé con ver televisión. Y siempre peleábamos por el inglés y yo llegué como a odiar el idioma y a ponerme el capricho que yo no le iba a dar gusto a él de aprenderlo.

Pero me recuerdo que una vez, eran como las siete de la noche y yo estaba siempre con mis novelas, cuando él pasó así enfrente de mi y agarró el control. Y le dije yo, '¡ayyy, otra vez!!' Entonces él me miró bien serio y me dijo, 'sí,' dijo, 'pero esta es la última vez que te lo voy a decir.' Y puso la televisión en mudo...Entonces yo le dije '¿Qué quieres?' así enojada. Y me dijo 'Te voy hacer una pregunta,' dijo. '¿Qué?' le dije. 'Tú ¿quieres a Marquitos?' dijo. Y yo me le quedé viendo, y le dije, 'Claro que sí,' le dije, 'bien sabes que sí lo quiero al niño,' le dije. 'Sí,' me dijo, 'pero yo lo que te quiero decir es esto,' dijo. 'Que

So I thought this money (for classes) is less money for his dream or for my son's education. So that's why I never demanded to go to Ocean College, and I always got by with the television, I always got by with watching television. And we were always fighting about English, and I began to hate the language and I got myself into this frame of mind where I wasn't going to give him the pleasure of seeing me learn it.

But I remember that one time, it was like seven at night, and I was watching soap operas as always, when he came in front of me and grabbed the remote. And I said to him, 'Ohhh, not again!!' So then he looked at me very seriously, and he said to me, 'Yes', he said 'but this is the last time that I am going to tell you.' And he put the television on mute...So then I said to him: 'What do you want?' angry like this ((making an angry face)). And he told me, 'I am going to ask you one question', he told me. 'What?' I told him. 'Do you love Marquitos?' he said to me. And I kept looking at him and I told him, 'Of course I do,' I told him. you know very well that I love the boy,' I told him.

un día...ahorita tiene tres años,'
dijo, 'pero un día el niño va a
crecer,' dijo, y tú nunca vas
a aprender el inglés y lo que
va a pasar, 'dijo, ... 'cuando sea
un *teenager*,' me dijo, 'tú', dijo,
'cierra tus ojos,' dijo, 'y ponte
esta fotografía en tu mente,'
dijo. 'Tú vas a estar sentadita
aquí donde estás, viendo tus
novelas de español, a la par va
estar él sentado, con el teléfono,
hablando inglés, y haciendo
negocios de droga...Cuando
le preguntes qué está haciendo,
él va a pensar, "mi mami es una
tonta, no sabe inglés." '...Y yo
miraba al niño y se me hacía un
nudo en la garganta de llorar.

Entonces él me explicó como
trabajaba y me dijo, 'tú lo
oyes y lo lees.' Entonces yo de
primero me costó, lo hallé difícil
estar poniendo atención como
lo pronuncia e ir leyendo a la
misma vez. Y algunas palabras
que él las sabía traducírmelas al
español rapido. Entonces yo lo
que hacía que a veces agarraba
un cuaderno y un lápiz, y cuando
me ponía a ver televisión, si
miraba palabras difíciles las
escribía y ya las buscaba en el
diccionario.

Y sí, ahora yo lo puedo ver
porque Marquitos cuando yo
le pregunto así...yo estaba
acá sentada, y él estaba con su
amiguito en el teléfono y estaba
hablando despacito y me miraba.
Y luego yo, yo como lo miré
sospechosa, en el momento que

'Yes,' he told me, 'But what I want
to tell you is this', he said. 'That one
day...now he is three years old,' he
said, 'but one day the boy is going
to grow,' he said, 'and you are never
going to learn English, and what
is going to happen,' he said, 'when
he is a *teenager*, you, he said,' close
your eyes,' he said, 'and put this
photograph in your mind,' he said.
'You are going to be sitting right here
where you are, watching your soap
operas in Spanish, and he's going to
be sitting right next to you with the
telephone, speaking English, and
making drug deals...When you ask
him what he's doing, he's going to
think, 'my mom is a fool, she doesn't
know English.'...And I looked at
the boy, and I felt a lump of tears in
my throat.
So then he explained to me how it
worked and he told me 'you hear it
and you read it.' So then at first it
was hard for me, I found it difficult
to be paying attention how to
pronounce it and to keep reading
it at the same time. And some
words that he knew he'd translate
them into Spanish for me quickly.
So then what I'd do sometimes,
I'd grab a notebook and pencil,
and when I sat down to watch
television, if I saw difficult words,
I would write them down and then
look them up in the dictionary.

And yes, now I can see it because
Marquitos, when I ask him
something like that...I was sitting
here, and he was talking to his little
friend on the telephone, and he was
looking at me. And then I, I looked
at him suspiciously, when I saw
he was about to answer I put the

yo vi que él iba a contestar puse la television *mute,* apreté mudo. Y cuando yo apreté él habló y dijo, '*let me talk my mom.*' Entonces le dije yo, '¿Qué me vas a decir?' '¿Me oistes?' (dijo). 'Sí te escuché' le dije. '¿Qué me vas a decir?' Entonces, entonces ya me dijo que dice Pedro que si puede venir mañana a la casa. 'OK,' dile que sí.

Pero sí, ahora él así dice que se siente *scary* porque '¡ay no!!' dice, 'que tú sabes el inglés,' dice.

television on mute, I hit the mute. And when I hit it, he said, '*let me talk my mom*' So then I said to him, 'What are you going to tell me?' 'Did you hear me?' (he said). 'Yes, I heard you' I said to him. 'What are you going to tell me?' So then, then he told me that Pedro wants to know if he can come to our house tomorrow. 'OK,' I told him yes…

But yes, now he says that he feels *scary* because 'Oh no!!' he says, 'You speak English,' he says.

The case of Camila would be seen by most SLA researchers as a problem of motivation or investment.[1] Clearly Camila had no incentive to invest in English since she had decided to invest in her Spanish family role instead. The fear that her husband instilled in her was enough to change her motivation to learn English. But what was the nature of that fear? Sociocultural theory would take into account the social and historical context in which her story unfolds: her past traumatic experiences in El Salvador, where she was threatened with death if she did not have sex with one of the government's military, her present anxiety that she might not be the perfect selfless wife and mother. It might also focus on Camila's slow discovery of her own identity as a responsible mother and her decision to take her acquisition of English into her own hands for the sake of her son (Norton 2000). But sociocultural theory could not explain the role that telling the story played in Camila's change of identity. After all, this is Camila's version of the events and a good story at that. She had told the story the year before in English to her English substitute teacher Jack, who had been so taken by the story that he repeated it to Julia, the researcher. The next time Jack came to substitute again, he gave Camila a large, hard-cover dictionary to help with her language learning, telling her in Julia's presence that the gift was 'on account of her story.' Now, six months later, in the course of an ethnographic interview that she chose to conduct in Spanish, Camila told the story once again (unsolicited) to Julia, this time in Spanish. In her final report on her study, the researcher characterizes Camila as 'one of the most dramatic and compelling storytellers I have ever met'. So the question that SLA theory leaves unexplained is: What is the relationship between the construction of the story and the construction of Camila as a multilingual subject?

2 Reframing the questions

In a first analysis, we can say that all four cases have to do with language learners attempting to take up a position in a context that is outside their usual field of action and whose constraints they accept or oppose: 20-year-old John is expected to be a social actor in a foreign country in a way that goes against his Australian upbringing and he just cannot perform the role. Twelve-year-old Hanif finds himself outside the ritualistic environment of the German classroom, and, when he is expected to conform to Mr N.'s social code of behavior, he uses German to challenge Mr N.'s authority. The adult ESL students, in the artificial context of an ESL classroom, find themselves positioned by the teacher as actors both in the classroom communicative routine and in the underlying ideology of the textbook. They use English either to accept this position or to oppose it. Thirty-six-year-old immigrant Camila at first resists the pressure to become an English learner in the foreign environment of her host country, but finally decides to learn English and use it to become an active agent in the raising of her son.

We have seen how SLA theory can explain these learners' objective successes or failures in their acquisition and use of a foreign language, but they cannot capture the subjective dimensions of their behavior. For example, they don't explain the violence of John's emotions at not being able to cross that threshold, the pleasure experienced by Hanif's tactics of resignification, the conflict of meaning-making practices in the ESL classroom, and the role of shame and motherly pride in Camila's story. In what follows we examine each of these issues.

2.1 John: the symbolic power of the habitus

Let's go back to John's difficulties in France. The first thing we notice is the highly emotional tone of his statement: *I hated it . . . It felt like . . . It still feels the same . . . I really feel . . . It's too traumatic . . . I mind.* He can speak French but he can't get himself to act French. The passage from feeling to action goes against the grain of his Australian upbringing. The discrepancy between who he considers himself to be and who he is expected to be at that particular moment is experienced as traumatic. John's case shows that our behavior is strongly channelled by the way we have been socialized in our original language and culture. Bourdieu (1991, 1997) shows how upbringing, schooling, and other forms of socialization are in fact processes of 'symbolic power' or 'symbolic violence' through which people are inculcated into more or less permanent ways of being and behaving that he calls *habitus*.[2] This inculcation, as we saw in Chapter 2, is done through the body, hence John's emotional tone.

> We learn bodily. The social order inscribes itself in bodies through this permanent confrontation [of the habitus and the field], which may be more or less dramatic but is always largely marked by affectivity and, more precisely, by affective transactions with the environment.
> (Bourdieu 1997: 141)

> Guided by one's sympathies and antipathies, affections and aversions, tastes and distates, one makes for oneself an environment in which one

feels 'at home' and in which one can achieve that fulfillment of one's desire to be which one identifies with happiness.
(ibid. 150)

John's emotional tone is accompanied by a moral sense of what is 'good' and what is 'bad' behavior. The social contexts with which John's habitus interacts are endowed with different kinds of symbolic resources or 'capital' and therefore afford different 'profits of distinction' through various verbal behaviors. Obviously, being considerate and respectful of someone else's space is a personal quality that is valued among middle-class Australians; it has given John a sense of pride and self-worth.

Bourdieu and Passeron (1977: 42–3). distinguish between primary habitus, acquired at home during primary socialization, and secondary habitus, acquired at school and in other pedagogic contexts. The latter, although aimed at being durable, is more amenable to change or modification according to the field, in part because it is multiple. In France John experienced to a painful degree the distance between the secondary habitus he feels he is asked to adopt and the primary habitus developed through his own Australian upbringing.

The reason why the primary habitus is so durable is because it is the product of a historical sedimentation (Damasio would say 'neural pathways') of attitudes, beliefs, and worldviews that have been reinforced over time. It is through the living bodies of individual speakers that history, says Bourdieu, is 'incarnated' in the social structure. In primary socialization, the individual's biographical history is made to conform to the history of the group through family upbringing, schooling, professional training, etc. In secondary socialization and especially in cross-cultural encounters, individuals' histories might clash with the history of another society's social structures.[3] Because these different histories operate on different timescales—the lived timescale of personal memory versus the historical timescale of a whole society—John's struggle to decide which course of action to take can be seen as the struggle between two different timescales.[4]

Thus, John's problem can be seen as going beyond one individual student experiencing 'culture shock'. When two interlocutors meet, or when a non-native speaker of English encounters a native English speaker, it is not only two communicative competences that interact with one another, but two social positions, two symbolic capitals, two histories.

2.2 The power of ideal cognitive models

Now let's listen to what John says. He speaks of refusing to 'invade the space' of the secretary—strong words indeed for something as trivial as entering a departmental office. His choice of metaphors and their repetition are correspondly powerful: *violating someone else's space, invading another person's space* evoke rape and military aggression. The dominant metaphors in John's ideal cognitive model (ICM) of himself seem to be A PERSON IS A SPACE,

UNSOLICITED HUMAN CONTACT IS AN INVASION, with their entailments: a person's space is sacred, entering that space without permission is taboo.

It is possible, of course, that John the narrator was amplifying, dramatizing for the benefit of his interlocutor, an experience that he had lived in a much more confused way at the time. He might have felt then a slight discomfort that he retrospectively attributed to his good Australian upbringing, thus placing himself in a more favorable light vis-à-vis a fellow Australian than if he had admitted his ignorance of French cultural mores. Of interest is less whether the feelings described here were the ones he experienced at the time, than the meaning John gave them retrospectively in English to a fellow Australian. The metaphors he used give us a glimpse into John's symbolic self, formed of the ICMs he has been raised with and that give meaning to his life (see Chapter 2). While John as an embodied self lived through the experience, John as a multilingual subject reflected on that experience with the help of the ICMs offered by his native language. Had he told the story in French to a French speaker, it is doubtful he would have positioned himself in the same manner, in part because the French language does not offer the same metaphors regarding 'personal spaces' and their potential 'violation'.

The social and moral interdiction against entering someone's space without that person's consent is repeated three times in this short extract; it foregrounds the symbolic power exercised by the English phrases inculcated during the student's primary socialization. No doubt such an inculcation was in the form of injunctions and taboos of the kind: 'you must ask for permission before entering someone else's room' and 'you shouldn't invade someone else's space'.[5] These performatives then acquired a life of their own, as John seems to be ventriloquating his parents or teachers, and their words seem to have the power to stop him dead in his tracks at the door of a French secretary's office.[6]

Thus, John's problem was not merely behavioral, based on the proper manners he had been socialized in, but a symbolic taboo that defined his very existence as a social actor. He felt that entering the office without permission was *an invasion*, that made him into someone he was not, that is, *an invader*, and that he just *couldn't be an invader like that*, it was too *traumatic*. Only the prospect of symbolic death and disappearance as a well-brought up Australian can explain such strong emotional language. It is reminiscent of Watson, who felt that speaking French was '*undermining his very being*' (Excerpt. 1.2) and of Dorfman (1998: 61), who, when he was three years old, considered the Spanish of his father to be such a threat to his existence that he had to '*build himself a space of his own where Spanish could not enter*' in order to preserve his biological, social, and linguistic self.

But couldn't John have changed the symbolic equation by asking for permission to come in, even though this was not the French way of behaving? In other words, to what extent can language learners as social actors resignify the context in which they use the foreign language? We explore this possibility below with the case of Hanif.

2.3 Hanif: language as resignifying practice

The way Hanif recycled the words of his German teacher, Mrs Wilson, to fleetingly change the balance of power in his English class evokes the disruption in the symbolic order that we came across in Kristeva. We encountered in earlier chapters the notions of heteroglossia (Introduction, section 3.3) and intertextuality (Chapter 3 section 3.4), that is, the idea that every speaker's utterance contains the voices of others, and that therefore, as Bakhtin (1981: 293–4) said, every utterance is a reaccentuation, or resignification of other people's words:

> As a living, socio-ideological concrete thing, as heteroglot opinion, language, for the individual consciousness, lies on the borderline between oneself and the other. The word in language is half someone else's. It becomes 'one's own' only when the speaker populates it with his own intention, his own accent, when he appropriates the word, adapting it to his own semantic and expressive intention. Prior to this moment of appropriation, the word does not exist in a neutral and impersonal language (it is not, after all, out of a dictionary that the speaker gets his words!), but rather it exists in other people's mouths, in other people's contexts, serving other people's intentions: it is from there that one must take the word, and *make it one's own*.
> (emphasis added)

Making other people's words one's own while retaining their 'otherness' requires distance, reflexivity, irony, and a certain dose of humor. This is precisely what Hanif and his peers displayed in Mr N.'s class. We could say that the students reaccentuated the coercive rituals of Mrs Wilson's class for their own purposes. They resignified German into *Deutsch* in order to challenge the authority of the teacher and the rules of conduct of the institution.

Both Mrs Wilson's classroom ritual and the students' subsequent resignifications are highly symbolic actions. If ritual is, as Rothenbuhler (1998: 27) defines it, 'the voluntary performance of appropriately patterned behavior to symbolically effect or participate in the serious life', Mrs Wilson's classroom choral drill can be seen as a purposeful performance, patterned to fit the grammatical objectives of the lesson, and designed in such a way as to enact the disciplined life of academia, or the bonding of the classroom community. In class, the students were forced to perform a ritual they had not voluntarily chosen, nor did they endorse the teacher's view of the serious life of academia. One would think that the difference between German in the classroom and German outside the classroom is the difference between ritual language, that is, an ahistorical linguistic paradigm addressed to no one, and living historic language addressed to other teachers and peers outside the German class. Interestingly, however, once outside class, they used *Deutsch*, that is, the ritualized phrases from the textbook, to impress Mr N. and gain a profit of distinction vis-à-vis the other students. Thus, as Rampton suggests, one could rightly ask whether such a behavior should not be considered a 'successful' outcome of ritualized language pedagogy.

What Rampton makes apparent is that the students have replaced one German symbolic ritual by another, namely the use of German as part of a classroom ritual by the use of German as a condensation symbol that Rampton calls *Deutsch*. This mythic use of *Deutsch* serves to contest the teacher's authority and express the students' resistance to the physical constraints of schooling. *Deutsch* emulates German and resignifies it with endless variations. This process of de- and resignification is a symbolic power struggle as to whose sign will be accepted within a given discourse community. Mr N.'s tit-for-tat rejoinder 'Schnell, schnell…exactly…vite, vite' seems to be an effort to enter the symbolic game and regain control of the situation. Thus, Hanif has rebelled against Mrs Wilson's symbolic order of *Deutsch* only to impose it tongue-in-cheek on Mr N., not in order to make ritualized *Deutsch* into living German.

Looking back at John's case in light of Hanif's experience, what were the possibilities for John to resignify the situation he was in? How could he both abide by local customs and retain a sense of personal integrity? John's case has been seen by researchers as the dilemma of language learners who find themselves betwixt and between cultures: either they behave in the foreign language the way they have been socialized in their native tongue, or they adopt the rules of use set up by native speakers of the foreign language. But if, as Kristeva suggested, the subject positions itself anew in every act of enunciation, an opening is created each time for a third position.

Like Hanif, John could have capitalized on being positioned between two languages. The concrete threshold and the thetic border on which John found himself opened up for him an opportunity to resignify his subject position. Being multilingual, he had a range of options: he could have requested permission in French to satisfy his Australian need to be polite, but with a disclaimer like: '*Est-ce que je peux entrer, comme on dit dans mon pays* [may I come in, as they say in my country]'; or he could have uttered his request in English (for example 'May I come in?') to satisfy the Australian etiquette but then continue in French to show that he was willing to use the French language but not French pragmatics–He could also simply have entered the office, and then explained in French to the secretary that he didn't want to 'barge' into her office without her permission–the point being in each case to remain faithful to one's symbolic self without offending one's interlocutor. Growing into a multilingual subject is precisely establishing a distance vis-à-vis one's usual habitus and explicitly reflecting upon it through a judicious use of contextualization cues (such as code-switching, ironical tone) that highlight the complex and contradictory nature of the context. In Chapter 7, I refer to this ability as 'symbolic competence'.

Furthermore, the very story that John told his professor was only one possible version of what happened to him in France. Because it was told within a culture and in a language that he shared with his interlocutor, namely Australian English, he could expect that his version of events made sense, indeed seemed absolutely natural to an Australian interlocutor, and that the professor would identify with his plight. However, this professor was not only Australian, but a bilingual, English- and French-speaking Australian, who knew that there is no equivalent in French for *personal space* nor for the *invasion* of that space. For a French person, the phenomenon has no name and thus no social existence. This does not mean that the French are incapable of discretion or tactfulness, or of respecting the privacy of a secretary dealing with another student, only that they don't have the concept of *invading someone's space*. If, for example, John had started thinking and speaking like a French speaker, he would have had the opportunity to 'see' this event in a different way, through a different system of signs. One could say that John, the character in the story, lacked the symbolic tactics used by Hanif to resignify and thereby regain control of the situation; John, the narrator, was hostage to an idealized cognitive model of self based on the English language.

2.4 ESL students: symbolic violence and oppositional tactics

The pedagogy of Mrs Wilson's class is radically different from that of the ESL class in Case 3. In the first, an audiolingual method was in action, in the second, communicative language teaching (CLT). Rampton (2002), following Bernstein, makes the point that ritualized language teaching and CLT are based on two quite different philosophies of the subject.[7] Ritualized language teaching is based on the presumption of irreducible cultural differences and asymmetries of power between teacher and students. These discrepancies cannot be bridged by rational dialogue or exchange of information; they can only be resolved through activities that achieve a sense of communal emotional experience, such as choral responses and the predictable performance of the word. Mrs Wilson's class was based on such a performance of the most constraining kind. By contrast, CLT is based on the presumption of a commonality of needs among autonomous individuals, and the acknowledgement of individual differences, that can be ironed out through dialogue and negotiation of meaning. This was presumably the case in the ESL class, a class based on the concept of communicative competence. But was it really?

The ESL class illustrates one of the difficulties inherent in CLT. On the one hand, the living language with various historical inflections on the part of students and teacher retains a semiotic diversity that calls for dialogue and negotiation of meaning. On the other hand, the monolingual discourse of the textbook, presented as ahistorical truth and embedded in the vocabulary and the grammar selected for instruction, clashes with the multilingual habitus of the students in the class. If, in addition, the teacher's habitus converges with that of the textbook writers and their dominant ELT ideology, the power differential between teacher and learners does not allow much space for resignification or reaccentuation on the part of the students. In this class, the various foreign students were positioned as participants in a dialogue that was severely constrained by the pedagogic goals of the activity. The fact that the students from Mexico, Venezuela, and Ivory Coast tried in vain to contest the ideology of the lesson and make their voices heard shows that even a communicative classroom can be conducted in a ritualistic fashion. In such classes, expression and negotiation of meaning become a ritual or ostensible display of symbolic power.

ESL teachers and learners in non-English-speaking environments might have a greater opportunity to question the ideology of the textbook. For example, Sullivan reports on one English classroom in Hanoi, where the (American) textbook called for a discussion of health food. The Vietnamese teacher commented in English: 'About *health food*, we don't have that concept. All food is healthy: rice, vegetables, meat.' Where the text read: '*A healthy diet can extend your life*', the teacher remarked to the class with a smile: 'As for extending your life, that is not for us to decide, is it?' (Sullivan 1996: 234). What the Vietnamese teacher was doing was taking myths such as *health food* and *a healthy diet*, whose power of persuasion lies precisely in their ahistorical, biological/natural truths, and demythifying them by giving them a historical reading, that is, a reading that relativized the truth of their propositions. By problematizing their self-evidence, he opened a space of alternative, historically and locally contingent meanings that put into question their symbolic power.

Thus in these two examples, as in Hanif's case, we see various tactics at work that attempt to resist the semiotic monolingualism of the target language and introduce heteroglossia into the classroom game. These tactics were more or less successful in disrupting the dominant symbolic order. Echoing on the sociological plane the argument Kristeva made on the semiological plane, the sociologist de Certeau offers a way of conceptualizing these tactics. In his *Practice of Everyday Life* (1984), he explores what social actors actually do to resist symbolic power or, rather, to divert resources for their own benefit—under conditions they have not (at least consciously) created, and forced to speak a language whose structures and style are not of their choosing. He is particularly interested in immigrants, children, and minorities who have to live in a space whose rules have been determined by others, according to time schedules imposed by others, and who have to obey rules of speaking established by the social conventions of others. Lacking an authority and a social locus of their own, these non-natives or not-yet-fully natives use things or words according to circumstances, in ways that echo the tactics of the resourceful tricksters in fairy tales (Chapter 1). The goal of such 'scattered practices' (ibid. 48) is the subject's psychological, emotional, and physical survival on the terrain of others. We have found examples in the writings of Tawada (Excerpt 1.6) and Chiellino (Chapter 3 section 3.3). In this chapter, Hanif, the ESL students, and, as we shall see, Camila all use tactics to construct themselves as multilingual subjects.

De Certeau distinguishes two ways of making use of linguistic and social space: strategies and tactics. He calls *strategy* 'the calculation (or manipulation) of power' by people and groups who either occupy a recognizable place of their own in society (in a business, an army, a school, a scientific institution, a profession), or who strive to acquire a place of their own, for example through the study of or apprenticeship in a foreign language. By learning another language, one gives oneself a certain independence with respect to the variability of circumstances, for example, one can find employment abroad, or a better paying job, or run a better company. Thus, language learning as a strategy is 'a triumph of place over time' (ibid. 36) because knowledge of the language can transform the uncertainties of history into power and autonomy. The same can be said of the strategies learners use to gain knowledge of the language. They are meant to facilitate 'appropriation', 'mastery', and 'proper' use of the language—all proprietary, and hence spatial, metaphors of learning. Second language acquisition research strives to find ever better strategies for language learners to gain their own, autonomous space in the foreign language.

By contrast, a tactic is 'a calculated action determined by the absence of a proper locus. The space of a tactic is the space of the other' (ibid. 37). Those who use tactics do so because they don't have and can't even dream of having their proper place. They are keenly aware that they are operating on the terrain of the other: they don't identify with the goals of the school, the dreams of their parents, the promises of politicians. They don't have the options of planning general strategies, because they know their future is uncertain. They can only do what is needed to get by. De Certeau calls tactics 'an art of the weak' (ibid.).

Taking advantage of opportunities, seizing possibilities, poaching on the verbal practices of the native speaker, creating surprising meanings, are all tactics we have encountered in the testimonies of multilingual speakers in the last few chapters. If they are 'an art of the weak' it is because they are used by language learners such as Hanif and the ESL students who are in a state of linguistic or cultural inferiority and do not occupy a secure subject position. Because they do not contest the need to acquire the dominant language, they offer less a resistance to the dominant symbolic order than an opposition to its claim at being the only game in town. In essence, they contest the belief that monolingualism and monoculturalism is the natural state of native speakers.[8]

What tactics do is insert into the semioconformity or monolingualism of rules, conventions, and expectations precisely an unexpected, mischievous semiodiversity, also called heteroglossia. In the case at hand, the majority of the ESL students introduced in the interpretation of the film a plurality of interpretations that the teacher could have profitably drawn upon to diversify the monolingual bias of the textbook.

2.5 Camila: the power of narrative structure

As in John's case, Camila's experience cannot be understood without taking into consideration the fact that the events narrated were not necessarily experienced in the way they are told. They are a construction by a narrative self that positions herself in a particular time and place vis-à-vis an interlocutor for a particular purpose. The fact that this story had been told several times in the past explains Camila's careful orchestration of the events in order to make her point. That point can be found both in the structure of the narrative and in the genre in which Camila chose to cast it.

Let's take a closer look at the structure of her story. It starts, like all stories (Labov 1972) with an orientation that sets the stage for the subsequent events and justifies telling the story as a valid response to the researcher's query: 'Why did you start watching television in English?' This orientation also serves to legitimize the 'turning point' of the story (i.e. the husband's intervention) by describing the circumstances that led up to it. The decisive event itself is recounted in three different scenarios: the account of the original event (1) serves as a template for an imagined future scenario (2). This projected scenario in turn scares Camila so much that she resignifies it step by step, almost word by word, when she recounts the success scenario (3) of how she learned English. The elements that recur in each scenario are transcribed in bold characters.

(1) The original scenario

> But **I remember** that one time, it was like seven at night, and **I was watching soap operas** as always, when **he came in front of me** and grabbed the remote. And I said to him, 'Ohhh, not again!!' So then **he looked at me** very seriously, and he said to me, 'Yes', he said 'but this is the last time that I am going to tell you.' And **he put the television on mute**...So then I said to him: **'What do you want?'** angry like this.

(2) The imagined future scenario

> **'You are going to be sitting right here** where you are, watching your soap operas in Spanish, and **he's going to be sitting** right next to you **with the telephone, speaking English,** and making drug deals...**When you ask him what he's doing,** he's going to think, "my mom is a fool, **she doesn't know English."**...'

(3) The success scenario

> And yes, **now I can see it** because Marquitos, when I ask him something like that...**I was sitting here** and he was **talking to his little friend on the telephone,** and **he was looking at me.** And then I, I looked at him suspiciously, when I saw he was about to answer **I put the television on mute,** I hit the mute. And when I hit it, he said, *'let me talk my mom'*. So then I said to him, **'What are you going to tell me?'** 'Did you hear me?' (he said). 'Yes, I listened to you' I said to him. **'What are you going to tell me?'** So then, then he told me that Pedro wants to know if he can come to our house tomorrow. 'OK,' I told him yes...But yes, now he says that he feels scary because 'Oh no!!' he says, **'You know English,'** he says.

These three scenarios have exactly the same structure:
— Camila is sitting watching television
— Marcos/Marquitos enters the scene
— Marcos/Marquitos looks at Camila
— The television is put on mute
— Camila questions the man/the boy
— Camila's English is a decisive factor in the outcome of the story.

This common script makes the variations all the more striking. Scenario (3) rewrites scenario (1) in dramatic ways. Rather than her husband 'putting the TV on mute', it is now Camila who 'puts the television on mute'. While Marcos was the one who 'looks at Camila very seriously', it is now Camila who looks at the boy 'suspiciously' when he looks at her. While Camila asked her husband what 'he wants', Camila now asks the boy what 'he has to tell her'. The narratorial self remains in control at all times, from 'I remember that one time' in (1) to 'yes, now I can see it' in (3).

But even more noteworthy than the parallels between (1) and (3) is the mapping of the actual scenario (3) onto the imagined scenario (2). Let's compare the wording of scenarios (2) and (3).

(2) *Marcos*	(3) *Camila*
You are going to be sitting right here	I was sitting here
He's going to be sitting…speaking English with the telephone	he was talking to his little friend on the telephone
making drug deals	
You ask him what he's doing	I said to him 'What are you going to tell me?'
'She is a fool, she doesn't know English'	'Oh no!! you know English'

We can clearly see Camila closely fitting the events in her success scenario onto the deterrence scenario painted by her husband in story (2). The empty space in scenario (3) is the triggering moment that possibly associates Marquitos' proficiency in English with his ability to do drugs. From the structure of the narrative itself, the slow crescendo of 'he said' and 'he told me', and the rhetorical staging that prepared it, it is clear that the turning point, in the center of the narrative, is the specter of 'negocios de droga' or drug trafficking. This is the closest her husband can get to revive in her the traumatic memories of rape, violence, and extortion she experienced in El Salvador and to scare her into learning English. The power of deterrence of the three words *negocios de droga* is of quasi-mythic significance. Interestingly, these are the words she does not repeat in rendition (3), this is the taboo scenario she does not wish to conjure. The words left unspoken raise the suspense level of the story and invite the listener to fill in the blanks.

The punch line is cleverly related to the original question 'Why did you start watching television in English?'. In scenario (2), her decision to learn English, and the way she learned it are emphatically related to her husband.

The increased frequency of 'he said', 'he told me' leading up to the climax underscores his power and authority.

> Yes, **he told me**, but what I want to tell you is this, **he said**, that one day...now he is three years old, **he said,** but one day the boy is going to grow, **he said**, and you are never going to learn English and what is going to happen, **he said**, when he is a teenager. You, **he said**, close your eyes, **he said**, and put this photograph in your mind, **he said**...

It is her husband who raises the specter of drug trafficking. It is he who then tells her how to listen and read the captions and note things down in her note-book. It is on account of the way she tells the story, with her husband as the main driver behind her conversion, that her teacher will later give her the dictionary she will use to learn English. In turn, the dictionary will become part of the next iteration of the story she tells Julia. Thus, one could say that, even as Camila recounts her success as an autonomous individual, who puts the television on mute and takes her son to task, she casts herself as a loving, self-sacrificing, and vulnerable wife, who is dependent on the love and the care of her husband; she casts her husband as the strong man who looks after the long-term social well-being of his family; and she casts her son into someone who, thanks to his mom, will be well brought up like his father.

2.6 The power of narrative genre in the construction of the subject

That kind of domestic narrative, with its melodramatic he-said-I-said exchanges and its sentimental dialogue ('do you love Marquitos?'—'you know very well that I love the boy') conforms to a genre that is inspired by and mapped onto the Spanish soap operas Camila loves to watch on TV. Thus one has to be cautious before concluding that the author Camila was in reality a helpless Spanish-speaking woman, dependent on her husband for her survival and on her son for her self-esteem, and that she grew into an autonomous, responsible speaker of English. Based on this narrative, we can only say that Camila's narratorial self has cast the story of her acquisition of English in a genre that is culturally recognized and admired in her Latino community—a genre that, incidentally, her English teacher and the researcher (also an English teacher) found 'compelling' too.

By skillfully mapping her own narratorial self onto that of helpless heroines in telenovelas, Camila created a persona that matched the role her culture expected her to play. But in fact, as the researcher testified, Camila was one of the most cheerful and self-confident students in the ESL program, even though 'she consistently portrayed herself in life-history narratives as a victim who always got rescued by a helpful male figure' (Menard-Warwick 2004a: 15, 2004b). Her ability to map the real onto the symbolic is illustrated particularly vividly by this anecdote she told the researcher. When she was 17, she so loved a certain romantic novel titled *Maria* by J. Isaacs (a nineteenth-century Colombian novel commonly read in high schools all over Latin America), that she read it 'at least ten times'. She found the story so inspiring and she identified so much with the heroine that she composed two love poems of her own. She first wrote them on a separate sheet of paper, but 'because [she] liked them' (*como me gustaron*) she went and copied them directly into the book, thus blending her own subject position with that of the female protagonist in the book.

This case shows the power of symbolic forms, namely genre, to influence not only the kinds of stories we tell, but the kind of subject we choose to construct for ourselves. The multilingual subject Camila presented here was particularly attractive to interlocutors such as ESL teachers. It was also one of the ways in which she could reconcile her proud Salvadoran subjectivity as a dutiful spouse and a responsible mother, and her new subjectivity as a learner of English. As communicative practice, genre is 'adapted to the dominant power structures in the field to which it is addressed' (Hanks 1996: 244). Some genres are more self-contained or finalized than others. For example, a judge's verdict is maximally finalized, bounded, and closed. By contrast, the meaning of a conversational narrative such as John's is incomplete without its reception by the listener, and, in the case of Camila, without its repeated reception by multiple listeners. Besides finalization, genres are characterized by two other dimensions of communicative practice, that is, regularization and officialization. Speakers 'regularize their discourse by fitting it to the field of their current practice' (ibid.). In the same manner as John studded his account of his stay in France with phrases he knew would resonate with his Australian professor, Camila used a style of narrative that was bound to appeal to English teachers and SLA researchers. In addition, speakers build their authority as speakers by associating themselves with dominant structures, by 'officializing' their discourse. Public speakers do this by using a professional title or dropping names of important people. Camila, by refer- ring to her husband as a powerful figure who can foresee trouble and make her take action, enhances her own quasi-official status as a narrator.

Hanks (ibid. 246) sums up a view of genre that has to be kept in mind when discussing the way Camila positions herself as a multilingual subject in her story:

> Genres, then, are a key part of habitus. Through routine use, genres become natural themselves, that is, they become so familiar as to be taken for granted. Their special features are invisible to actors who experience the world through them. Through habituation and infused with the authority of their agents, genres make certain ways of thinking and experiencing so routine as to appear natural.

Camila's story is not an improvised response to the researcher's question, but a reaccentuation of past actions that she had already narrated to others or that she had heard recounted or fictionalized by others, in particular through the Spanish-language telenovelas she watched on TV.
(Wortham 2000, 2001)

3 Doing language as a multilingual subject

Let us now return to the questions we left open at the end of each case study. We were struck by the highly emotional tone of John and Camila's stories beyond their propositional content—John's visceral rejection of French behavior, Camila's deep fear that something might happen to her son if she doesn't learn English. We noticed that in each case the very discourse of the narrative contained clues to myths and memories of injunctions or interdictions that got experienced anew upon pronouncing or hearing certain utterances. The evocation of the words *'invading someone's space'* was enough to make John's body revolt; the mere mention of *negocios de droga*, that unlike the English expression 'doing drugs', evokes not only addiction and health risks, but extortion, violence, and death, was enough to bring Camila to tears. The original event (proper upbringing for John, armed violence and death for Camila) was in each case evoked in the home language. John's memories of the taboo against invading someone else's space were recalled in English in the context of a sojourn in France. Camila's memories were recounted in Spanish in the context of an immigration to the US. Both John and Camila showed a heightened sensitivity to words and their symbolic value, as they were both away from home, he in France, she in the US, and language played a prominent role in their sense of self at the time.

John and Camila's narratives raised the question of narrative truth. How do we know what Camila's real motivation was to learn English, or what the real reasons were for John's culture shock? It became evident that autobiographical narratives yield a more complex truth than informational statements of a more bureaucratic kind. The discourse dimensions we have explored: mythic language, performatives, genre, add a social and historical depth to the truth of utterances; they redefine truth as truthfulness and verisimilitude. There can be no single truth regarding the multilingual subject as social actor, especially since events lived in one language might be remembered and relived differently when recounted in another. The truth of utterances will always require interpretation and judgment.

Finally, we asked how the protagonists in each of these case studies positioned themselves as social actors vis-à-vis others within differential relations of power and authority. The cases examined in this chapter all point to the power that speakers have in the symbolic construction of their social reality. Speakers who learn, speak, or write more than one language have additional symbolic resources through which they give meaning to things, persons, and events. If, according to Foley, culture is symbolic action, that is, 'a system of public meanings encoded in symbols and articulated in social action in particular places and with particular histories and times' (Foley 1997: 16–17), then multilingual subjects have multiply embodied understandings of social reality and a broader and more varied range of options than others to act on these understandings. Ultimately, they have the choice of foregrounding either their familiarity with the dominant language, or their multilingual sensibility. If they focus on the latter, their broader and more complex understanding of people and events can increase their opportunities for reflection on self and others and for a reappraisal of commonly held assumptions and beliefs.

Notes

1   Researchers have explored motivation in SLA under varied notions: attitude and orientation (Carroll 1962; Gardner and Lambert 1972; Spolsky 2000), appraisal (Schumann 1997), investment (Norton 2000: 10), engagement (van Lier 1996: 48; Pennycook 2001), or motivation (Dornyei 2001).

2   The habitus is defined as a cluster of 'inculcated, structured, durable, generative and transposable dispositions' (Bourdieu 1991: 12). The first three features are well known. Habits of mind and behavior are inculcated in early socialization, they reflect the social structures in which they were acquired and are so ingrained in the body that they last a lifetime and are rarely amenable to conscious reflection and modification. This habitus is constantly maintained and reproduced during a lifetime through its interaction with specific social contexts or *fields,* which it both shapes and is shaped by. The last two features in Bourdieu's definition of the habitus, *generative* and *transposable,* refer to the role that the social actor plays in creating, shaping, and perpetuating the very context that, in turn, shapes his or her habitus. For example, John as a social actor is not only the product of his early socialization. By acting, reacting to, and interpreting events like an Australian, he is actively, albeit unwittingly, 'reproducing' and perpetuating Australian attitudes linked to the English metaphor of *respecting someone's space.* When in Australia, he contributes to reinforcing the very culture which has socialized him; when in France, his habitus can become the object of conscious reflection, as it no longer concurs with its original conditions of existence. The generative and transposable nature of the habitus allows for the possibility of a gap to emerge in the very process of generation and transposition—a gap between the original context of the habitus and other, less convergent contexts. It is in this gap that Bourdieu sees the possibility of social change.

3   This is particularly clear in Camila's case (Case 4). Taking the initiative to learn English originally went against Camila's socialization as a selfless Salvadoran wife and mother.

4   The notion of timescale comes from the French social scientist Fernand Braudel (1969). In his study of how systems and societies change over time, Braudel distinguished between different speeds and levels at which changes occur in societies, political institutions, and individuals. Applied linguists working in a post-structuralist, ecological tradition, such as Blommaert (2005) and Lemke (2000, 2002), have applied the notion of timescale and level of consciousness to the way an individual experiences events. For the multilingual subject the use of different languages is associated with events on different timescales (for example, experienced during infancy, childhood, or adolescence, or by proxy through stories of ancestors) and on different levels of consciousness (explained with reference to local, historical, or geopolitical events) that all coexist in an individual's subjective apprehension of reality.

5   The work of Pavlenko (e.g. 1997, 2002, 2005) confirms that for middle-class Anglo-American speakers *privacy* and *personal space* are sacred values (see also Nuckolls 1997; Bellah et al. 1985). For the differences between the French and the American perceptions of self, see the work of Laurence Wylie and Jean Francois Brière (1995), Raymonde Carroll (1988) among others, who have studied proxemics and the economy of personal space in French and North American cultures.

6   Note that, at the time the event happened, John might not have verbalized his interpretation of it in exactly the same words that he used in his statement here. The taboo might have been effective beyond its original wording and the student might have felt nothing more than a visceral repulsion at 'barging into' someone's office, without being able to explain why. His unsolicited comments several months later to his professor suggest that language retained its performative power far beyond its original iteration. Alternatively, his ascription of his behavior to the lofty principle of 'respecting someone else's space' might be seen as an a posteriori verbal construction for the benefit of his compatriot interlocutor, that served to reinforce their shared values about Australian politeness, and to justify his awkwardness in a French environment. In both cases, the taboo is a symbolic interdiction linked to a very specific English metaphor.

7   Bernstein (1996: 58) makes the distinction between performance-based and competence-based pedagogies. The tensions inherent in performance-based pedagogies are linked to the sense that linguistic, social, cultural, or ethnic 'otherness' may be problematic. These tensions are resolved through collective rituals, such as choral drills, or repetitive routines that are conducted with such psychic and emotional intensity that they can create a sense of bonding among the ritual participants. By contrast, in competence-based pedagogies, such as communicative language teaching, pedagogy is about a personal relationship between teacher and students. Social control of the class is exercised in a 'therapeutic' manner, in which discipline is internalized by the student and monitored by the teacher-as-partner.

8   We shall see more of this in Chapter 6, when we examine the productions of language students on the Internet. This happens also in classrooms all over the world. Canagarajah (1999) gives a good example of the tactics employed by his Tamil students, who resent the communicative approach used in their English classes, and who, by diverting the textbook (that doesn't belong to them) for their own, illegitimate purposes, resignify the content of the lesson in the form of graffiti in the margins of the legitimate text. Tactic users exercise their tacit 'practical sense' (Thompson 1991: 13) to survive as social actors in the space of the other.

5

The multilingual narrator

In the previous chapter, we discussed the tension between conventional membership categories, such as national, social, and cultural identity, imposed on social actors by analysts from the outside, and the subject positions available to the speaking subjects themselves. We saw how bi- or multilingual speakers use the linguistic resources available to negotiate subject positions in their exchanges with others.

In this chapter we examine how multilingual writers construct their experience and themselves as multilingual narrators. How do they use the semiotic resources offered by their various symbolic systems? How do they create new meaning through metaphors and conceptual blendings? What intertextualities do they establish with prior discourses and how do they resignify or reaccentuate them? We ask these questions first of published writings by bi- or multilingual authors that were read in a freshman seminar on *Language and Identity* given at UC Berkeley a few years ago. We then examine some autobiographical essays written by multilingual students at the end of that seminar. Whereas in Chapter 3 we looked at language learners' essays for how they represent and enact the symbolic 'subject-in-process', in this chapter we examine similar essays for how their authors construct themselves as multilingual narrators in line with the texts they have read.

The four student authors considered here are first-semester college students, fresh from high school. English is their second or their foreign language. They have been exposed to other languages besides English and the language of their parents. They have read in class some autobiographical and semi-autobiographical works by bilingual authors writing in a language that is not their native language.[1] These readings served to illustrate various kinds of narrative style. Bulgarian author Canetti's chronological narrative written in German, *The Tongue Set Free* (1979), illustrated the representation of an autobiographical self. Polish author Hoffman's highly reflexive English prose in *Lost in Translation* (1989) highlighted the construction of a multilayered narratorial self. These two authors inspired some students to construct linear, reflexive narratives akin to the linguistic autobiographies assigned in Hinton's class (see Chapter 3). In this class, however, the assignment focused less on the chronological telling of events than on the multilingual experience itself. I reproduce it once again:

> Write a one-page essay on what it means to be multilingual and multicultural. Choose the genre, the style, the code or mix of codes you prefer. Remember that being multilingual does not necessarily mean that one uses several languages as fluently as do monolingual speakers of each language. There are various degrees of multilingualism, as there are various degrees of identification with multiple cultures.

The four writings discussed here were inspired by non-linear literary forms: Malaysian poet Shirley Geok-lin Lim's English poems (1994) thematized the necessity and the impossibility of translation. Jewish Czech author Kafka's parable (1917/1971) written in German illustrated the change of identity that accompanied a monkey's acquisition of the human language. Arabic author Abdelfattah Kilito's allegory (1994), written in French, featured the bilingual person as a lost traveler in search of his tribe. Swiss/British author Christine Brooke-Rose's experimental novel *Between* (1968), written in a mixture of several European languages, epitomized the self as an acutely conscious multilingual narrator.[2] Some of the student authors were then interviewed individually and asked to comment on their essay. The interviews included such questions as: For whom did you write this text or who do you wish would read it? Why did you choose to write it in this particular manner? Why did you switch languages at this particular juncture? Which part of your writing do you like best?

I should note at the outset that, although the students were asked to write these texts as class assignments, and thus could be expected to have written them for the instructor, several of the authors insisted they had written them primarily for themselves, with no particular addressee in mind: 'like a diary' (Sean), 'I kind of imagined it just for myself' (Jocelyn). Zoe claimed she wrote it both for herself and for her boyfriend: 'It was kind of at him and it was kind of at me. It's my deepest secret but I'd love everyone to know'.[3]

The students' essay style was loosely inspired by the readings mentioned above, even though the assignment was not to imitate or emulate any particular text. In other words, this was not an *à la manière de* exercise, but, rather, a piece of creative writing to express personal experiences and memories. Specifically, in the essays below, while Jocelyn recognized having been indirectly inspired by Lim's poetry, Estella, Sean, and Zoe acknowledged that their essays were direct echoes of Kafka's, Kilito's, and Brooke-Rose's texts respectively.[4] To each student's essay, I therefore juxtapose portions of the texts read during the semester in which the students saw an inspiration for their own. At the end of the chapter, I discuss the opportunities and the risks of establishing such intertextual relations.

1 Exterior and interior landscapes of the heart

1.1 *No Man's Grove* and *Learning English*

The following two poems by Lim served as an introduction to the course's theme of language and identity. Lim grew up as a Chinese Malaysian from Malacca, and was educated in English. She now lives in California. About herself she writes:

> For many Malaysians of my generation, the language we loved and were most at home in was not our mother tongue, be it Urdu or Hindi or Mandarin or Cantonese, but the tongue of the white man we were educated to fear and admire, English. The Irish nuns who taught me to read Tennyson, themselves children of colonialism, did their jobs well. I not only learned to read, but I also learned to love; I not only learned to imitate, but I wished to belong. For this personal outcome it is not the Irish women I have to thank, but the English language itself and its manifestations in literature…Idealizing the language, I do not mean to idealize the English-language user…I do not believe in the hegemony of English in the international scene; I would always want the wonderful babble of polylanguages about me, for I grew up in a world where I spoke three languages and heard another ten on either hand.
> (Lim 2003: 170–1)

The two poems below are taken from the collection *Monsoon History* (1994).

No Man's Grove

> Crossing the China Sea, we see
> Other sailors, knee-deep in padi,
> Transformed by the land's rolling green.
> We cannot enter their dream.
>
> The sea brings us all to jungle,
> Native, unclaimed, rooted, and tangled
> On salt like one giant tree.
>
> We spring straight from sea-wave. We see
> But do not see grey netted pliants
> Shutting out the sun. Where sea and plant
> Twine, mammoth croakers crawl on tidal zone.
>
> Some will live in the giant's shade, bend
> To the rapidly rolling horizon.
> I choose to walk between water and land.
> (ibid. 37)

In *No Man's Grove,* the concrete details of plants, roots, and crawlers, the amphibious and polyvalent land- and seascape, the merging of sea and jungle, the narrator's access to other people's cultures through dream and metaphor, and her decision to occupy a boundary position between water and land—all create the dream-like atmosphere of a boundary existence where, in this in-between zone, plants and animals are each other's equivalents and sea and land mirror each other, forming an organic whole. The word 'grove' (small cluster of trees) in the title, rather than the expected 'land' (as in 'no man's land') reinforces the merger of land, sea, and vegetation. The narratorial 'I' in the last line blends the Chinese-Malaysian mindscape of the first three stanzas with her own autobiographical subject-position, living as she does now in the United States, where she remains, as she says, a 'stranger in a strange land' (ibid. 173).

Learning English

A change of heart.
An English phrase, a Western idea.
I couldn't understand
its meaning. A child,
I knew hearts did not change—
grew older unfaithful
forgetful, but were the same
father, mother.
Unfaithful
forgetful, but still father mother.

It wasn't like changing
shoes, one pair of shoes
for leather heels
tap-dancing semaphores
of excessive meaning.
Or like simple translation:
Ditditdit dahdahdah ditditdit.
It was like learning
to let go and to hold on:
A slow braking, shifting
gears, an engine
of desire on a downhill
slope, momentum of vocabularies
carrying the child
to foreign countries,
to families of strangers,
an orphanage of mind,
and technologies of empire.

It was more like cry,
a beloved country, and
see, traveler, on a hill,
by the wall, exchanging
what must be changed
forever, good-bye, farewell,

the different words working,
to say what is
unchangeable. Say, father mother.
(ibid. pp. xxiii–xxiv)

Through its repetitions and parallelisms from one line and one stanza to the next, *Learning English* establishes a historical continuity from one generation to the next, despite separations and farewells. A simple English idiom, 'to have a change of heart', untranslatable in her mother tongue, serves as a trigger for a reflection on the impossibility of translation between languages and on the permanence of emotional bonds beyond the rift created by the switch to another linguistic system. At the same time, it establishes intertextual links with other English texts, for example, in the last stanza, Alan Paton's *Cry the Beloved Country* (1960) and John Bunyan's *Pilgrims' Progress* (1678/2003), with its puritan notion of America as a city on a hill. Here again, the narrator assumes an active, albeit separate position, as an English speaker, as if dialoguing with herself, with the reader, and with the English language. The last line, with its injunction 'Say, father mother', could be addressed to the reader or to the narrator's alter ego or to other learners of English to remind them of what remains permanent across the different codes. Lim's poems served as a backdrop to Valerie's poem in Chapter 3. They have inspired Jocelyn's essay below.

1.2 Jocelyn's text

Jocelyn, 19, was born in Maryland of Korean parents. She considers Korean to be her native tongue, but she does not know it well. English is the language she identifies with. She wrote at the beginning of the term: 'English is me... I am glad for my English personality. I am secure in English. Safe.' Jocelyn had six years of Spanish. She wanted to take French but 'my mother made me take Spanish because it's more practical'. Having moved from the East Coast to California, the way she constructs herself is changing. In her first autobiography of the semester she wrote about her move to California:

Among so many Asians, among so many Koreans, I felt less Korean 'Ga-jah'. Fragments of Korean conversation surrounded me. What had been FOB [fresh off the boat] behavior before was now normal. Others' proficiency in Korean made me feel less Korean, more and more americanized. White bread where there should've been wheat. Wheat is healthier, they say. Its flavor didn't appeal to me before, but now I appreciated it for its texture, its distinctness.

Among so many Asians, among so many Koreans, I felt more Korean. 'Ai, juh nahmjah nahl-lah-ri tgat-chi...' the girl down the hall would say. Occasionally I would have to stop and ask, 'What does that mean?' I was not fully competent in code-switching. Now I spoke snatches of Korean with my hallmates. A deeper connection with those hallmates, a deeper connection to my culture.

Jocelyn's changing representation of herself and her position across several languages and cultures can help us understand the short essay she wrote at the end of the term on what it means for her to be multilingual and multicultural. Her autobiographical essay is written like a poem in prose—an internal landscape centered around childhood memories of the Korean New Year's ritual in her family. I have retained Jocelyn's unconventional spelling of Korean words and added the footnotes.

Cranes

New Year's Day. *Saebae.*[1] The colored arm stripes swooping down in elegant descent to the hardwood floors. *Saebok mahnhee bahdoo saeyo*[2] murmurs as the elders smile benevolently over the glossy black heads of the future reflected in the hardwood floors. Rice cakes falling the dog swoops to the floor, bowing not left out to bring in prosperity for the new year. *Saebok mahnhee bahdoo saeyo*[2] zechoes from the older children to the small ones who bow too fast, slur the words and whisper to the hardwood floors reflecting their smiles and confusion and bright colored arm stripes. The cranes on the brightly colored *hanbok*[3] flock to the floors to bow *saebok mahnhee bahdoo saeyo* luck and prosperity.

1 *Sebae*: a New Year's day custom of bowing (greeting/showing respect) to the elders.
2 *Saehae bok manhi baduseyo*: We wish you to receive much good luck in the New Year.
3 *Hanbok*: Korean dress/outfit for either men or women. Traditional dress.

The subsequent interview a few weeks later took place in English. R is the researcher, J is Jocelyn.

R: What did you have in mind when you wrote this?
J: It's one of my favorite memories from home and from my childhood. I just remembered all the times that I've done this and had images in my head and I thought of using the phrase *Sae...seyo*, and the cranes, then it just all fell together really quickly. In the house where we used to do this there were hardwood floors and then we would put cushions on them. It's very clean looking and natural, which is like the more traditional way, but it was also confusing because the floors reflect and so it could be several things at once, for example when the children bow, they don't really understand what they're doing and because of the reflections, it kind of adds to their confusion.
R: Why did you write the Korean words in the Roman alphabet?
J: I think it flows better because it's all in lines. Korean isn't smooth it has the blocks and things. I can't even write Korean that well. Which is maybe why I didn't write it out in Korean but in English lettering which is kind of like what I am.
R: What is your favorite sentence in this essay?

J: I like the one with the children but then it's kind of sad because they don't really understand.

R: What about the cranes?

J: Some of the *hanbok* have designs of cranes on them. There is one I really liked it's really pretty; it has cranes lining the entire arm in all different colors.

R: You have cranes on the *hanbok* of the children. Is it the cranes or the children who flock to the floors to bow?

J: It could be either.

R: What were you trying to say in this essay?

J: When I read this I imagine something at the same time peaceful and chaotic...it's really peaceful because the elders are just very benevolent and they sit there calmly and the hardwood floors and everything is very simple, but then maybe on the part of the younger generation it's really chaotic and the children are running around and the dog is trying to scramble for food and all the colors and reflections add to the chaos.

Like Lim's *Learning English*, Jocelyn's text is triggered by a traditional Korean greeting, *saehae...baduseyo*, associated with an image of family gathering and a cultural symbol, cranes. Around these three pillars of embodied memory (words, image, cultural symbol), she constructs a scenario that captures the reconciliation of the old and the young generation, peace and chaos, children and animals in the traditional ceremony of a Korean New Year's Day. The reconciliation of opposites brought about by this tradition is expressed through the symmetrical structure of the essay with its rhythmic repetition of the Korean New Year's greeting, and the alternation, in almost every line, of the words *floor* and *hardwood floors*, reflecting the past, the present, and the future around which the dog, the cranes, and the children bow, flock, and swoop in brightly colored smiles and confusion. As in Lim's poem, in which SEA IS LAND, and PLANT IS SEA, the overarching metaphors here are OLD IS YOUNG and PEACEFUL IS CHAOTIC which embrace two opposite notions, enabling the reader to see one in terms of the other. In both cases, the use of the present tense gives a feeling of time suspended. However, unlike the Malaysian poet, the student narrator does not occupy any explicit subject position in this narrative. Jocelyn chose to conceal her narratorial position—a choice consistent with her reluctance to highlight her dual identity as a Korean and an American and her desire to identify at that stage in her life mainly with her English-speaking self.

We may also give this essay an additional reading, based on the notion of conceptual blend. As we saw in Chapter 1, we give meaning to our world by mapping our experience onto previous experiences, onto the experiences of others, or onto abstract notions that we blend to make new meaning. Jocelyn's testimony on how she felt moving to California and being surrounded by other Korean-Americans is constructed discursively as a parallel mapping of one experience onto the other (cf. the repetition verbatim of 'Among so many

Asians, among so many Koreans, I felt...'). In her essay, Jocelyn's mental space can be seen as circular; the shining surfaces of the children's hair, the hardwood floors, the ritualistic greeting repeated three times, the bowing and swooping, constitute so many circles of images and counter images that establish continuity from generation to generation. The title blends the Korean mythical bird, the crane, with the children's dresses and with the children themselves.[5] Here Jocelyn's essay seems to resignify the symbolism of the crane in the Korean imagination—a bird with which children would play, but also a migratory bird—to express the invisible threads that link her back to her culture through the visual and auditory channels (the crane design, the sound of the Korean phrases), the embodied gestures and ritualistic behaviors, while at the same time prefiguring metaphorically her take-off as a multilingual subject.[6] The code-switching itself delineates the perimeter of a linguistically and culturally hybrid emotional landscape, where the spoken Korean language remains bounded and preserved but within the matrix of English. Like the idiom 'a change of heart' in Lim's poem, the traditional Korean New Year's formula *saehae...baduseyo* (awkwardly spelled in the essay) provides Jocelyn prime access to memory, images, and emotions (see Chapter 2), at the same time as it enables this daughter of immigrants to move on to the English self she now identifies with.

2 Metamorphoses and reincarnations

2.1 Kafka *A Report for an Academy*

Kafka was an assimilated Czech Jew living in Prague around the time of World War I. Although he could understand the Yiddish spoken by the Prague Jewish community and spoke Czech outside the home, German was the educated language spoken by his family and friends. It was the language he was taught at home and at school. It is also the language Kafka wrote in, a language that was for him, as he said, a 'learned' or 'paper' language.

In November 1917 Kafka published in German in the Zionist journal *The Jew* a short story titled *A Report for an Academy* (Kafka 1971). This report, narrated in the first person by a fictional well-known variety artist named Redpeter [*Rotpeter*], is a satire of an official speech traditionally delivered upon invitation to the assembled members of the Austrian academy by prominent scholars and artists. The speech is supposed to relate how they became the famous personalities they are now. In Redpeter's case, it is the story, told in perfectly literate high German, of an ape who decided to become human and who became a successful artist. It begins like this:

> Honorable members of the Academy,
> You have done me the honor of inviting me to give your Academy an
> account of the life I formerly led as an ape.
>   I regret that I cannot comply with your request to the extent you
> desire. It is now nearly five years since I was an ape...I could never

have achieved what I have done had I been stubbornly set on clinging to my origins, to the remembrances of my youth. In fact, to give up being stubborn was the supreme commandment I laid upon myself; free ape as I was, I submitted myself to that yoke. As a consequence, however, my memory of the past has closed itself off from me more and more.
(ibid. 250)

He then goes on to recount his animal life in the jungle of Sierra Leone, his capture by the hunters of the German Hagenbeck circus, the gunshot wounds he received, his incarceration in a cage too small to stand, too narrow to sit, crushed against a locker, his exhaustion and desperation, and, finally, his decision to escape by the only means available, namely, by ceasing to be an ape.

Immer an dieser Kistenwand—ich wäre unweigerlich verreckt. Aber Affen *gehören* bei Hagenbeck *an* die Kistenwand—nun, so *hörte ich auf*, Affe zu sein.
(Kafka 2002: 304)

[All the time facing that locker—I should certainly have perished. Yet as far as Hagenbeck was concerned, *the place for apes was in front of a locker*—well then, *I had to stop being* an ape.]
(ibid. 253, emphases added)

Note that this metamorphosis itself is a linguistic feat. From *gehören [an]* (to have a place) to *hören auf* (to stop), there is in German only a difference of a few letters, yet metaphysically the difference is between life and death.

The ape starts learning the body language of his captors, he imitates their every gesture, is rewarded for his progress. He manages the sociopragmatics of the human handshake, the smoking, drinking, and grunting of the sailors on board. One day, as he has at last managed to gulp down a whole bottle of vodka and to throw the empty bottle dramatically behind him, not as a desperado, but 'as an artist', the word 'Hello!' bursts forth from his lips—his first human word. Thus starts his career as a human artist. His linguistic breakthrough is the first milestone on the path to becoming a fully assimilated speaker of German. He takes German lessons and wears out many language teachers. He makes spectacular progress. He earns honorary doctorates. He becomes indistinguishable from a human member of the Academy. The only bad habit he has is to remind visitors of his origins by lowering his pants in public and openly displaying the wound he received during his capture.

Through a typical blending of mental spaces, this story was immediately understood by the readers of the time as a satire on the assimilation of Jews in German-speaking Czechoslovakia.[7] After World War II, it was put on stage at various German theaters and was read as a metaphor for the plight of immigrants and the problems of identity associated with their acquisition of the dominant language. Since the 1990s there has been a dramatic increase in the number of performances of the 'Report', for example, in Vienna, Weimar, and

Berlin, and many other German cities, featuring Turkish and Kurdish actors in the role of the German-speaking ape.[8]

Besides this rather transparent blend of an ape learning the human language and a Jew or immigrant learning German, this story can be blended with the many stories of Monkey, the Great Pretender, mischief maker and havoc wreaker par excellence, who in various trickster narratives always plays an ambiguous role, robbing Peter to give to Paul while pretending to serve both. In Kafka's story, the first human behavior that the ape learns is the human handshake, the traditional sign of man-to-man honesty and trustworthiness, a pledge to keep's one word. 'The first thing I learned was to give a handshake, a handshake betokens frankness, well, today, now that I stand at the very peak of my career, I hope to add frankness in words to the frankness of that first handshake' (Kafka 1971: 251). But of course we have to take such a statement with a grain of caution as the learner is an ape, who by definition cannot be trusted. Our suspicion extends to Redpeter the narrator. We may perhaps even distrust this whole story, since monkeys are notoriously playful and unreliable, and their language is 'gibberish'—defined by the *OED* as the 'nonsense chatter of an ape or monkey'. Kafka's monkey parable was avowedly the inspiration for Estella's text.

2.2 Estella's text

Estella, 19, was born and raised in Southern California of Korean parents. She considers her mother tongues to be Korean and English, even though she now hardly speaks any Korean at all. She says she grew up speaking exclusively English in public and Korean at home with her parents and grandparents, but she makes it clear that she didn't like Korean. She started French at age 14 and slowly became totally enamored with that language. She is now taking advanced French in college. She has written her autobiography in the form of a memo from her subconscious to her conscious mind.

To: Conscious Mind
Re: Identity

As your subconscious...I feel obligated to warn you that your attempts to break yourself away from half of your identity can have harmful effects on both of us. First and foremost, you will not become any more American by becoming less Korean. The latter is impossible, because it is an inseparable piece of you. This should be obvious, given your physical appearance and your inability to shed certain habits such as calling our mother only by the Korean word 'Uhm-ma' when speaking directly to her. Even people whose legs are amputated experience a sort of 'phantom' pain which seems to originate in the now-absent limb. The most you can do at this period in your life by learning French is merely to add another piece of identity to yourself. It is not a prosthesis or another leg, to take the place of your Korean-ness. I do think it is wonderful that you have found this new language and culture, but it can only add to the store of treasures you have accumulated in life, it will not make you forget the others.

How did Estella re-accentuate the Kafka story? The ape's obligation to give up his identity as an ape in order to survive becomes in Estella's essay the desire to stop 'stubbornly' clinging to her Korean roots, and embrace French. French has fulfilled Estella's desire to 'break herself away' from her Korean home culture, while learning a foreign language which, she said, her mother held in high esteem. But Korean leaves a phantom pain, a physical appearance and an inability to shed certain habits such as displaying her link to her mother in Korean (analogous to Redpeter displaying his wound). Proud of her achievements in French, she can't forget her origins. The metaphor of the phantom pain captures the fundamental trauma of separation from the Other (see Chapter 3) and the impossibility of ever fully uniting her Korean world and her English world. E is Estella, R the researcher:

R: How did you come up with the phantom pain?
E: If I were to try and sever the part of my identity that's Korean I would feel there would be something lacking in that area and I would feel maybe pain or guilt or regret. I feel [that phantom pain] a little bit more when I speak to my parents in English because I can't speak in Korean and so they try to speak in English but they can't because they're not as fluent as I am so there's that blockage of communication and it's when I feel regret or guilt that I hadn't tried to learn Korean so that I could communicate with them.
R: But the language spoken at home by your parents was Korean?
E: Yeah, but they weren't home that much when I was little.
R: So the language you heard most was English?
E: Yeah from a very young age, at school or with babysitters.
R: And why haven't you taken Korean in school?
E: They offered Korean classes at my high school too but I didn't want to take Korean, maybe it was part of *severing myself* from being Korean. Maybe I learned French to *fill that void* that I might have felt subconsciously by the absence of the Korean *as I tried to separate [myself from it]* and so maybe I thought *it would fill that* and in a way I thought it did because I was so enthusiastic about learning this language and even about its culture and just more and more of everything French . . . I chose French because I thought it would be more sophisticated to learn than Spanish . . . It might not be a prosthesis nor even another leg but it might almost be like an accessory, like a really nice hat or something.
(emphases added)

For Estella, French has symbolically filled the emotional void opened up by her rejection of Korean. This rejection itself, as the narrator of the testimony explains above, stems from the impossible obligation to choose between Korean and English in a society that cannot deal with ethnic diversity in any other way than through hyphenation, that is, Korean-American. Estella now and then slips so much into a French persona that she confesses espousing other political views in French classes than those she normally holds in English. Her example of the death penalty reinforces the idea of physical pain and duress.

> E: When I read *L'étranger,* [Camus] was talking about the death penalty and how people were being executed, I remember thinking violently against the death penalty, but later on when you read about it in the American newspapers you just associate it with national security or the word justice. I don't sense anything metaphysical when I read about it in the newspaper. I don't know, it's just a different mode of thought like your brain kind of switches modes. Normally I'm somewhat for the death penalty but in French class I found myself going totally against that and I remember thinking if this were in English I would probably be able to sustain my own personal argument but here I feel like I should be more liberal…just the words that come to my mind when I talk [in French] it's easier to think against the death penalty. I don't know it's hard to explain…You feel more liberal…liberated in French.
>
> R: Is it because *peine de mort* sounds different from *death penalty*?
>
> E: That might have something to do with it…maybe…peine de mort sounds worse.

The bodily metaphors Estella uses in her essay and in her interview to express her missing link to the Korean language—*amputation, prosthesis, phantom pain*—are not uncommon in language-learning memoirs. Canetti began his *The Tongue Set Free* memoir with a memorable scene in which the child is threatened to have his tongue cut off; later, he calls German 'an implanted mother tongue' (see Chapter 3). Derrida, a French Tunisian Jew, who was forbidden to speak his home languages in school (Hebrew and Arabic), calls his French monolingualism a 'monolingualism of the Other' and a 'prosthesis of origin' (Derrida 1998). The very physical, painful loss of language as a part of oneself gets transposed, in Kristeva's sense, from the body to the writing. Both Canetti and Derrida (like Hoffman and Rodriguez) write in a language that they don't feel is theirs, but that they make theirs through writing. Similarly, in her subsequent interview with the researcher, Estella associates the recovery of her Koreanness with the preparation of the writing assignment itself, that is, the concrete symbolic shaping of the subject through words.

> R: And when did you suddenly realize that French could not take the place of Korean?
>
> E: Um probably the night before I wrote this.

One should not romanticize the conversion back to an exclusively Korean identity that such a statement seems to suggest. In fact, a year later, she is confident that her two allegiances can be reconciled.

E: One thing that has changed for me is that my love of French has grown quite a bit since writing that passage. Given what I wrote in my memo, I'm not sure how I should feel about it, or how my subconscious feels ☺. But I definitely don't think that Korean and French are mutually exclusive and I'm sure some arrangement can be worked out.
(personal communication)

3 Survivors and tricksters

3.1 Kilito *Dog Words*

Dog Words written by the Arab francophone writer Kilito is a tongue-in-cheek allegorical reflection about language and identity, how one creates the other, and how the act of speaking a different language threatens to strip the speaker of his or her self. A Bedouin, lost at night in the desert, must find his clan at any price. Because he figures that human habitations are guarded by dogs who will respond to other dogs, he is compelled to imitate the barking of dogs to find his way home, but discovers after a while that he has forgotten his own human language in the process or that his own tribe doesn't understand him anymore. The story begins thus, followed by excerpts:

> Quick, what does a Bedouin do when he loses his way at night in the desert? What stratagem does he use to find human habitation, and therefore find himself? (p. xxi)...Taking his cue from the monkey, he resorts to a rather simian ploy: he starts barking (incredible but true)...One must bark in order to find one's way; in order to become human one must first turn into a dog (p. xxii)...[But] what if, upon finding his tribe, he did not find his language? What if he could only bark in response to their questions? What if he were no longer capable of using the language of his family, this language grown so familiar from his days in the cradle, if not before, this other language that he learned by imitating the movement of his mother's lips?...How then would his tribe react? (p. xxiii)...What now? No matter what he does, he will be seen as an animal. When two languages meet, one of them is necessarily linked to animality. Speak like me or you are an animal...Our hero will soon discover all of this at his own expense. The strangers, whose language he does not speak, mistake him for an animal, not necessarily a dog (he has stopped barking in their presence) but a monkey. A monkey imitating not the language of dogs but the barking of foreigners. As long as he does not speak like them, he is considered a monkey. He knows himself to be a monkey, and an asthmatic one at that...It is the effort that marks him as a monkey and mimic. There is no such thing as an effortless imitation. The monkey, who is none other than our recent wanderer, tries to get rid of his simian character in order to be seen as one of his human interlocutors...He imitates because he is *not* those that he imitates, he imitates what he cannot be, a fact of which he is well aware...An

imitation, even it if attains perfection, will never abolish the difference
that occasions it in the first place...

On the other side of the mirror the interlocutors—the monkey's
audience—are in an enviable situation. They have nothing to hide, they
appear as what they are, they act in broad daylight, in the noonday
sun (the one that casts no suspicious shadows). The monkey, on the
other hand, is a born hypocrite; he always hides something, an entirely
disavowed shadow zone goes with him everywhere. What he hides is
not what he shows. Let us not forget that he was once lost at night in the
desert, and that he is now lost among people, all because he is a mimic,
because he dissimulates.
(pp.xxvii–xxviii)

But whatever became of our noctural wanderer? He has followed his
trajectory, barking all the while. He is perhaps in a place abandoned even
by its dogs (canine deserters do exist). If that is the case, he will bark all
night to no avail.

As he writes these lines, the author is suddenly struck by a very
disturbing possibility. What if, as he writes about dogs, he suddenly finds
himself transformed into one? What if, in speaking about animals, he
were to lose his tongue (or rather his tongues, since he speaks several
languages)? What if, all of a sudden, he started barking? This risk is
shared by the reader, who is no longer immune, and risks opening his
mouth to produce, not phonemes and morphemes, not distinctive and
significant units, but rather bark after identical bark. If this possibility is
a strong source of anguish, just clench your teeth, put your hand on your
mouth, and think about something else.
(p.xxx)

We have here a cunning, avowedly multilingual, narrator who engages in
what if scenarios of the most outrageous kind. His meandering digressions
make the readers lose the little suspension of disbelief they were ready to grant
the narrator, and yet they cannot but recognize themselves in that story and
enjoy the various incarnations of humans into dogs and dogs into monkeys in
the interest of human survival. Sean chose to emulate Kilito's style and appropriate the story for the construction of his own narratorial self.

3.2 Sean's text

Sean, 18, was born in Peru of a Spanish mother and a Chinese father. Spanish
is the language of the family. The family moved to the US when he was six.
There he learned English in school and in the street, and suffered from not
knowing the language of his father's family, Cantonese. In the US, his Spanish
slowly deteriorated, but he made it his own again by taking Spanish classes
in high school. However, he never learned Chinese, in part because of the

high expectations from his father's family that he should. He has tremendous guilt feelings because of this, but hopes that one day he will connect with the Chinese language and with the culture of his father's family.

Sean has written his essay in the third person as a direct continuation of Kilito's allegory, which he resignifies to match his own autobiographical situation.

> Ah, but what if the Bedouin finds a foreign tribe where the faces seem familiar? The fires are out, the traveler knows better than to expect hospitality. Yet as the men begin to line the outer fringes of the tribal grounds, our traveler senses a *déjà vu*. These people look familiar...as if he were related to them. Slowly, this realization dawns on them too, and they warily open the way to their homes. Still, this Bedouin, a young boy of maybe six, finds himself far from home and the place where he grew up. He doesn't understand the grunts these people make; grunts are all he can understand, to him their language is a series of odd sounds that somehow make sense to these strangers. And because their language seems different, he can't shake the notion that they seem both inferior and animalistic. Yet the faces around him tug at him. He feels bad, he wants to understand, he thinks he should understand. So he tries for a middle ground; maybe he learns sign language, maybe he learns a few words, but mostly he feels guilty for producing nothing but barks. Defensive, the Bedouin adapts by appreciating the tongue he is familiar with. Since the others define him as much by what he is not, as by what he is, and he is constantly bombarded with proof that he is not part of this new tribe, he learns to take pride in the difference—not what he is missing, but what he has that they don't. Eventually, he will go back to his own tribe (after all, day must come), but until then he simply remembers. He keeps alive his unique tongue, knowing that eventually, somehow, he will find his way home. He may have to bark through another night, but the comforting language of family will be waiting.

Here are Sean's glosses:

R: How did the dog story resonate with your own?

S: It sounded very familiar, particularly the part about the transformation: how the language becomes dog sounds and how at some point they're not quite sure whether the person is human or an animal—all that really resonated with me. I remember walking in with relatives the first day when we moved. I was six, I couldn't really understand what was going on in Chinese and English neither of which I could understand...For all intents and purposes it was gibberish to me.

R: How do you see your relationship now to your different languages?

S: Language never seemed like something that I am, but something you could go out and grab a piece of.

R: Do you remember at what point Spanish ceased to be just your mother tongue and became your own?

s: When I started taking Spanish classes in high school, I remember all of a sudden being proud of the fact that I could do it, it was not just a means of communicating with my mom, it was a skill of mine, something I took pride in.

r: And you still intend to take Chinese?

s: Yeah although I'm afraid that it won't be the same as with Spanish. People who speak Spanish tend to have a certain playfulness, friendliness to their personality, but with Chinese...

In his essay, the student author has constructed a narratorial self in the interstices of Kilito's. More clearly autobiographical, less tongue-in-cheek, but no less moving, it takes as its point of departure the elements of the original story: the lost Bedouin, the lost tribe, the barks, the long night, but also the feelings expressed: the disorientation, the rejection, the longing. All these get translated into a new frame in which it is now the tribe that grunts and is therefore incomprehensible; guilt and shame get added to the mix, as well as compensatory pride on the part of the protagonist. Sean's essay ends on a promissory note characteristic of the mythical quest genre: lack-errance-trials/tribulations-attainment and liquidation of lack (Propp 1968). We find this folk tale genre in many immigrants' stories and Hollywood films. It is a familiar narrative genre in American culture. For example, the testimonies collected from Asian-American students by Hinton (1999), some of which are excerpted in Chapter 3, are presented by the researcher in the form of one such narrative under rubrics such as: language of the home, language shock/language loss, feelings of shame, journeying, struggling and searching for identity, waging internal conflicts, rediscovering and reclaiming the heritage language, and, ultimately, embracing the benefits of bilingualism. Sean's story falls into that genre. It represents in that respect a significant departure from Kilito's playful allegory that belongs, rather, to a classical Arabic tradition of texts 'whose cursory movement seems to lack direction but whose overall economy manages to contain a vast and substantial array of information' (Elmarsafy 1994: p. xxi). Resignifying stories of others entails, as we discussed with Camila's story in Chapter 4, not mere reiteration in different words, but a recasting into a social genre more appropriate to one's culture.

4 The avatars of the multilingual narrator

4.1 Brooke-Rose *Between*

The Swiss/British writer Brooke-Rose was born in Geneva from a half Swiss, half American mother and a British father, and was brought up in Brussels. She was bilingual with French as her dominant language, and did some translation from the German during the war. She married a Polish poet, studied and taught in London for twenty years, then in Paris for another twenty, and is now retired in the south of France.

The experimental novel *Between* is a non-linear narrative that thematizes travel and translation. It recounts the multilingual and multicultural displacements of an unnamed female French-to-German interpreter, who constantly travels through Europe to various conventions, conferences, and congresses. The novel is a collage of dialogues in various languages, reported thoughts and prior voices, descriptions of various locales and anonymous acolytes. Its circular structure is captured by the opening and the closing paragraphs of the novel. It starts thus:

> Between the enormous wings the body of the plane stretches its one hundred and twenty seats or so in threes on either side towards the distant brain way up, behind the dark blue curtain and again beyond no doubt a little door. In some countries the women would segregate still to the left of the aisle, the men less numerous to the right. But all in all and civilization considered the chromosomes sit quietly mixed among the hundred and twenty seats or so that stretch like ribs as if inside a giant centipede. Or else, inside the whale, who knows, three hours, three days of maybe hell. Between doing and not doing the body floats.
> (ibid. 1)

It ends, 180 pages later, with the following passage, in which the protagonist experiences/remembers/imagines/recounts (we don't always know which) one of her many interpreting jobs in Avignon, that blends the different kinds of traveling—between languages, places, cultures, people—into one big physical metaphor of suspended time.

> But all in all and civilization considered the chromosomes lie quietly mixed among the hundred million others or so that multiply in geometrical progression while nobody does anything at all.
> So that the hum of voices echoes loud in the Palais des Papes as the mayor speaks into a microphone bidding everyone welcome to this ancient city of Avignon, the acoustics of the stone palace carrying the words unheard into the high ceiling as the members of the Congress on Tradition and Innovation unless perhaps The Role of the Writer in the Modern World burble on almost excluding the introduction of Dame Janet McThingummy and Madame Helène Chose-Truc as well as Monsieur le maire's speech on hands across the frontiers over floating stomachs that move about and shshsh! Que cherchez-vous madame? A travers la cour. Au fond à droite. Ah, la sortie? A gauche madame. Oui il fait bon dehors, une belle soirée, comme toujours ici. Vous avez senti le froid dans ces murs de pierre ? Or else inside the whale and out in simultaneous wonder. Und haben Sie noch einen Wunsch? Madame désire encore quelque chose? No, nothing at all, just personal effects.
> Between the enormous wings the body floats.
> (ibid. 180–1)

These two passages are typical of the novel's echoic, circular style, where voices mesh and float into one another without any particular attribution or sense of ownership, and where the highly reflexive use of language creates its own pleasurable context. The protagonist's dizzying shuttle between languages, countries, conferences, lovers, is reflected in the myriad linguistic code-switchings the narrator engages in throughout the novel between Czech, Slovak, Hungarian, German, French, Spanish, Italian, Portuguese, within a matrix of English.

One question that recurs at regular intervals throughout the book is the crucial question of identity and loyalty of the multilingual protagonist. The female interlocutor raises that question in dialogue with Siegfried, her German lover and fellow interpreter, who responds with a quote from Goethe's poem *Erlkönig*.

— Ideas? We merely translate other people's ideas, not to mention platitudes, si-mul-ta-né-ment. No one requires us to have any of our own. We live between ideas, nicht wahr, Siegfried?
— Du liebes Kind, komm, geh' mit mir. Gar schöne Spiele spiel' ich mit dir.
— We have played those games before mein Lieb.
— Why don't you marry me?
— You know why.

In this decentered narrative without attributions of utterances or actions, the narrator disappears behind the language itself, that becomes a 'schönes Spiel'—a dazzling language game without an owner. Zoe was fascinated with this style of writing, as we can see in her essay below.

4.2 Zoe's text

Zoe, 19, was born and raised in the Czech Republic. Her mother tongue is Czech. She learned English, French, and German in high school. She came to the US at age 18, and entered UC Berkeley. For Zoe, 'each language has somewhat of a different resonance': Czech resonates with 'love and family', French with romance, play, and banter, English with professional fluency. But what she mostly enjoys is the multiple physical relation she entertains to all of them: 'speaking English', 'dipping' into French, 'slipping' into German.

Zoe's text is a reflexive dialogue between the Czech narrator and her Czech boyfriend on both sides of the Atlantic. Directly inspired by Brooke-Rose, it attempts to capture the highs and lows of their multilingual love affair through ample use of intertextuality and heteroglossia.

Chérie, I love you.
Nádherná solidarita založená na nedorozumění.[1]
A musty old apartment. Smells like cat. I think I love you. Here, have the keys.
I'd like you to be able to come and go as you please.

Lásko miluju tě, jseš nejskvělejší bytost, kterou jsem kdy poznal.[2] I LOVE
YOU BABY. And the feeling is gone…replaced by musty old cat smell
and keys to come and go as I please. Why do you say it? Do you feel that
I can only understand I love you? Proč mi neříkáš kočičko, lásko, zlato
pojd' na to, at' to stojí za to.*usměv*[3] Even a simple du bist mein Alles[4]
no matter how mangled. Anything that doesn't conjure up cats. And
marriage proposals. And a feeling that, well, if you don't rob the state,
you rob your own family. Koneckonců, kdo neokrádá stát okrádá vlastní
rodinu.[5] Oh wait, that didn't go as well as it should you ever feel the need
for a friend, appelez-moi.[6]

My bonnie is over the ocean, my bonnie is over the sea and we're like
little kids again. Only well then we don't know each other and nothing's
a problem until you make it one. Well and if I wasn't leaving on that
jet plane and you weren't l'autre et ainsi l'enfer, on aurait pu avoir
quelque chose de magnifique.[7] Instead, it's all about I love you baby, and
apartments that smell like cats and which I can never leave. And I sit
here typing away, as if I really care about all those strangers calling me
liebchen, kočičko, drahoušku, kotě,[8] but see at least they don't tell me
they love me…Tak to budeš moje česká milenka, jo? No jasně, a budeme
se mít strašně rádi, jo? No jasně, miláčku. Dobrou. Nebála by ses v noci
ve věži?[9]

---

[1] (Czech) Beautiful solidarity founded on misunderstanding.
[2] (Czech) Darling I love you, you are the best person I have ever met.
[3] (Czech) You don't say, love, dearest, let's do it, so it's worth while. Smile.
[4] (German) you are my everything.
[5] (Czech) After all, he who does not rob the state, robs his own family.
[6] (French) call me (formal second person plural).
[7] (French) [if you weren't] the other and thus hell, we could have had something magnificent.
[8] (German) darling, (Czech) dearest, honey, little cat.
[9] (Czech) so you want to be my Czech lover? By all means, we will love each other, right?
Of course love. Good. Would you be afraid to spend the night in a tower?

Zoe's text showcases the various narratorial positions available to the multilingual subject in increasing degrees of distantiation and artfulness. The
text starts with a dialogue of intimacy and closeness between the self and her
Czech boyfriend in the playful cohabitation of French, English, and Czech
(lines 1–5). At the boyfriend's abrupt switch from 'I love you' to 'I LOVE YOU
BABY', the multilingual dialogue unravels. English takes over in lines 6–7,
Czech remains only a memory of intimacy (lines 7–8); even German would
be better than this all-pervasive English (line 8). The narrator becomes more
distant as she ventriloquates in English a popular Czech saying dating from
the Communist era in the CSSR. When the original Czech saying appears in
line 12, it has the effect of a bombshell. The boyfriend is insulted, and the
narrator resorts to a citational utterance ('should you ever feel the need for
a friend') and a French formal formula ('appelez-moi') to distance herself

from the damage done (lines 13–14). In the next five lines, English becomes the language of sadness, loss, and nostalgia, while the playfulness indexed by French and the tenderness indexed by Czech are rallied, as if to ease the pain (lines 15–19). The last three lines of the text provide a final ironical twist. As Zoe explains in her interview, these are direct quotes from an exchange she had with an unknown Czech interlocutor on the Internet.[9]

In this text the narrator and the boyfriend, and, somewhat marginally, the anonymous Internet correspondent take on various subject positions, depending on the language they speak and how that language is positioned vis-à-vis the others. Like Brooke-Rose, Zoe plays with disembodied narratorial voices, and uses the same grammatical features to index both closeness and distance, intimacy and alienation, and to maintain this ambivalence throughout. The subsequent interview between Zoe and the researcher yields a much-needed gloss to this postmodern-style essay.

R: So what did you have in mind when you wrote this?

Z: He had the tendency because I am in America and he's Czech once in a while to say I love you instead of the Czech, and it used to drive me insane. The simple translation of the words [into English] completely changes the meaning and completely changes my relationship to him. I love you doesn't connote love to me, because I've had American boyfriends that I never felt love for but who felt love for me and who would say I love you...

R: What about the capital letters in I LOVE YOU BABY?

Z: The word baby just sounds so bad. *Chérie* I can do, *chérie je t'aime*. But I love you baby is just I love you baby bend over type of thing...pardon my vulgarity...

R: Why German in Du bist mein Alles?

Z: To me it's preferable that he uses some sort of neutral language rather than a language where the words are already associated with specific meanings.

R: What's the value of French?

Z: It's more of a game when we speak French to each other. It adds a little bit of distance and a little bit of fun, but at that point in time [when I used the formal *vous* in *appelez-moi*] it just created too much distance.

R: What is the meaning of 'if you don't rob the state...'?

Z: My parents had told me that about robbing the state versus the family, [they said] it was a communist thing, and I brought it up in some conversation with [my boyfriend] and he told me I didn't know what I was talking about and I shouldn't discuss things I don't understand, and so I just kind of threw that in because it was something that was somewhat rankling.

R: In 'should you ever feel the need...' you omitted a *should,* was that on purpose?

Z: I put in a conscious deconstruction of the sentence and consciously um chopped the first part, yet kind of made it flow into the other...maybe just to stop the self-reflection and to turn it into something much more impersonal and much more um offensive, like taking the offensive instead of being put into the defensive...

R: What did you mean to say by writing 'my bonnie is over the ocean, my bonnie is over the sea'?

Z: That's a song I learned English with. It's a reflection about the fact that I'm here and he's there and there is a sea between us...on the other hand it's using language to imply things that I mean but because I know that he knows what the next lines of the song are, it's easier just to leave it implied than to actually state it and make myself vulnerable, so again I can hide behind the language and use that and discount it in the next sentence...

R: Where did 'nothing's a problem until you make it one' come from?

Z: I think this was actually something he may have said to me in Czech and I've translated it into English and threw it back in his face.

R: Why do you switch then to French ?

Z: I was struggling with...how do I spell *appelez*, does it have one l or two...it was actually it was just *l'autre* and the distance, that switched me into French. And I finished the sentence off in French because that just seemed the most appropriate at the time and um because I know that he can understand me in whatever language I speak.

R: And what about this quotation from Sartre?

Z: I wanted to just let him know that well ok if you're going to distance your-self from me with language, then I can do the same. If you can't relate to me on my linguistic basis then you are obviously further away from me than I can relate to and that idea just glid into the idea of Sartre...

R: What is the significance of Czech in the last sentences?

Z: I was talking to a person I had just met on the internet that was a Czech guy living in San Francisco and we were talking about how I was Czech...and all of a sudden he's like so oh you're Czech cool do you want to be my lover (*tak to budeš moje česká milenka, jo?*) but it was annoying because he was using the terms of endearment that my boyfriend would use...it was depressing because I was having a relationship that was linguistically more authentic to myself with complete strangers than I was having with him...That was the funniest question: so you want to be my Czech lover? Hey you wanna be my lover? I've never met you but hey you want to be my lover, based on the fact that you're Czech and you're 19?

R: What about 'Nebála by ses v noci ve věži'?

Z: Instead of saying do you want to come up to my place, he says would you like to spend the night in my tower, and I thought that was quite a poetic way of saying it. I love that line and I thought it would be appropriate to use that as a metaphor for my relationship to Czech and English, because this text is really about the conflict between the two and the untranslatability between the two.

Zoe's essay and her narrative in this interview offer an extreme case of the way the multilingual subject exploits the semiotic resources of code, stance, and subject position to construct and enact her multilingual experience. At the end of the interview she transforms the line out of the Czech film *Kolya* (in which a lonely violin teacher tries to seduce girls by asking them to 'spend the night in [his] tower') into a 'turning point' (Bruner 2001: 32), which serves retrospectively to justify her whole narrative, that is, the conflict between Czech and English.

When asked whether she felt there was such a thing as a linguistic identity, Zoe brought up metaphors of appropriation and ownership.

> z: Being able to say things in more languages changes your relationship to each specific one... If I didn't speak English and I didn't speak French and I didn't speak German, it would never occur to me that I could have words that are linked to specific emotions that are untranslatable into other languages.
>
> English is the language I use on the whole the most, I have the widest vocabulary in English. It is the language that I can best manipulate to suit my views but I don't consider a language mine until I can actually feel I own the words, and I don't, in English. I'm not very grammatically proficient at French to say the least but I can express myself in a good enough manner and I feel confident enough about my French that I can say yes I own that language, although I don't always get the subjunctive right and the spelling and all that, but I do feel that I own the words to the extent that I can make them say what I want to say.

Ironically, the subjective ownership of French gives Zoe also the freedom to disown it, that is, to use it in order to distance herself from it. As Zoe remarks, the multilingual subject is not necessarily the person who speaks many languages with equal mastery or with native or near-native proficiency, but is more often than not someone who resonates to each language relative to the other, and who has a more acute awareness than usual of the social, cultural, and emotional contexts in which his/her various languages have grown and of the life experiences they evoke.

5 Discussion

The juxtaposition of student essays and the texts that inspired them gives us a glimpse into the way each of the multilingual authors crafted a narratorial self that was both unique and constrained by the cultural conventions of genre. As Bruner remarked, autobiography is less a 'remembering' than a 'self-making and world-making' (2001: 25; Bruner and Weisser 1991).

In each case, it seems that the authors resonated to a theme, a genre, a style and tried it out on themselves for size. First let us look at the theme they chose. Like Lim, Jocelyn started out with a phrase and an image, and built a New Year's scenario around it along the theme of the reconciliation of opposites; the poetic genre and its historical present seemed appropriate for this timeless family portrait preserved in memory for future generations. Estella resonated to the theme of the ape become human under extreme physical duress by casting her essay in the form of a stern memo featuring her dual self under equally painful conditions. Sean was attracted to the theme of rejection and possible redemption found in the Kilito narrative; he reaccentuated this theme to his own multilingual situation. Zoe was seduced by the theme and the style of Brooke-Rose, and resignified the tribulations of the protagonist of *Between* in the form of a playful cohabitation of multiple languages, each associated with her own life experiences.

In each case the authors had to decide how they would organize their multilingual experience: around harmony (Jocelyn), separation (Estella), a thwarted search for wholesomeness (Sean), or language games (Zoe). The original question, what does it mean to be multilingual and multicultural? is answered, then, differently by each narrator. For Jocelyn and Estella it means a subjective tension between two distinct cultural identities and an attempt to resolve the present by recasting the past. For Sean and Zoe, it means finding or rediscovering a linguistic bridge to a lost family or a lost lover. Each of these essays represents a thematic transposition or reaccentuation of an experience constructed differently by another multilingual author.

Second, let's look at the genre and the style they chose to write in. The students' narratives make sense to us because we are familiar with the genres in which they are cast. The family vignette, the memo, the quest/redemption narrative, the surrealist stream of consciousness are all part of our repertoire of genres with which we construct ourselves as subjects. Some are more familiar to our culture than others—for example, the quest narrative feels more truthful to most American undergraduates than the surrealist stream of consciousness—and they contribute to making us into the cultural subjects we become. Within genres, certain styles (metaphors, collocations, etc.) are common to members of a given culture and make their narratives comprehensible, because they make the telling legitimate and trustworthy. For example, Estella's metaphor of the *phantom pain*, semantically linked to *amputation* with such phrases as *breaking yourself away from half of your identity* (memo) or *severing myself from being Korean* (interview), is made possible by the English language in which she expresses herself. These are recognizable ways of talking about cultural identity in the United States (see Excerpt 3.12). Estella might have constructed a different narrative self had she used a different linguistic system and a different style, as she experienced in French classes regarding the death penalty. But telling her story in the commonly accept generic idiom ensures her the empathetic recognition of American readers and makes her readily recognizable to herself as an American narrator. In Jocelyn's essay, such collocations as *bright(ly) colored arm stripes*, *benevolently smiling elders*, *cranes swooping or flocking to the floor* are part of a conventional genre recognizable to anglophone readers as typically 'Korean'.

But didn't the authors say they were writing these essays for no one but themselves? As Bruner (1986, 1991, 1994) and Bruner and Weiss (1991) argue repeatedly, all narrators tell their stories both for themselves and for others, even if these are only imagined others. On the one hand, they do write for themselves, because as Roman Jakobson remarks, 'language is a system not only for communicating, but also for organizing attention' (cited in Bruner 2001: 32). 'Narrative', writes Bruner, 'is a form of organizing experience...autobiography is not only about the past, but is busily about the present as well' (ibid. 28–9). In that respect, our student narrators were organizing, casting, recasting a multilingual experience they were grappling with and trying on various theories of self: looking back and consecrating the past (Jocelyn), projecting themselves into the future (Estella), searching for a lost family link (Sean), or making multilingual intimate relationships comprehensible to themselves (Zoe). These theories of self imply 'theories of growth or at least transformation' (Bruner 2001: 27), that were expressed in the interviews.

However, despite their claims to the contrary, autobiographical narrators also write for others. Part of the socialization into becoming a speaker of culture is learning how to tell one's story in ways that are understandable to others, and for this, one has to abide by the socially accepted conventions of the genre. 'The shape of a life is as much a function of the conventions of genre and style in which it is couched as it is, so to speak, of what 'happened' in the course of that life' (Bruner and Weisser 1991: 129). Part of the narrative genre is the insertion of a 'catastrophe' or crucial event that triggers the sequence of events and justifies the telling of the story (see Camila's story in Chapter 4). In their study of the autobiographical narratives among members of the same family, Bruner and Weisser (1991) found that each narrator chose a different 'turning point' that served as the organizing principle in his or her narrative. A turning point is an event, an utterance, an action that is taken as a metaphor for rationalizing all other events and legitimizing their telling. Here Zoe clearly organized her narrative around the switch from Czech to English in the boyfriend's utterance I LOVE YOU BABY. The emotional shock caused by this code-switch forms the turning point around which all other utterances in her essay are organized. For Sean, it is the sudden transformation of the warm family language into grunts of rejection. The choice of a turning point generally corresponds to a deep version of self that plays itself out at each telling, but not without variations. As Bruner and Weisser (ibid.131) write, 'Once one commits oneself to a particular 'version', the past becomes that version or becomes inflected toward that version,' but 'we can tell or write our own autobiography in one mode or genre and later read or recall it in terms of another or several others.' For example, Estella, from her own admission, would write her essay differently now. Such variations are elicited to a large extent by the person of the reader or interlocutor, the language(s) used, and the circumstances of the telling.

One issue that Bruner and his colleagues do not address is: what happens to genre when a narrator tells in a foreign language for a foreign readership a story that was experienced in another language in quite a different cultural community? Beyond the linguistic code, which genre will make the story comprehensible? Which rules of telling will obtain? We realize the importance of genre when we see what generic subjects the students constructed for themselves upon reading the texts at hand. The three seasoned prose narrators in the Kafka, Kilito, and Brooke-Rose stories were writing for quite a different readership and had been shaped by quite a different narrative tradition (Jewish, Arabic, and European respectively) than the young American student narrators. Their prose is characterized by self-conscious irony and a heightened metalinguistic awareness. Kafka's *Report* and Kilito's *Dog Words* end on a verbal pirouette, and Brooke-Rose's *Between* definitely has no turning points. These characteristics get lost in Sean and Estella's texts, that pick up on the themes of these texts, but not on their style. Sean and Estella's style reflects, rather, the narrative tradition in which they have been trained in American schools, that includes the account of losses, struggles, and the prospect of happy endings. By contrast, Brooke-Rose's surrealist style is in part retained in Zoe's essay, that is more in line with the different schooling she received in the Czech Republic and the different narrative traditions she has been exposed to there. However, she too introduces a turning point that gives a narrative dynamic to her essay that is not found in Brooke-Rose's *Between*.

Looking back to the construction of these students as multilingual subjects, they were given the opportunity to craft a subject position with the resources offered within the realm of the symbolic [1] and [2]. As bilingual youngsters having grown up in families that spoke another language than English they wielded the grammatical and lexical structures of English and other languages to refer to their autobiographical experience (symbolic [1]). But they also patterned those structures to represent the more subjective realities of memories, fantasies, projections that make up their symbolic selves (symbolic [2]). In fact, this work of representation, that, as we saw, had elements of the poetic and the literary, had a performative effect on the authors themselves, as if writing about themselves in that manner created scenarios of possibility they could actualize later.[10] The phrases and metaphors that triggered their essays (a Korean New Year's saying for Jocelyn, a 'phantom pain' for Estella, 'foreign grunts' for Sean, a lover's switch from Czech to English for Zoe) served as condensation symbols that captured a cluster of emotions and feelings that could be expressed only indirectly through metaphors and parables. In turn these condensation symbols opened up a realm of human possibilities that the authors were discovering as they were writing about them. Indeed, by her second year Estella was attending Korean as well as French classes, Jocelyn decided to enroll in Korean classes, Sean became determined to learn the language of his Chinese paternal family, and Zoe decided to eschew her known languages altogether and venture into Japanese. Her avatars on the Internet offer a glimpse of what happens to the multilingual subject in the virtual realm of cyberspace, which we explore in the next chapter.

Notes

1   In *The Translingual Imagination* (2000), Kellman calls such authors either 'ambi-linguals', if they write authoritatively in more than one language, for example, Beckett (French/English) or Dinesen/Blixen (English/Danish), or 'monolingual translinguals' if, as is more often the case, they write in only one language but not their native one, as is the case with the authors cited in this book: Canetti, Chiellino, Esteban, Hoffman, Kafka, Lim, Makine, Sarraute, Sartre, Tawada.

2   Other readings in this course included: Kaplan (1993), Rodriguez (1982), and selections from Danquah (2000), as well as poems and essays by Jean Arceneaux et al. (1980) and Chiellino (1992, 1995).

3   All names are fictitious. The texts and portions of the interviews are reproduced here with the students' permission.

4   This assignment was the third of three given during the term. The first two were (1) a 2- or 3-page linguistic autobiography; (2) a 2-page account of a significant event in your life as a multilingual person. I am grateful for the inspiration that Leanne Hinton (2001) gave me for the first assignment.

5   During our interview, Jocelyn explained the cultural significance of cranes. Cranes thrive over the vast area of Siberia and migrate down to the Northern Korean peninsula and the Yangtze River in China during the winter. In the Korean tradition, the crane symbolizes longevity and noble character through the beauty of its graceful body, white purity, and noble dignity. Along with clouds, mountains, and pine trees cranes are often the subjects of poems, paintings, writing, and music. Cranes were embroidered on the formal robes of scholars in the earlier Korean dynasties. In modern times, they appear on fabrics, gifts items, vases, and dishes to represent long life, happiness, and abundance. Jocelyn remembered being read as a child the well-known short story 'Cranes' written in 1953 by the Korean author Hwang Sunwon, which captures the mood and aspirations of the Korean people at the end of the Korean war. In the story, which takes place along the 38th parallel that was to divide North from South, cranes, tied down by children to serve as playmates, are ultimately freed to fly high up into the sky and to migrate to distant lands.

6   Two years after writing this essay, Jocelyn decided to take Intermediate Korean in her third year in college.

7   In a letter to his friend Max Brod dated June 1921 (Brod/Kafka 1989) he refers to attempts by Jews to learn German as 'mauscheln', the German word for 'speaking like Moses, i.e. like a Jew':

> Das Mauscheln im weitesten Sinn genommen…[ist] die laute oder stillschweigende oder auch selbstquälerische Anmaßung eines fremden Besitzes, den man nicht erworben, sondern durch einen (verhältnismäßig) flüchtigen Griff gestohlen hat und der fremder Besitz bleibt, auch wenn nicht der einzigste Sprachfehler nachgewiesen werden könnte.
> (ibid. 336)
> (Jewish talk [*Mauscheln* or the use of German by Jews], in the broadest sense…is the loud or silent or even torturous appropriation of a foreign property, which one has not acquired, but has stolen through a relatively rapid sleight of hand, a language that remains foreign property, even if not a single speech error can be detected.)
> (my translation)

8 For a more comprehensive analysis of Kafka's story, see Kramsch (2008a).

9 For a more comprehensive analysis of this essay, see Kramsch (2003b).

10 Given that they had already written two other aubiographies in a more straight-forward report style, most students chose to write this, their third essay, in a style that invited a metaphoric reading. We should not conclude that multilingual subjects are intrinsically more literarily gifted than others. The self-conscious, semi-serious, semi-parodistic stylization we find in these essays only demonstrates that, as psycholinguists have shown, multilingual individuals tend to have greater metalinguistic and metaphorical awareness (Bialystok 1991; Bialystok et al. 2005; Baker 1993), a greater ability to grasp the arbitrariness of the linguistic sign and its relationship to reality (Ianco-Worrall 1972), and a sharpened capacity to decenter, i.e. to take on a perspective other than their own (Genesee, Tucker, and Lambert 1975).

6

The virtual self

After examining how multilingual subjects position themselves as narrators in spoken and written communication, we turn now to one of the major changes in our late modern era, that is, computer mediated communication, and the new forms of subjectivity offered by the electronic medium. We first consider how computer communication, by changing the relation of speaking subjects to time, space, and other speakers, is changing their relation to themselves. We then examine concrete examples of the use of computer mediated communication to learn foreign languages and we listen to what youngsters say about their experience networking on line. We finally draw on recent theories of identity in the age of the Internet to discuss the opportunities and the risks presented by the virtual reality of cyberspace for the multilingual subject.

1 From personal diary to electronic blog

We saw in the last chapter how Jocelyn, Estella, Sean, and Zoe wrote about their experience with various languages and claimed to have written these essays 'for themselves', even though they had written them upon the request of a teacher as a classroom assignment. They had typed these texts on their word processors and handed them in, but retained a sense that they were like personal diary entries—a dialogue with the self. For example, Jocelyn did not feel the need to translate the Korean phrases she wrote, nor did Zoe feel obliged to translate the Czech sentences, since they themselves understood all these languages. Estella and Sean took it for granted that the reader would recognize the Kafka and Kilito subtexts in their essays. Zoe's text in particular is as opaque to an outsider as a personal diary entry intended only for the eyes of the writer. The subsequent interviews clarified much of the unspoken assumptions that an external reader could not possibly know. We examined these writings in their performative aspects, noting that they not merely represented but also constructed the unique multilingual experience of their authors. The struggle with various symbolic forms and codes and their subjective meanings was, we said, what made possible the emergence of the multilingual subject.

Now what would happen if these four authors had not typed and printed these essays to hand in to the teacher, but had posted them on a blog, or shared them with others in an electronic chatroom, or text messaged them to friends, or posted them on Facebook? It is easy to think that, because the computer can be used as a typewriter, the passage from the diary to the blog affects only the transmission, not the content of the message. But is that really the case? By changing a diary into a blog, you change the number of intended readers, the speed of transmission, the scope of dissemination, the format of the text: shape of the paragraph, size, color, and shape of the font, visual inserts, and tolerance to typographical and other errors. It also makes your diary more interactive: by making your diary public, so to speak, you open yourself to the evaluation of your text by others outside the bounds of any institution, you solicit their responses, which you can then incorporate in any future diary entries—a virtual co-construction of the self in dialogue with others. To what extent is the virtual subject constructed in computer networks in the same way as the symbolic subject we have encountered throughout this book? What becomes of the multilingual subject when it goes online?

2 Three models of language, three modes of subjectivity

From a diary to a conversation to a blog, the change of medium brings about a change of focus and value. Following Graddol (1994), we can identify three models of language description, each of which focuses on a different aspect of language and its associated symbolic value: the written and print medium, with its emphasis on form and information; the spoken medium, with its emphasis on dialogue and interaction; the electronic medium, with its focus on link and connection.[1] Each offers a different way of constructing the multilingual subjectivity.

Model 1, a 'modern' or structuralist model of language derived from the study of written Latin, focuses on the material substance of language, the grammatical and lexical structures of the sentence, that can be analyzed and taught as building blocks to communication. This model is heavily influenced by writing and print technology and the way print has made possible the standardization of language. Meaning in this model is predominantly seen as referential meaning, as information that is enclosed in written or spoken texts and that is retrieved, sent, and exchanged. It is a transmission model of language still espoused by many language teachers. Because language in this model is very much subjected to the rules of usage imposed by dominant institutions such as the educational system, academia, and professional standards, it forms part of the symbolic order that, as we saw in Chapter 4, human beings are socialized into. Communication in this model depends on everyone agreeing to use words to mean the same thing, codified within the standard language promoted by educational institutions. The language learner herself is an idealized, standardized, non-native speaker anxious to abide by the rules of the standard native speaker. One way people have found to free themselves from the constraints of this symbolic order has been the diary. A diary allows its author to write for herself, to construct for herself an idealized alter ego that becomes the recipient of all sorts of intimate confessions: dreams, doubts, and desires that remain unseen, uncensored. The diary is a safe place to express the subjective feelings that Kristeva attributed to the realm of the semiotic.

Model 2, a social model, sees language as embedded in its social context, and communication as dialogic interaction between speakers and listeners, and by extension between readers and texts. In this model, form and meaning vary according to the setting, the situation, the intentions, and the purposes of the language users. Because language in this model is seen very much as a tool for social interaction, it is constrained by the norms of the social group. It is based not just on attested rules of usage (grammar, vocabulary) but on observable rules of use (pragmatics of conversation, text genres, discourse conventions). One way in which people have freed themselves from this social symbolic order is by diversifying and relativizing its constraints. Through such concepts as heteroglossia and intertextuality, Kristeva has shown that the social group (and the symbolic order it imposes) is much less homogeneous than Lacan seemed to suggest. Not diary, but conversation is the genre of choice for a multilingual subject here. Conversation, or dialogue, allows speakers to construct for themselves a new subject position with every new interlocutor and with every linguistic choice, as we have seen in the cases discussed in Chapter 4.

Model 3 is a 'postmodern' model of language as it informs media texts. This model takes a broader view of language as symbolic system. Born out of media and cultural studies, it is concerned with signs rather than words and how signs connect with other signs. Music, pictures, clothing, belong to signifying practices or processes of human communication of which the linguistic system is only one: 'the boundary between language and non-language is blurred' (Graddol 1994: 17). We could call this model of language an ecological model.[2] It is concerned preeminently with texts, not with sentences as model 1, nor interactions as model 2, but rather, it sees text as a combination of many semiotic systems (words, typographical conventions, layout, photographs, graphs, diagrams) that are socially and jointly constructed by many people. Texts are viewed as speaking with many 'voices' (ibid. 18). Communication in this model is a site of struggle to be heard, noticed, and understood, and to 'maximize the acquisition of symbolic profit' (Bourdieu 1991: 76). In this model, authenticity and authorship acquire a new meaning, as Graddol remarks:

> [T]exts are not simply read and understood, but *consumed, used, exploited* . . . a text will take on a different life, new functions and new meanings, *according to the social activities in which it is embedded* . . . The postmodern language user cannot be said to have particular ideas, intentions and meanings which then become encoded in language, since language users are not the authors of their own meanings: they use the

words of others, their utterances and texts are populated with other voices, and they cannot guarantee how their texts will be received and interpreted.
(Graddol 1994: 19, emphases added)

This model, with its emphasis on the social use of texts in social interactions, shifts from a focus on authenticity and authorship to a focus on agency and connection (Kramsch, A'Ness, and Lam 2000). It is often associated with electronic communication.

As is the case with the print and the spoken media, the electronic medium has an overlay of symbolic values: the value of creating links, making connections, recognizing patterns, and manipulating signs. The blog is the quintessential manifestation of this connectionist model: it is as unencumbered by standard rules of usage as the diary, as interactive as a conversation, and through the compression of time and space offered by the computer it enables users to shape and manipulate public opinion. If the first two models imposed their own constraints on the speaking subject—standard usage on the one hand, norms of interaction on the other, this model imposes a global connectivity that is at once exhilarating and threatening for the autonomy of multilingual subjects and the delicate balance of their languages. We shall see in section 5 below how language learners deal with this postmodern condition.

3 From self offline to self online: what has changed?

In each of these three models, language is linked to technologies for the production and reproduction of semiotic systems—the pen or the printing press, tape recorder, telephone, television, computer—with their concomitant political economies; each has its own conventions and constraints, its own gate-keeping mechanisms, its own ideological overlays.[3] Since they represent different stages in the development of technology, each technology seems to build on the previous one, reframing, amplifying, or attenuating aspects of communication found in previous technologies. Moreover, each new technology offers aspects of the previous ones. For example, one can use the computer as a word processor, or as a tool for face-to-face conversation (interactive video or Skype), or as a television. Thus there is a temptation to think that computer-mediated communication (CmC) is different from spoken or written communication only in degree, not in kind.

Proponents of the first two models of language would agree that CmC is not intrinsically any different from, say, communication via a telephone or a TV, because they view the technological object and the individual subject as two separate realms—according to the modern 'man–machine' dichotomy. It is not the electronic medium that changes things, they say, but human users. The subject that sits at the computer is the same as the one bent over a sheet of paper or speaking into a telephone. Like written communication, CmC has its conventions that language users need to abide by. They too must authenticate the electronic 'spoken' or written texts they read on the screen, they too must become authors if they are to make sense of the (virtual) world online. Computer learners do this by learning the language variety of their electronic interlocutors, the rhetorical conventions of electronic genres, and by interacting with people and written texts online. The computer, they argue, fosters the same kind of language use as before, only now with a broader readership that has easier and speedier access to texts. It is a facilitator, an enhancer of a textual literacy that is fundamentally the same as our traditional print literacy (Warschauer and Kern 2000).

By contrast, those who espouse the third model take a different view. If texts are indissociable from the 'activities in which they are embedded' (see Graddol quote above), they argue, and if language as semiotic system is inseparable from the events it encodes, then the computer as semiotic medium is itself part of literacy events. It is not a neutral technological object that we can use for our individual or institutional purposes. My use of the computer as a typewriter or a database or as a way to network is itself an historic event, embedded in a network of discourse practices and institutional constraints. By talking about 'browsing' through various 'spaces', 'surfing' the net, opening various 'windows', sitting in electronic 'cafés' and 'chat rooms', and 'interacting' with 'people' in various 'meeting places', we are already creating a continuity between the real world of cities, beaches, houses, and cafés, and the virtual worlds created by the computer. By saying, 'it is not the electronic medium per se that changes literacy practices, but its enlarged readership, its speed of delivery, the multiple scales of the texts, their ease of access', we talk as if readership, time, scale, access, were not constitutive of the medium, as if the medium were only the hardware. The change in technology does not seem to change the activity itself, nor ourselves in the process. But in fact, the computer is both the product and the producer of the connectionist view of language and communication held in model 3. It is transforming the multilingual subject into what Mitchell has called the networked self or Me++, as we shall see in section 7 below.

The fundamental difference between the subject experienced offline and the online subject lies in the kind of knowledge they can have both of the world and of themselves. In their textbook for MIT's entry level subject in electrical engineering and computer science *The Structure and Interpretation of Computer Programs*, Abelson and Sussman (1985) make it quite clear that 'the computer revolution is a revolution in the way we think and in the way we express what we think' (1985: p. xvi). While we have been used to viewing knowledge as declarative and language as referring to how the world is, computer knowledge is procedural, that is, it acts upon the world, models it, manipulates it, in an attempt to solve its problems. 'The essence of this change is the emergence of what might best be called *procedural epistemology*—the study of the structure of knowledge from an imperative point of view' (ibid.).

As MIT literary scholar and computer scientist Janet Murray (1997) explains, a digital environment has four essential properties.

1 *Procedural authority*. We tend to forget the quintessentially procedural nature of the computer, invented to solve problems by drawing on an unlimited, relational database. The computer gives access to a mutable, kaleidoscopic world of possible connections that seems to have no center. Unregulated, unauthored, juxtaposed, and multiple versions of reality and degrees of simulation make the Internet into a system of interrelated actions, without the coherence established by one autonomous, holistic subject.

2 *Distributed authorship*. Indeed, the connectionism of cyberspace is enhanced by the interactive network of users itself. The virtual space of the computer encourages collaborative virtuosity, collective responses, and multiple addressees, *commedia dell'arte* role-plays, in which Goffman's (1981) distinction between authors, animators, principals, ratified and non-ratified participants becomes more difficult to uphold.[4]

3 *Spatial agency*. The attractive feature of the medium is the sense of spatial agency it confers upon its users (Kramsch, A'Ness, and Lam 2000; Lam 2003). Unlike authorship, that requires the imprimatur of those who control the distribution of texts (publishers, distributors, academia), agency is gained at the click of the mouse. The ability to find, retrieve, recycle, recontextualize, and otherwise manipulate and disseminate data, without any outside interference is for many a source of empowerment and pride (Lam 2000). Some have associated the pleasure derived from such bricolage (see Chapter 1 Note 4) to an aesthetic experience (Lanham 1993; Murray 1997).

4 *Encyclopedic search*. The computer is an environment that can not only manipulate existing symbols such as words and texts (word processor, hypertext technology), but also model, that is, represent, reality and thus recreate it (multimedia technology). Through its capacity to model the complexities and paradoxes of the world, it can leapfrog analytical modes of understanding, shift perspectives, and simulate reality, and has therefore endless potential for storytelling and art (Murray 1997: 284; Heath 2000; Hull and Katz 2006).

The result of the procedural epistemology that humans have created through the use of computers is a virtual culture, that is redefining not only how we know, but who we are. As Sherry Turkle, a clinical psychologist from MIT, writes: '[On the Internet], we are encouraged to think of ourselves as fluid, emergent, decentralized, multiplicitous, flexible, and ever in process' (1995: 263–4). This sounds like the subject-in-process we saw in Chapter 3, except that the computer has dramatically changed the very time/space axes of the subject's existence. The autonomous self as conceptualized by Damasio and Neisser and semiotically grounded by Kristeva, whose body is inscribed in history, whose personal memories and fantasies are based on individual neural pathways and actualized in interactions with others, is slowly being replaced by a networked self, whose cognition and emotions are distributed across an electronic web of global connections, and for whom time and space have been collapsed through a keyboard on a computer screen. If the self is a decentralized network, how can it 'think of [itself] as fluid, emergent and decentralized'? Who is there to do the thinking? And in which language?

The virtual self we encounter in this chapter is all the more intriguing as it retains close ties, of course, to the symbolic self we have been examining in this book: a self that, sitting at his or her computer terminal, perceives, emotes, feels, remembers, projects, and fantasizes based on the verbal and non-verbal symbolic forms he or she apprehends on the screen. These forms are particularly conducive to dreams of escape, anonymity, and performative power and to the imagined identities that we have encountered in youngsters learning a foreign language (Turkle 2001). We have associated these forms with the construction of a symbolic self, but what is the nature of the virtual self? In the following section, I examine what kind of virtual personas students build for themselves in electronic chat rooms and telecollaborative exchanges. I then reflect on the thrills and threats of virtual environments for the integrity of the multilingual subject.

4 Multilingual chats online

The use of synchronous chatrooms where language learners practice the language and learn to use it in interaction with others has become a favored pedagogic activity in foreign language classes. Researchers report greater motivation to communicate and increased volume of communication, greater willingness to self-correct and to learn from one another—all beneficial effects for the development of communicative competence. In addition, researchers have noted a greater propensity to play with language, to code-switch and foreground language form.[5] Here we examine some of these data from the perspective of the construction of the multilingual subject.

The following excerpts are taken from two intermediate college-level foreign language classes that use the MOO (Multiuser Object-Oriented synchronous, text-based Internet database) chatrooms of networked computers to get the students to practice the language for communicative purposes (see also von der Emde, Schneider, and Kotter 2001). I use here MOO data collected by Warner (2001) and Kern and McGrath (2008) at UC Berkeley. In each class, 15–20 students have been placed at computer terminals. In the German class, students have been asked to improvise the role-plays assigned in the textbook. In the French class, they have been given no other constraint than to chat freely with one another in French. The excerpts below are taken from exchanges that took place in the first few weeks after the beginning of class, when students did not know each other well yet.

Excerpt 6.1
Intermediate learners of German are assigned to role-play a restaurant script

1 Freak says, „Wo bist du, Kellner"
2 Freak says, „Schnelllllll".
3 Schmu says, „Bestellen Sie jetzt etwas zu essen."
4 Freak says, „ja?"
5 Schmu says, „oder, moechten Sie eine Speisekarte?"

6 Freak says, „ich habe ein Spieskarte."
7 Schmu says, „na gut. Was moechten Sie zu essen?"
8 Schmu says, „SCHNELL!"
9 Freak says , 'I'm not really trying to be an ass. It's a game, right?'
(Warner 2001).

[1. Freak says, 'Where are you, waiter?'; 2 Freak says; 'Quick!!!!!!'; 3 Schmu says, 'Are you ordering something to eat?'; 4 Freak says, 'yes?'; 5 Schmu says, 'or do you want a menu?'; 6 Freak says, 'I have a menu'; 7 Schmu says, 'OK. What do you want to eat?'; 8 Schmu says, 'QUICK!'; 9 Freak says,' 'I'm not really trying to be an ass. It's a game, right?']

In this pedagogic role-play, the students exploit the spaces between the identities of German waiter/German customer imposed by the assignment and the more fluid subject positions afforded to them by the medium. In the pseudonymity of the electronic chat room, cultural authenticity gives way to playful banter. The visibility and recyclability of the utterances on the screen lead to the possibility of animating identity types ('impatient waiter' modeling himself on 'impatient customer') (see Note 4), and of parodying and reaccentuating the utterances of the interlocutor (line 8 where the customer's *quick!!!!!* is reaccentuated into *QUICK!*). The participants seem to enjoy typing German words while retaining American cultural frames (in the insistence on speedy service)—a procedural game that is less likely to happen in face-to-face interaction in the classroom under the watchful eye of the teacher. Here, the students feel free to play with the very frames of the assigned role-play while using standard German. But the real risk of playing with frames has to be reduced by flagging the make-believe nature of the frame. Here, the risk was apparently so great that Freak felt compelled to switch to English in line 9, to make sure that no threat to Schmu's real face had occurred. The subjects being constructed here have to navigate various degrees of reality and surreality. The next exchange follows immediately upon Excerpt 6.1.

Excerpt 6.2
Same German role-play activity 'At the restaurant'

1 Freak says, „Ich moechte mehr Rotwein und Fleisch."
2 Schmu says, „was fur Fleisch moechten sie?"
3 Schmu says, „Kuh, schwein, oder Pferd?"
4 Freak says, „Rumpsteak mit Pilzen und Karotten aber nicht Pilzen und nicht Karotten."
5 Schmu says, „gut gut, ich bringe es schnell, ohne Pilzen und Karotten".
6 Freak says, „gut".
7 Schmu says, „hier ist es!"
8 Freak says, „Ich warte."
9 Schmu says, „und wie ist Ihre Wein?"
10 Schmu says, „HA ich bin schnell!"
11 Freak says, „that means I'm waiting".
12 Schmu says, „ja".

13 Freak says, „Ja. Bist du nicht so schnell."
14 Schmu says, „pshaw".
15 Schmu says, „hier ist deiner Fleisch ohne Pilzen und Karotten" (Warner 2001).

[1 Freak says, 'I would like more red wine and meat'; 2 Schmu says, 'what kind of meat would you like?'; 3 Schmu says, 'cow, pig, or horse?'; 4 Freak says, 'rumpsteak with mushrooms and carrots but not mushrooms and not carrots'; 5 Schmu says, 'OK, OK, I will bring it quickly, without mushrooms and carrots'; 6 Freak says, 'OK'; 7 Schmu says, 'here it is!'; 8 Freak says, 'I'm waiting'; 9 Schmu says, 'and how is your wine?'; 10 Schmu says, 'HA, I am quick!'; 11 Freak says, *'that means I'm waiting'*; 12 Schmu says, 'yeah'; 13 Freak says, 'yeah, you are not that quick'; 14 Schmu says, 'pshaw'; 15 Freak says, 'here is your meat without mushrooms and carrots'.]

Whereas the role-play had up to then followed the rather traditional textbook script, Freak in line 4 tries to break the expected frame by ordering the canonical menu item but without most of its components. His use of 'ich warte' in line 8 playfully ignores Schmu's display of prompt service in line 7 and impersonates an impatient customer, but it also puts him in an ambiguous subject position. For, the German phrase 'ich warte', unlike the English equivalent 'I'm waiting', could be understood as a sign of patience ('I am not in a hurry, I can wait'). In line 11, by reiterating this time in English 'that means I'm waiting', Freak seems to be offering a simple translation of his previous German utterance in line 8, but in fact, he is giving the German phrase retroactively the English connotation of impatience. He is thus sending the message 'I'm really playing at speaking English even when I speak German within a German role-play.' In the rarefied cultural environment of a German classroom in the US, the electronic medium seems to increase the possibilities of playing one linguistic code against the other and of trying on subject positions that are both German and American at the same time.

Excerpt 6.3
Intermediate level college French students

1 Gilles says, « vous n'etes pas des students mais des stupidents ».
2 Corinne_C says, « tu es mechant ».
3 Gilles [to Corinne_C]: « je blague voyons!! ».
4 Emily_Y says, « oui il blague »
(Kern and McGrath 2002).

[1 Gilles says, 'you are not students but stupidents'; 2 Corinne_C says, 'you are mean'; 3 Gilles (to Corinne_C): 'hey I am kidding'; 4 Emily_Y says, 'yes, he's kidding'.]

In this brief exchange, we note that Gilles's 'kidding' is effective only because of the written nature of the medium and the code-switch in line 1 from French to English. The switch retains the real English word 'students', silently read or subvocalized as '*studants*', modeled after the association with the French word '*étudiants*' that has currency in the real world of the French class. But '*studants*' then gets retextualized in the surreal space of the MOO into a hybrid Franglish '*stupidents*'. This space of play is textually expressed through the insertion of the two letters *p* and *i* to coin the neologism *stu-pi-dents*. Thus we have here multiple levels of play, not with the French language itself, but with the interstices between French and English, between spoken and written language, between French imagined as English, and English imagined as French. The fact that Gilles needs to explicitly index the play frame in line 3 'Hey, I'm kidding!!', reinforced by Emily's 'yes, he is kidding', illustrates again how labile the frame 'This is play' can be and how easily ritual insults in the virtual world can be mistaken for insults in the real world.

Excerpt 6.4
Intermediate college level French students enter the chatroom

1 Marina says, « salut tous ☺. »
2 Doug says, « On chat. »
3 Doug says, « ☺ ».
4 Dina says, « eh bien…»
5 Doug says, « Ou "chatte"…»
6 Marina says, « chatte veut dire qqch de vulgare Doug! »
7 Doug says, « Eh…je pensais que ce pourrait etre le cas.'
8 Doug says, « alors, c'est quoi le mot correcte pour dire « chat »? »
9 Dina says, « mais non! c'est une petite chatte mignonne!☺ »
10 Tony says, « on dit tchat ».
11 Marina says, « je crois qu'on peut bien dire chat…euh…peut-etre… »
12 Doug says, « Ah oui, c'est ca. »
13 Tony says, « on va 'tchater' je crois ».
14 Marina says, « merci Tony ».
15 Doug says, « tchatcher… » (Kern and McGrath 2008).

[1 Marina says, 'hi to all ☺'; 2 Doug says, 'we chat/cat'; 3 Doug says, '☺'; 4 Dina says, 'well…'; 5 Doug says, 'or "female pussy cat"…'; 6 Marina says, 'pussy means something vulgar Doug!'; 7 Doug says, 'eh…I thought it might be the case…'; 8 Doug says, 'so, what is the correct word to say "chat"?'; 9 Dina says, 'no! it is a nice little female cat! ☺'; 10 Tony says, 'they say tchat'; 11 Marina says, 'I think we can say chat…eh…maybe…'; 12 Doug says, 'yes, that's right'; 13 Tony says, 'we will tchat I think'; 14 Marina says, 'thanks Tony'; 15 Doug says, 'tchatcher…']

In line 2 Doug proposes an ambiguous definition of what the group will engage in: '*on chat*' can mean 'we chat' or 'we cat'. This ambiguity might not have been intended, because it was probably subvocalized by Doug as English *chat* as he typed it, and thus represented a code-switch, but it is impossible to say for sure from the written form of the word. Upon reading this written form, Doug himself seems to resignify English *chat* as French *chat* since he offers the feminine form of chat in line 5. The space created by this discrepancy between speaking and reading, between a written English word potentially pronounced like French, and a French word potentially pronounced like English, opens up unintended typographical possibilities. In line 5, the French word *chatte* (female cat, pussy cat, or pussy) remains within the rules of French spelling and fits phonetically within the expectations of the on-going discourse, but it opens up new spaces for free semantic variation. What Doug has done, in a sense, is transform the French reality of male and female cats into a hybrid hyperreality of English chats that also simulate French cats, but he risks breaking the rules of English decency in the process.

Excerpt 6.5
Assignment: 'Write with a partner about your plans for the Christmas break'

1 Janice dit, « Preetha: tu a visite singapour pendant les vacances de noel? »
2 Cameron (to Franz), « ou est-ce que tu veux aller? »
3 Preetha dit, « oui, pendant 3 jours ».
4 Sabine dit, « je n'ai rien a dire ».
5 Marcus dit, « Comme elle est belle...je ne peux m'en detacher, je serre plus fort la main
6 de maman, je la retiens pour que nous restions la encore quelques instants, pour... »
7 Justin dit, « Janice, est ce que Molly est dans un autre classe de français maintenant? »
8 Janice dit, « Justin, oui je vois son nom dans la liste... »
9 Cameron dit, « moi je ne l'ai jamais vue ».
10 Marcus dit, « Je n'y arrive pas bien. Je ne parviens a revoir que son visage assez
11 flou, lisse et rose...lumineux...».
12 Franz dit, « Cameron, ma femme etude d'etre une coutouriere et new york est le
13 meilleure ville en etats unis »
14 Marcus dit : « c'est mon emerveillement qui surtout me revient...tout en elle etait
15 beau. C'etait cela etre belle ».
16 Marcus dit : « O; est doffoco;e de retrpiver ce qie cette [pi]ee de cpoffeir avaot de so.
17 fascomam » [CK : *il est difficile de retrouver ce que cette poupée de coiffeur avait de si fascinant.* (Marcus has moved his hand into an incorrect position, one key to the right.)].
18 Sabine dit, « Mark, tu es vraiment bizarre ».
19 Eve dit, « Marcus, de qui parles-tu? ».
20 Marcus dit, « c'est de Nathalie Sarraute, *Enfance.* J'en lis maintenant ». (Kern and McGrath 2008)

[1 Janice says , Preetha, 'have you visited Singapore during the Christmas break?'; 2 Cameron says (to Franz), 'where do you want to go?'; 3 Preetha says, 'yes, for three days'; 4 Sabine says, 'I don't have anything to say'; 5 Marcus says, 'How beautiful she is…I cannot take my eyes off her, I press harder the hand of my mother; 6 I hold her back so that we can stay a few more minutes, so that…'; 7 Justin says, 'Janice, is Molly in another French class now?'; 8 Janice says, 'Justin, yes, I see her name on the list…'; 9 Cameron says, 'I have never seen her'; 10 Marcus says, 'I can't manage to see her. I can only recover the rather vague contours of her face, 11 smooth and pink…a shining face'; 12 Franz says, 'Cameron, my wife is studying to become a seamstress and New York is the 13 best city in the United States'; 14 Marcus says, 'it is my amazement that I mostly remember…everything in her was beautiful. 15 This is what it meant, to be beautiful'; 16 Marcus says, it is difficult to 17 recover what was so fascinating about this Barbie doll'; 18 Sabine says, 'Mark, you are really bizarre'; 19 Eve says, 'Marcus, who are you talking about?; 20 Marcus says, 'it is by Nathalie Sarraute, *Childhood*. I am reading it now.']

This extract has a surrealist, even absurd, Ionesco-like feel to it because of the clever insertion by Mark of literary quotes from Sarraute's *Childhood* (1984: 80–1) and the bizarre intertextuality that ensues. It capitalizes on the typographical layout of MOO utterances on the screen, that the computer is programmed to present in quotation marks preceded by the name of the speaker. Thus Mark's utterances become visually indistinguishable from those of the narrator Sarraute as if they were part of that conversation. His voice meshes with hers in the typical heteroglossic, double-voiced experience Bakhtin identified in Dostoyevsky's fiction (Bahktin 1986). The cleverness stems not only from this tightly controlled ventriloquation, where the literary quotes closely fit into the ongoing conversation, but by the actual—deliberate or not?—typographical displacement by Mark of one letter on the keyboard in lines 16–17. This displacement creates a physical space of disjunction that throws off his interlocutors. Their indignation illustrates the unsettling feeling experienced by language users when genres are blurred and the real clashes with the surreal in the hyperreality of the online classroom.

The extracts above show a significant amount of language play, a phenomenon that has been shown to be conducive to second language acquisition.[6] As Cook notes, all play transforms reality—with or without role-play or computer, because it foregrounds form and fiction.

> A good deal of authentic or natural language is playful, in the sense of being focused upon form and fiction rather than on meaning and reality…What is needed…is a recognition of the complexity of language learning: that it is *sometimes play and sometimes for real, sometimes form-focused and sometimes meaning-focused, sometimes fiction and sometimes fact.*
> (Cook 2000, emphasis added)

But in online chat rooms, the procedural nature of the computer makes language learning into both play and reality, both fact and fiction *at the same time*, depending on whether you look *through* the frame or *at* the frame. In this environment, the taboos of language learning are suspended: grammatical and spelling errors, code-switchings, code-mixings, non sequiturs slip in, that foreground signifiers and weaken the links between utterances and their intentionalities, thus bringing semiotic 'play', or looseness, into the system.[7] In the moving, fluid, relational realm of cyberspace, there seems to be an increased temptation to exploit the transitional contact zones between languages, between spoken and written language, between authoring and animating words (see Note 4), and to use these contact zones for greater manoeuver and creativity. As such, it seems to offer particularly interesting possibilities for the construction of a multilingual subject if reflected upon later in class.

5   The intercultural communicator online

If online chat rooms seemed to offer a propitious site for getting 'out of gear' and enjoying the 'play' of asocial talk, intercultural communication with real native speakers brings back the necessity of attending to the real world in all its linguistic and cultural complexity. In that respect it brings students back to the serious business of language learning as goal-oriented communicative practice. However, here too, as we see below, unexpected gaps or divergences open up between what is meant and what is said that can be disconcerting to the participants. In intercultural communication these gaps can leave them angry and resentful, as they expect the computer to act as a transparent conduit for their well-intended messages.

Telecollaborative projects have become a popular activity in US foreign language education. They are intended to put language learners in direct contact with native speakers from the target country.[8] They usually consist of three to seven-week email exchanges between American undergraduates at the intermediate/advanced levels of language instruction and learners of English abroad. Such telecollaborative projects are notoriously difficult to organize and they present an intercultural challenge for both students and instructors. I examine here an excerpt from Ware's (2003) study of an asynchronous email project between intermediate-level students of German at a university in the southwestern part of the United States and intermediate-level students of English at a university in northeastern Germany (see also Ware and Kramsch 2005).

The students, in groups of five, were asked to initiate their online contact during the first week of the exchange by posting on the small-group bulletin board their comments on the results of a language and culture survey they had all filled out prior to the beginning of the project. They were left to choose which language they wanted to use, English or German. The group from which this excerpt was taken comprised two Americans (Rob and John) and three Germans (Marie, Ida, and Steffi). All members of the group had previously posted their first assignment, and they all used their foreign language to do so. Now they are waiting for Rob's contribution. Rob's posting is responded to by Marie, and the following exchange ensues, to which none of the others contributed, but to which they had access via the bulletin board. As we shall see, this exchange offers glimpses of the rich historic context in which Rob and Marie, as authors, live and post their messages, but it simultaneously highlights the uncertainties about the reality and authenticity of Rob and Marie as narrators, and Rob and Marie as computer users. In the discussion I use different fonts to indicate that distinction: Rob and Marie are the living authors; *Rob* and *Marie* are the narrators; ROB and MARIE are the computer users.

```
Current Forum: Group 3
Date: Tue Mar 5 2002 4:37 pm
Author: Rob
Subject: Tuesday, March 5


Well, I guess it is already Wednesday the 6th for you
guys. I am not sure to which one of you I am supposed
to be writing to, but I guess that will clear itself
up in time. I am not sure I will be able to hold an
interesting discussion today because I have had a very
bad and long day and have a lot of work to do. Are you
guys excited about doing the email exchange thing?
Do you have much contact with Americans? There was an
American army base in the town I was in (Wuerzburg)
and so many people there thought that all Americans
were so loud and obnoxious. I soon learned that
there were many American bases throughout Germany
and unfortunately many similar Americans. I learned
German fast and with a good accent just so I would
not be related to them. But I am not sure how all that
is in der ehemaligen DDR, I mean, with the American
bases. Do you dislike being called that? If so, what
do you prefer, if anything? Many people in the US are
proud to be from certain states (like Texas) or even
from the North or the South. We are such a big country
that we need to divide ourselves up in order to define
ourselves and relate to others.
```

Rob, the narrator, clearly has problems with footing and finding the proper narratorial voice, as he bravely attempts to establish a common ground for an informal exchange among strangers. His convivial form of address ('you guys'), his hedges ('I am not sure', 'I guess'), his disclaimer ('I am not sure I will be able to hold...because...'), his attempt to distance himself from 'ugly Americans', his efforts not to sound judgmental about the division of Germany by equating it with the division of the US into states—all these are attempts to reduce the distance between him and far away strangers. He wavers between various subject positions: a plain 'good guy', a fellow student, a good (rather than an 'ugly') American, a proud American.

But we must also look at ROB, the computer-competent student. If the medium is, indeed, the message, we must factor in his avowed lack of interest in 'that email exchange thing', because, for him, a computer assignment is boring. We must consider the non sequiturs, the monologic style, the ease with which he can fill the screen with words to quickly get rid of an unwelcome assignment. ROB is, in Bruno Latour's (1999) words, ROB-WITH-A-COMPUTER—a different kind of person than ROB-WITH-A-VOICE, or ROB-WITH-PEN-AND-PAPER. To this we have to add the fact that Rob is writing in English and that Rob-writing-in-English is a different signifying self from Rob-writing-in-German (cf. Chapter 1). For example, the register that he would use with his American peers ('you guys') has a different flavor when addressed to and read by non-English speakers. The colloquial 'you guys', addressed to complete strangers would be perceived by Americans as a sign of friendliness and outreach, but could be taken by German readers to be merely a typical American marker of informality, not necessarily friendliness, so that it might be read as indexing Americanness, not necessarily friendliness. Thus, in the relational and ecological sense we discussed above, *Rob* the English narrator becomes a different subject from Rob the author (cf. in Chapter 5, Estella's changed self-perception when she speaks French). The medium, and the symbolic uses to which it is put in Rob's life, inclines ROB to post things on the screen that Rob might not say or might say differently in face-to-face conversation.

```
Current Forum: Group 3
Date: Wed Mar 6 2002 12:55 pm
Author: GERMAN, LERNERIN D <None>
Subject: East—West—conflict

Hi Rob,
this is Marie. I read you letter today and I have
been a little suprised. You have made the experience,
that the Germans think or thought the Americans are
abnoxious? Why that? Because of the role they played
after 2nd worldwar? Actually the US was a occupation
power after the 2nd worldwar. Do you experienced any
anger or something like that?
Now a little history lesson: After 2nd worldwar the
former 3rd empire was splitted up by the Allies into
two parts. Western Germany was controlled by the US,
France and England. The Eastern was controlled by
Russia. The ideas of order weren't not the same in
each part of Germany. So they argued with each other,
then came the wall and the cold war (is this the right
word?) So there can't be any army-base in the eastern
```

part of Germany. Nowerdays there are also no army-
bases in the East.

I have no contact to Americans. In former times I had
a pencilfriend in America. Her name was Jamie but I
think we don't fit together. She had some strange ideas
about the world I couldn't handle with.
[...] Well, I was born in the former GDR. Now I'm
just a German girl. We have also federal states like
you in the US. I live in the new federal state of
Mecklenburg/Vorpommern.
[...] After the wall broke down many of eastern
Germans lost their jobs. Today we have the highest
number of unemployed people. We never knew that in
our former state. The social system in the GDR was
bad but there weren't enemployed people. That's
just one reason for bitterness here. To my point of
view the reunification was just fine. Now there are so
many abilities for me. I'm really happy and glad.
Everything in the GDR was strictly organized. [...]
Today it is possible to do what you want. Just having
a little American dream. [...] Today it is like in
America maybe. We are allowed to do what we want, to
go where we want and to say what we think. We are just
glad. There are allways good and bad things. To my
mind it was the best that could happen to us.
[...]What do you think is Bush a warhawk. We had
a little discussion in class about. Write me you
opinion.
Greetings Marie

In her response, Marie, too, can be seen alternately as an author (Marie), a
narrator (*Marie*), and a computer user (MARIE). *Marie* presents herself as a
new Westerner, a born-again American, free to voice her opinions and to ask
others about their opinions, free to criticize or at least to express the criticisms of others. But her voice is ambiguous. On the one hand we have the
autobiographical Marie, born and raised in the GDR, with her ambivalent
feelings about the social and economic consequences of the reunification for
Germans living in the East and her avowed bad experience with a former
American penpal. On the other hand we have the narratorial *Marie*, conscious of the Americanness of her interlocutor and anxious to sound both
factually informative (through her little history lesson) and ideologically con-
genial (through her praise of her new democratic freedoms). Like *Rob*, she
seems keen on establishing common ideological ground (her 'What do you
think...?' echoes *Rob*'s 'Do you dislike...what do you prefer...?'). But then
there is also a computer user MARIE, who behaves differently on the computer

than she would in real-life, face-to-face conversation. This MARIE obviously enjoys the medium and has pleasure expressing herself in English. For her, the computer assignment is new and exciting. The length and chattiness of her contribution can be seen as a sign of her excitement at using this sexy new technology, her eagerness to practice her English, or to show off her new 'Americanized' identity, or to do small talk in the hyperreal, carefree way she feels is encouraged by the electronic medium. Expressions like 'Now I am just a German girl' or 'Is Bush a warhawk?' index a certain theatrical coyness, a rhetorical pose, that is made possible by the narcissistic freedom of cyberspace. But her display of enthusiasm for the German 'American dream' sounds a little artificial after the depiction of the unemployment rates caused by the German unification. So where is the real Marie?

```
Current Forum: Group 3
Date: Wed Mar 6 2002 4:59 pm
Author: Rob
Subject: Re: East—West—conflict


Dear Marie,
Thank you very much for the little history lesson,
but unfortunately I was already aware of that. My
only question was whether the American army bases had
moved into the old eastern part of Germany since die
Wende. Maybe because you did not grow up around any
of these bases, you do not have the same experiences
as the people in West Germany do with the soldiers.
And yes, I met many people that did not like Americans
at all...As I said, I learned to speak German very
fast and with a good accent, so that later I was able
to avoid these problems. As far as Bush is concerned,
I would apologize for his being elected as our
president, but, as I was in Germany at the time of his
election, I was not able to vote and therefore am not
guilty of his being elected. Now that he is president,
all I can do is hope that he does what is right
instead of criticizing him.
```

Rob feels obviously peeved at the history lesson despite the mitigating diminutive 'little', especially coming from a woman and a foreigner. He does not take *Marie*'s admonition as being, possibly, some phrase that comes from her environment, or a role she is playing, or the expression of an exuberant young East German excited to be sitting at a computer. His answer is addressed to the autobiographical, the 'true' Marie, whose statement he has taken at face value. In his response to what he takes to be an attack against his elected government, he feels obliged to tow the party line, even though he later admitted that he didn't know why he wrote that, because he doesn't even support

Bush's policies. So he too, displays a narratorial or virtual self that is not necessarily the same as his own, authorial self.

```
Current Forum: Group 3
Date: Thu Mar 7 2002 12:11 am
Author: GERMAN, LERNERIN D <None>
Subject: Re: East—West—conflict


Good morning Rob,
it's about 7 and it's my birthday.
Probably my English knowledges are to blame for the
misunderstanding, I´m sorry, I wouldn't teach you.
Your answer in order to Bush sounds a little bit
sulky. I don't want to attack you. Or was it just
ironic?
My English seems to be that bad that I maybe can't
hear those fine differences.
Have a nice day
Marie
```

Marie is struggling with the truth value she is expected to attribute to *Rob*'s statement. Surely he must be sulky, that is, offended or on the defensive (the German equivalent being *schmollend* or *eingeschnappt*). In turn, her own statement 'I'm sorry' is ambiguous: Is it a real apology? The display of an apology? A coy simulation of an apology? The real and the virtual collide. In the absence of further clues, the conversation feels like the blind leading the blind, to the distress of the parties involved.

```
Current Forum: Group 3
Read 16 times
Date: Thu Mar 7 2002 4:56 pm
Author: Rob
Subject: Re: East—West—conflict


happy birthday, and no, your english is not bad at all.
```

This last statement, in its brevity and inconclusiveness, shows the perplexity of well-intended participants when conducting 'real-life' exchanges in the hyperreal environment of online communication. From then on, Rob participated very little in the conversation. Marie, by contrast, continued to write more prolifically than any of her peers on either side of the exchange. After the online exchange ended, the researcher attempted to clarify the misunderstanding by asking Rob and Marie for their perspective. Rob did not respond except to post the following message that refers to a passage from Marie's postings.

```
Current Forum: 27.3 Vergleiche Verhandlungen
```

```
Now a little history lesson: After 2ⁿᵈ worldwar the
former 3ʳᵈ empire was splitted up by the Allies into
two parts. Western Germany was controlled by the US,
France and England. The Eastern was controlled by
Russia. The ideas of order weren't not the same in
each part of Germany. So they argued with each other,
then came the wall and the cold war (is this the right
word?) So there can't be any army-base in the eastern
part of Germany. (Marie)
Ich glaube, dass jeder Germanistik Student etwas
davon lernen konnte. Wir sollen alle unsere
Geschichte kennen. [I think that every student of
German can learn from this. We should all know our
history.]
```

Marie replied over email to the researcher's invitation to interpret what had happened. She leaves open the possibility of multiple interpretations.

```
Hi, Mrs. Paige,
...I wanted to avoid misunderstandings. I felt like
I had to explain everything, because I wanted him
to understand what I was trying to explain. I had a
long time to think about it and in the end I can't say
what made him angry. I read the letter once, twice,
again and again. I cannot say...my big explanations
maybe? My writing sounds very teachful, don't you
think so? I wrote him so many things, he had already
known, because he had spend time in Germany before.
You told me, that he is very proud on his knowledge
about Germany. Could this be the reason? Write me your
opinion.
```

If we compare Rob and Marie's final comments, we can see that *Rob*'s narrative ends on a moral, that he posted publicly in German to all members of his group and that gives this whole exchange the meaning of a cautionary tale.[9] This kind of closure is in line with the way Rob perceived the 'true' reality of an exchange that engaged real people with real feelings and reactions. By contrast, *Marie*'s response retains the inherent ambiguity of what was both a real and a virtual exchange.

There was a great deal of controversy among the participants as to the meaning of the event. This in itself is evidence of the ambiguity of subject positions afforded by the electronic medium. The semiotic gaps that opened up in this exchange were unanticipated and incomprehensible to the participants. They are analogous to those we witnessed in the online chat rooms, except that, here, both teachers and students expected the medium to offer cultural 'authenticity' and reliable 'truth'. That this was not the case and that it prompted frustration and distrust instead is due in no small part to the fundamental ambiguity of the medium, its fluid time-space, and its lack of boundaries. This ambiguity can be captured along three axes of space, time, and reality that directly affect the way the multilingual subject is constructed.

5.1 Space: presence–absence

Unlike real space that is characterized by either the presence or absence of two living sign users who share a common acoustic, visible, or palpable material communicative base, virtual space is characterized by both presence and absence. The sign producer is co-present with the computer in the real world, and the signs are visible on the screen, but sign producer and sign receptor are absent to each other.[10] Not only are they absent, but the signs on the screen are not necessarily their own (see Excerpt 6.5), rather, they are a collage from various sources, for example, forwarded email messages, input from multiple recipients, or inserts from multiple texts; their words can be altered, amplified, interspersed, they no longer point to or stand for their original authors. Language users are co-present only in a liminal utopian space that has features of the liminal spaces we encounter in literature or myth—spaces of transgression, semiotic exuberance, and fluidity. For instance, we noted *Rob*'s desire to pass for a German, *Marie*'s desire to pass for an American, we noted MARIE's verbal exuberance online, as well as the semiotic uncertainty experienced by both partners and exacerbated by cultural differences. In the chat rooms we noticed a propensity to play with signifiers, to engage in word magic, bricolage (see Chapter 1 Note 4) and in potentially subversive, anti-authoritarian language practices (Lam 2003; forthcoming).

5.2 Time: reversibility

By contrast to real time that is irreversible and heterogeneous, i.e., that is experienced differently at different times in different places, virtual time is both irreversible and reversible. What has been 'uttered' irreversibly in real time is endlessly reversible and reproducible by clicking on the 'undo' icon on the screen, and endlessly iterable by clicking on the 'copy' icon. The words of others can be borrowed, recycled in different contexts, reattributed, and scrutinized, and texts can be blended into one another. Language can be assembled, disassembled, dissected, analyzed; a text can be erased, corrected, embedded in and linked to other texts through a hypertext technology that might add to, subtract from, or otherwise change its 'intended' meaning. We saw a dramatic example of this in chat room Excerpt 6.5, but we saw this also in the Rob–Marie exchange, as *Marie* picks on *Rob*'s textual juxtaposition of 'in der ehemaligen DDR' and 'American army bases' and its factual untruth, and sets the record straight, instead of attending to the spirit of Rob's message. The fact that Marie's answer appears on the bulletin board, for all to see, right underneath Rob's message, makes the discrepancy between Marie's and Rob's versions of history particularly glaring and oppositional. The easy intertextuality afforded by the infinite reproducibility of prior postings, rereadable at any time, has to be factored in when trying to understand, for example, the controversial use of 'warhawk' by *Marie* as a potential echo of *Rob*'s controversial use of 'die ehemalige DDR [the former GDR]'. Both phrases are ideological condensation symbols (see Introduction, section 4) that, publicly and officially posted and reproduced on the screen at every reading, are bound to arouse conflicting emotions.[11]

Not only did this telecollaborative exchange eliminate the usual time and space boundaries but it transformed what looked on the screen like a unique and autonomous encounter between two individuals into a repeatable, networked event, in which time had become as visible and divisible as space—a time-space. It transformed a one-to-one, irreversible event into a one-to-many happening, an endlessly scrollable series of postings that became accessible on the electronic bulletin board to other ratified and non-ratified participants (see Note 4), who could stand by or eavesdrop on the conversation, even though they remained invisible. Much of what happened during this exchange has to be understood against this context. Having to understand a penpal from a foreign culture is already difficult enough; having, in addition, to save one's face and those of many other unknown participants in public raises the stakes inordinately. Rob's gradual disengagement had a lot to do with the fact that Marie made him lose face in front of four other members of his group. From Rob's comment in the end '*We* should *all* know *our* history' it appears that Rob was very aware of the public nature of this exchange and its possible interpretation by the group, whereas Marie seems to have carried on as if it were a private conversation.

5.3 Reality: from the real to the hyperreal

Although this exchange was meant to be authentic and informative, it was still not easy for Rob and Marie to know what truth to attribute to each other's statements. For instance, should *Marie*'s theatricality, *Rob*'s initial self-deprecating strategies be taken at face value? How was Rob to take *Marie*'s 'little history lesson'? How was Marie to understand *Rob*'s desire not to be an 'obnoxious' American? Referential language strives to enforce a clear difference between reality and fiction, between truth and verisimilitude. The strict separation between genres, say, between an information exchange and a role-play is meant to ensure that what happens in reality is clearly demarcated from what happens in the fictional world of myth or language practice. But here the genre was unclear, half cocktail-party talk, half role-play, with no clear rules of decorum.

Online communication makes it easy to blur the distinction between real communication and display communication, between having a conversation and 'doing' conversation. For example, we saw in the MOO chat rooms how the display of one's words on the screen, the multiple audience, and the public nature of the postings, can transform real communication into a display of communication. Even though the telecollaborative exchange between Rob and Marie was for real, one gets the sense that each of them was 'doing' being real: Rob later confessed he didn't mean what he posted about Bush, and Marie thought she had been too 'teacherly'. Affect, too, becomes display. Emoticons, such as the ones used by Doug and Dina in Excerpt 6.4 lines 3 and 9, are the visible symbol of emotions that are no longer necessarily linked to the corresponding feelings. In the absence of embodied contact, virtual signifiers take on a life of their own, they become a reality in their own right—a hyperreality.[12] In the following I consider two questions raised by computer technology for the construction of the multilingual subject online. The first emerges from the very hyperreality offered by virtual environments: *who* is the real me? The second is prompted by the use of networked computers and the scattered nature of virtual selves that they seem to encourage: *where* is the real me?

6 Who's the real me? Hyperreality and the construction of the online subject

Baudrillard, the postmodern critic and semiotician, has theorized the notion of simulacrum (Baudrillard 1983, 1995). He suggests that in late modernity signs have become disconnected from reality, they have become a hyperreality, in which simulacra have been substituted for the actual objects.[13] He gives as an example Disneyland, which is such a good simulation of real America that the distinction, he says, between the two disappears and America ends up being itself a hyperreal Disneyland. Indeed, the virtual world opened up by the computer can be seen to correspond to a hyperreality. Depending on the degree of reality we confer on what we see on the screen, we are more or less engaged with the symbolic and the real, or with the virtual and the hyperreal. If we use the computer as a typewriter or a telephone, our sense of reality might not be very different from what it is in face-to-face communication, but as soon as we use it to manipulate reality—to cut and paste, insert images, crop, reduce or enlarge, alter sequence order, frequency, timing, etc. we change the way we not only represent, but model and experience reality for ourselves and others.

The electronic environment of synchronous chat rooms and asynchronous email places both forms of the symbolic, symbolic [1] and symbolic [2], in brackets, that is, it surrounds them by a virtual frame. This frame encourages a double vision focused either on the content or on the frame (Lanham 1993: 5). We can either look THROUGH the frame to a world 'where facts are facts', or we can look AT the frame and how it constructs the very facts that are 'out there'. Scholars with a literary and poetic imagination (Lanham 1993; Turkle 1995; Murray 1997) stress the educational potential of this double vision. They show the creative benefits of oscillating between the two ways of positioning oneself, either in frame or out of frame. For someone writing on the Internet, for example, it means thinking: 'It's both me writing/talking and it's not me' or 'It's both me and a role that I'm playing' or saying 'It's me (with one's fingers crossed behind one's back)'. We recognize here the dual, authorial and narratorial, position taken up by literary writers.

Indeed, much of what we see afforded by the electronic medium is reminiscent of what we encountered when discussing the decentered nature of the multilingual subject, his or her semiotic flexibility and ability to play with signifiers, that is, speak French but think Russian (Excerpt 1.10), pronounce a German word but make it into a simulacrum of a Japanese word (Excerpt 1.6), ascribe unexpected meanings to shapes, sounds, and code-switches (Excerpts 1.12–1.14), speak English but talk Vietnamese (Excerpt 3.13). We recognize in the playfulness of electronic chat rooms the ambiguities of Self and Other and Other in Self to which the multilingual subject is particularly sensitive, as well as the art of the trickster in fairy tales, with his masks, aliases, alibis, and metamorphoses. We find in digital language on the screen not only the instrumental style characteristic of print literacy, 'the clear, brief, and sincere transmission of neutral fact from one neutral entity to another' (Lanham 1993: 83) that Kristeva would attribute to the symbolic, but also the high degree of rhetorical ornamentality (ibid. 82), verbal flatulence, and playfulness characteristic of the oral tradition and the semiotic.

However, because the computer interface erases its traces, it makes it easy to take the reality on the screen for reality *tout court*. For electronic readers it is tempting to take the virtual self as a hyperreal self, who, like its avatar in *Second Life*, ends up being more 'real' than its symbolic counterpart. In foreign language education, information processing technologies are mostly used as if they had no frame and as if they could give immediate access to knowledge and to real people. Thus educators such as Lemke (1998) fear that young computer users might not know the difference between the virtual and the real. It has been argued that the longer computers are in use, the more people will be able to make the difference and appreciate the simulation qua simulation (see Turkle 1995: 83). This is surely true of digital imaging technologies, computer games, and special effects, but, as we shall see in the next section, language learners engaged in computer-mediated communication tend to see the computer as a transparent medium between two real worlds. They do not think of words on the screen as being any different from words spoken in face-to-face conversation. Most computer users ignore the frame and see the computer as a transparent window onto reality.

So, to go back to the question asked at the beginning of this chapter: from diary to blog, what's the difference? As with any technology, much depends on what the computer is used as. As word-processor, it can serve to write diaries. As email platform, it can support electronic conversations. As Internet portal, it can serve to collect information. As blog, it can be used to network. However, in each of these uses, electronic technology not only represents reality, it manipulates, re-orients, transforms reality into a hyperreality that is in fact a simulacrum, co-constructed by multiple users. This simulacrum risks being substituted for reality.

In sum, the transformation of language practice from the reality of human scale environments to the hyperreality of cyberspace can be best expressed through paradoxes: from an experience of co-presence to an illusion of presence typical of the medium; from a unique and irreversible act to a reversible performance; from a historically and spatially bounded event to an event taking place in a relational time-space; from a 'true' reality to a true simulation. Since the subject is constituted through language and its contexts of use, online contexts are likely to constitute a multilingual subject that has to grapple not only with various symbolic forms, but with the degree of reality or hyperreality they represent. In this sense, online communication is both exhilarating and anxiety-producing, as it exponentially increases the freedom to be whoever one says one is and the uncertainty about the reality that words refer to.

7 Where's the real me? The thrills and anxieties of the networked self

We turn now to the construction of the self in the electronic networks available through synchronous and asynchronous instant and text messaging (IM and TM) and such Web 2.0 programs as Facebook, MySpace, Twitter, Second Life, and others. They offer exciting and also problematic possibilities for the construction of the subject through language.

Computer technology has been hailed as facilitating encounters in cyberspace[14] among language learners and between non-native and native speakers (Carrier 1997), in the forms of Facebook profiles, Second Life avatars, pseudonymic blogs, YouTube videos, Skype mugshots, and other real and simulated identities. Synchronous and asynchronous email exchanges, electronic chat rooms, text messaging, and telecollaboration in general connect computer users to one another through language in the hyperreality of the screen. The compression of time and space by global networks of communication is shaping generations of youngsters who have quite a different relation to others, to themselves and to communication in general. Overwhelmed by the sheer multiplicity and complexity of phenomena and participants, they are keen on gaining control by anchoring themselves in the variety of concrete, spatial metaphors offered by the computer industry: (web)*sites*, (chat)*rooms*, (My)*Space*, (Face)*book*, as well as *browsers*, *screens*, *windows*, and the indefinitely replayable linguistic *structures* of messages, postings, and mailings. The users of these spaces are both self-centered and gregarious, competitive and collaborative, craving for recognition, acknowledgment, confirmation of self-worth, and eager to participate and stay in the game, but they feel less and less able to really understand the overwhelming complexity of people and events. They feel at once empowered and anxious at the possibilities of their networked selves.

7.1 'Liberated' communication?

The creator of Facebook wanted to 'liberate communication' from many of the constraints imposed by society (Ellison et al. 2007). In the same manner as youngsters with a low self-esteem can benefit from networking on Facebook, MySpace, and other interactive websites, foreign language educators have hailed networked computers as enhancing the communicative potential of language learning and boosting learners' self-esteem (Kern 2000). Many students who are too shy to speak in front of a class feel liberated when posting messages online: the anonymity/pseudonymity of the medium, the possibility of editing, erasing, and scrolling messages, the ability to put on various fictional personas before sending them—all these features of CmC free learners from the usual social constraints of face-to-face communication. The ease of access without the time constraints of having to vie for the floor leads to a greater volume of language use, hence a greater opportunity to practice grammatical and lexical forms.

Furthermore, students feel free to experiment with different personas. They can give their imagination free rein. The total immersion and concentration afforded by the medium resembles, some say, the literary experience of yesteryear. It is akin to a sojourn abroad, but with lesser risk of face loss and social isolation. One of the most popular ways of constructing a self online is through TM and the personal web- and blogsite Facebook. TM and Facebook satisfy today's youngsters' desire to belong to a community, to participate and cooperate but on their own terms. Because they fear disappearing in the mass, they hunger for attention, visibility, success, and acknowledgement but at the same time they are keen on remaining in control by assuming that their discourse style is universal and by switching their computer on or off according to their needs of the moment.

As we have seen in the example of Rob and Marie, however, this seeming lack of constraints might get them into trouble in international telecollaboration. Because the genre boundaries that constrain face-to-face or eye-to-paper language have disappeared behind the universal frame of the computer screen, the foreign language Other is erroneously assumed to be doing the same thing as the Self only in another language (see Kramsch and Thorne 2002; Hanna and de Nooy 2003, 2009). We saw in the case of Rob and Marie how the use of a common language (namely, English) exacerbated the illusion that both were engaged in the same type of activity, which was clearly not the case: Rob was 'doing an assignment' or 'doing being American', while Marie was 'practicing being American' or 'doing being West German'. We also noticed in Rob's, but even more in Marie's postings, a certain narcissistic pleasure of verbosity that has been noticed in much electronic communication (Lam 2003; Ware 2003), and a feeling that in virtual communication, historical time is suspended. Thus Marie felt free to use the vocabulary item she had just learned in class, that is, 'warhawk', and Rob used the term he was proud of knowing, 'die ehemalige DDR', and practice these terms without really understanding, or even imagining, the historical connotations their use might carry for the other, even though they dutifully inquired.

So is the virtual self but an enhanced variety of the self identified by Neisser in Chapter 2? In a cyberspace environment, the self has similar ecological and interpersonal dimensions; as an embodied presence sitting at a terminal, it has the memories and fantasies of an extended self; as a user of symbolic forms, it certainly has the potential, as in real life, to be a reflexive and a conceptual self. However, the self online is now in a hyperreal ecological environment, where it interacts with hyperreal or imagined others, and where critical reflexion and conceptualization are less called for than control and connection. Cyberspace is by definition a multisemiotic, heteroglossic, multicultural space, where any link is possible and seemingly anything goes, but where is the real me?

No one is more optimistic about the benefits of CmC for the development of this new virtual self than MIT scientist William Mitchell. In his futuristic *Me++: Cyborg Selves and the Networked City* (2003: 62) Mitchell sees the virtual self as having quite a different subjectivity than the self before the advent of networked computers.

> In emerging network culture, *subjectivity is nodular*...I am plugged into other objects and subjects in such a way that I become myself in and through them, even as they become themselves in and through me...For this particular early-twenty-first-century nodular subject, disconnection would be amputation. I am part of the networks, and the networks are part of me. I show up in the directories. I am visible to Google. I link, therefore I am.

Because of the close link between self and machine in cyberspace, Mitchell uses the term 'cybernetic organism' or 'cyborg' to characterize the networked subject.[15] He writes:

> [I am not], as architectural phenomenologists would have it, an autonomous, self-sufficient, biologically embodied subject encountering, objectifying, and responding to my immediate environment. I construct, and I am constructed, in a mutually recursive process that continually engages my fluid, permeable boundaries and my endlessly ramifying networks. I am a spatially extended cyborg.
> (ibid. 39)

In addition to a literally 'extended self', the computer offers the possibility of presenting a variety of real, surreal, or simulated selves and of using them as so many hyperreal masks and alibis. 'As my body extends artificially from its fleshy core, its gender, race, and even species markers may fade. It may acquire *multiple, sometimes contradictory aliases, masks, and veils. Its* agents and avatars in particular contexts may be ambiguous or deceptive' (ibid. 61, emphasis added). IM and TM seems to offer a solution to adolescents' and young adults' need for affection, friendship, and recognition without the closeness that might put undue demands on their time and attention. For example, for young Chinese immigrants to the US, the difficulties they face due to racial and linguistic prejudice are alleviated by their intense use of TM with other Chinese youngsters around the world. Lam's transcriptions of Chinese high-school students' TM chats with peers around the globe in a mixture of English, Mandarin, Cantonese, and Shanghainese, offer dizzying insights into the possibilities of global connections in local settings. As Lam (2000), reports, these global exchanges not only boost the students' self-esteem, they also improve their English and help them do better in their local American schools.

In sum, hyperreality can liberate communication from the social and cultural constraints imposed by the real world and facilitate the acquisition and use of another language through encounters in cyberspace. This liberation can potentially foster the growth of a postmodern, reflexive subject that looks at language as well as through language. But it can also transform it into what Mitchell (2003) has called a 'nodular' subject or 'Me++', that depends for it very existence on the networks that link it to other nodular subjects. This dependency in turn can be the source of a widespread anxiety.

7.2 The anxieties of the networked self

The empowerment offered by CmC has a downside as it seems to foster but at the same time destabilize the subject's sense of self. One of the best examples of this is the highly popular social networking program Facebook. Created by Mark Zuckerman at Harvard, Facebook was born out of an undergraduate college experience of cohort bonding, but Web 2.0 in typical fashion it replaced the top-down access system by a horizontal user-created knowledge system that feeds on itself and was extended to other contexts and to adults. The intense connectivity offered by Facebook can be the source of great satisfaction but also of great anxiety, as we can see in the following two American student testimonies.

In fall 2008, Carolyn, an 18-year-old undergraduate student, confessed to me one day that she didn't really know who she was, so she started writing a 'diary' and sent it every night to family and friends. When asked why she should want to share her diary with others, she said she couldn't think of anything she would write in her diary that was not suitable to be shared with others, moreover, she would never have the incentive to write a diary if she couldn't send it to others and receive feedback. She admitted that she was trying to get a grasp on herself through her network of friends. They are around her at all times, she added, in her address book, lined up on her Facebook profile, and on the screen of her Blackberry. She explained:

Facebook not only links you to each of your friends, but because everyone who has a Facebook can post messages on your *wall*, everyone can act as voyeur to everyone else's interactions. '*Applications*' options like 'most lovable person contest', or 'compare people' (for example, who is cuter?) enable you to measure yourself against others, compare your judgment, your appearance, your qualities, yourself to others. Also, your friends' friends' Facebooks are accessible to you and so are the names of their friends. So the system opens up unlimited expansions of your network. You experience the power of having put so-and-so in contact with so-and-so and spawned friendships among your friends.
(personal communication)

Thus the spatial display of one's friends' photographs, all in similar frames, describing themselves under similar parameters (interests, hobbies, favorite books, music groups, movies, age, attachments, occupation) encourages visibility, comparison, competition. In Facebook culture, subject positioning has become a calibration of self, a reassurance that one fits into the statistical world of one's networks. Furthermore, because Facebook encourages chance encounters, serendipitous coincidences of 'friends', it has a gambling quality to it that makes it attractive to adolescents and young adults, as the next testimony shows, this time from a graduate student.

In that same semester, a 31-year-old graduate student wrote on *Found in Translation*, a language-focused group at UC Berkeley:

<u>I Facebook, Therefore I Am</u>
9 06 2008
I find myself needing to validate my existence through the site. *Who* I am—or who I seek to be seen as?—is constructed daily and diligently through my Facebook profile. My political views ('Obamaniac', the daily political articles posted on my 'Posted Items'), religious views ('Whateverist'), emotional states (through 'Status Updates', 'Wall' postings, tagged photos, 'Notes'), hobbies, interests and affiliations ('Groups'), and musical tastes ('ILike Dedications', 'Recent Plays') are laid bare for my friends' perusal. I am unclear at this point, I have to say, how much of this is for others, and how much of this is for me . . . for, Facebook is also a forum for self-construction, self-reflection—not to forget—narcissism on a grand, networked scale. I am not merely connecting with others; I am fashioning a self, *the self I want public*, the self I want 'out there.' I can control the 'digital' self I put out for 'public' consumption through a plethora of privacy settings: I can control who sees what in my profile, and—by extension—I *think* I control what people 'make' of me. How deluded that is is not something I have figured out yet.

Recently, I told a friend of mine a story of how a 'Friend' wrote a highly objectionable Wall Post on my profile. I told the story stuttering with indignation and anger. She stared at me like I was a kook, and said, 'That's Facebook, that's not real life, you know? Who cares what anyone says on FB?' I couldn't understand her statement...of course it matters, it's Facebook! It IS real life—isn't it? Well, at least it's a reflection of my real life—with the added benefits of privacy controls, the ability to untag, remove news from your mini-feeds, block stalkers or people you would like to avoid and—that most important of tools: 'Remove Friend.' It's like a policed, self- and Friend-fashioned life forged through multi-modal literacy. In this very individuated society, Facebook is my savior: it is my life, only better. When I am on it, I feel connected to humanity—and my own humanity—in ways I haven't in too long...The very point of Facebooking is social networking; therefore, in entering that world, one automatically forfeits at least a level of privacy. Privacy is no longer at a premium; *visibility* is.

As far as Facebook addiction goes, I am only one of millions of habitual Facebook users who visit the site daily or even hourly. It is hard to figure out *what* it is about social networking sites that makes them so addictive...

A friend of this blogger responded on the same blogposting:

> i completely associate with that...☺ I had to ban myself from facebook for two weeks coz the addiction was impeding the completion of my research essay: S...am finally back...after 48 hours of sleep deprivation...i handed in my assngmt n my first compulsion was not to come and watch tv or sleep. i marched into my room...switched on my lappy n i facebookd! after 12 days...it felt like eternity ☺ goood [*sic*] to know im not the only crazy one out there.
> (personal communication)

These blog postings are not isolated opinions. Nor is Facebook an isolated phenomenon. *Facebook* grew out of a culture where 'networking' is as impor- tant as academic learning. In the US, many guidance counselors will tell high school students: 'School is not only for acquiring academic knowledge, but for making friends,' thus underscoring the importance of popularity in American schools. The same mentality can be seen in the education to entrepreneur- ship in a capitalistic economy, where 'making friends', that is, establishing a network of stakeholders, is a prerequisite for successful business. Hence the need for 'communication skills', and for fostering 'participation'. Hence also the strong appeal of interactional and dialogic approaches to learning in American education. The current debate raging in Europe about what kind of education is appropriate to our times reflects the tension between an educa- tion traditionally designed to train the disciplined, critically minded citizen working for the common good within stable institutions (see Graddol model 1 above), and an education designed to train the risk-taking entrepreneur that relies on ingenuity and on friends and connections to achieve his or her individual goals (see Graddol models 2 and 3 above).

The testimonies of the two students above express as much elation as anxiety about who and where they can position themselves as subjects within the networks that they feel they control, but that, ultimately, control them. Cyberdependency can take various forms. The first is an addiction to the *agency* and the *control* that the computer seems to afford. The freedom to present oneself as one chooses, to see without being seen, to switch oneself in or out of connections at the click of the mouse, can give a sense of empowerment that is quite addictive. The second is the *relational dependency* that seems to be encouraged by Facebook and other networking programs. The ability to bring people together, to compare and contrast 'friends', to make new friends, to 'write on someone else's wall', that is, to post a message that all Facebook users can read, to become visible, read, acknowledged, responded to, taken seriously, can be addictive because, as Bourdieu said of rites of institutions, it 'tears [a person] from the clutches of insignificance' (Bourdieu 1991: 126). The third form of cyberdependency is the *risk-taking spirit* that seems to be inherent in computer use: testing the limits of the system, seeing how far one can push the popularity game in Facebook, finding new ways of exploring cyberspace can become addictive practices for the creatively-minded user. Finally, the never-ending construction of self associated with Facebook profiles can create a compulsion to constantly reinvent oneself. The self being created online is intricate, multi-modal, and multi-aspectual and in perpetual motion. Facebook users create their 'status' profile through writings, through simple bios, pictures, and videos, and through 'applications'. The unlimited editing capacity of CmC and Facebook wall-posting, the ability to erase what one has just 'said' with no consequences to anyone gives one total control over one's utterances until one clicks SEND. Like the control over one's status on Facebook, the unbounded, open-ended possibilities of the self can paradoxically endanger the autonomy of the subject (see below).[16]

Indeed, it seems that the computer gives its users a feeling of temporary empowerment that gets constantly undercut by the low self-esteem it engenders (if only because computer users will never know as much, or be as quick or as smart as the computer). These aspects of CmC and Facebook in particular are prompting educators to rethink the ultimate goals of language education (see Leith 2007; King 1996). In foreign language education there are calls for rethinking the goals of language instruction (see MLA Ad Hoc Committee 2007): is the goal to acquire native speaker accuracy, appropriateness, and fluency in the language (something that the computer can facilitate)? Is it not also to develop a critical understanding of one's relationship to others in all their linguistic, social, cultural, and historical dimensions, and of the very conditions of one's own growth as a multilingual subject (something for which the computer is an insufficient guide)?

8 The future of the multilingual subject online

What do virtual environments contribute to the construction of the multilingual subject-in-process discussed in this book? Both in its ability to manipulate symbols and to model reality according to the user's subjective needs, and in the access it gives to other virtual selves in a multitude of virtual contexts, the computer has the potential to enhance the multilingual subject's creativity, resourcefulness, and ability to exploit the symbolic gaps between form and meaning, between what is said and what is meant, reality and fiction, fact and simulation. Like myth, the virtual world of electronic communication can be liberating and can have liberating effects on the subjectivity of real subjects sitting at their computer terminals or texting on their Blackberries. But like myth, the virtual world of blogs, postings, Facebook profiles, and other symbolic manifestations of the self is an ahistoric world, or rather, as Barthes (1957) said of myth, it is a world where history (the way things came to be) has been transformed into nature (the way things are). We saw in the Introduction how photographs of real people being born, living, working, dying, or being killed under real conditions became, appropriately displayed on the walls of a museum, the hyperreal myth of 'The Family of Man'. Myth had highjacked a phrase from the English lexicon (family, man) and made it into a seemingly natural phenomenon, that elided any consideration of history, politics, and the conflicts of power. As Barthes wrote: 'Myth is speech *stolen and restored*' (ibid. 125). Indeed, the computer has highjacked reality and restored it in the form of a hyperreality that computer users are encouraged to take for reality. Thus, the virtual self is a mythical self—exhilarating and creative, but vulnerable to manipulation by the invisible powers of its own addiction.

It is necessary at this point to remember the difference between the computer scientists and engineers who created cyberspace and the cyberspace users of today. The imagination of MIT robot scientists, born and educated in modern, pre-digital times, was nourished by an experience and an awareness of boundaries of all sorts, for example, linguistic and genre boundaries, disciplinary boundaries, boundaries between man and machine, between one individual and another, one text and another. They invented a boundary-free space, where texts would no longer be autonomous and sacred, knowledge would no longer be the property of the individual knower or inventor, where procedural knowledge would be made available to every computer user to manipulate and process words, texts, and images (Vinge 2001). But their creativity itself came from the boundary. In a similar manner, the pleasures and pains we have encountered in the testimonies of multilingual authors and narrators come from their awareness of the boundaries between languages, experiences, cultures, and worldviews—and from their thetic position at the boundary of the symbolic and the semiotic. As we saw in Chapter 4, it is the boundary that creates the subject.

Computer-mediated communication entices us to assume that Self and Other are one, and that we all speak a common computerspeak—a return to the myth of The Family of Man. But, in fact, it confronts us as never before with the need for boundaries, so that we can discover the spaces between them where the multilingual subject can grow (see Kramsch and Thorne 2002; Hanna and de Nooy 2003). The virtual self does not have the social safeguards that constrain the possible meanings of authors and narrators in real time and space: the visible ICMs, frames, stances, contextualization cues, indexicals, and other explicit markers of subject position (see Chapter 5). The computer has given the self procedural authority and spatial agency, it has dramatically increased the potential for distributed authorship and inter-subjectivity, it offers borderless spaces for play and creativity—but at a price. The virtual self, together with others, must reinvent the contextual boundaries without which there can be no agency, authorship, or creativity—indeed, there can be no subject. The multilingual subject must reinvent the perceptible boundaries needed to generate the gaps where it can thrive: boundaries between its languages, between its body and that of others, between memories, present experiences, and imagined scenarios. But most of all it must reconnect to what makes language itself into a boundary. As music needs measure and painting needs perspective, so language needs grammar, spelling, conversational maxims, discourse conventions, genre, style, register, and an identifiable voice.

So at the end of this book, we come to the realization that the multilingual subject is not defined by its boundless freedom and agency, but, on the contrary, by the linguistic and discursive boundaries it abides by in order to, now and then, transgress them. The ability to decide how to attach oneself to the world does not come from a lack of boundaries, but from the choice of which boundary to transgress. As Haraway (2000: 316) succinctly put it: 'We are responsible for our boundaries; we are they...[this] means embracing the skilful task of reconstructing the boundaries of daily life, in partial connection with others, in communication with all of our parts...This is a dream not of a common language, but of a powerful infidel heteroglossia.'

Notes

1 Graddol's three models are related to Frederic Jameson's three dominant aesthetic periods of realism, modernism, and postmodernism (Jameson 1984).

2 I use the term ecology here to refer less to a concern for the biochemical preservation of the natural environment than to the diverse, complex, relational, and changing nature of human communication as it is seen now (see Kramsch 2002b; van Lier 2002, 2004; Leather and van Dam 2003). In this sense, it also refers to the computer's electronic database and the virtual world it creates.

3 For the politics of science see Latour 1999; for multimedia literacy see Lemke 1998; 2000, 2002; for the relationship of technology and ideology see Reinking et al. 1998; Haraway 1991; Latour 1999; Mitchell 2003.

4 In *Forms of Talk*, Goffman (1981: ch. 3) distinguishes various *footings*, or ways in which participants in an interaction can align themselves with others: as principals, they enact a social role given to them by an institution; as authors, they select the sentiments being expressed and the words in which are encoded; as animators, they animate words that are not necessarily their own. Goffman also distinguishes between ratified and non-ratified participants such as overhearers,

eavesdroppers, and the like. These distinctions apply to the participant status of all the students involved in the telecollaboration event discussed in section 5.

5   See Wrigley 1993; Noblitt 1995; Kramsch 1997; Muyskens 1998; Myers, Hammett, and McKillop 1998; Warschauer 1999, 2000; Kern and McGrath 2008.

6   See Kramsch and Sullivan 1996; Cook 1997, 2000; Crystal 1998, 2008; Lantolf 1997; Sullivan 2000; Broner and Tarone 2001; Belz 2002c. Going beyond the manipulation of linguistic structures, Cook (1997) sees the dichotomy between playful form and serious content, between fiction and reality, as being the very essence of language learning and as holding the promise of educational growth. 'Play is an exuberance of the mind, something which occurs naturally and authentically *when there is a space to be filled*' (ibid. 227, emphasis added). The notion of a space or gap to be filled has been a recurring theme of this book—gap between symbolic [1] and symbolic [2], between the semiotic and the symbolic, between social conventions and individual creativity.

7   Note that, unlike English that has three words for 'play' (play, game, gamble), other languages have all three meanings in one word: Russian *igra*, French *jeu*, and German *Spiel* have the combined meaning of play, game, and gamble. The French and the German words have, like the English, the additional meaning of space, as in a loosely fitted joint (*jeu*), or room for maneuver (*Spielraum*)—i.e. an interstitial void that is not so much to be 'filled' (Cook 1997), as it is to be grasped and exploited for one's own purposes (see de Certeau's tactics in Chapter 4, and the theme of the trickster in Chapter 1, whose purpose is to create disjuncture, disorder, and chaos (= void), in order to bring newness into the world).

8   See Kramsch and Thorne 2002; Kern 2000; ch. 8; Belz 2002b, 2003; Belz and Muller-Hartmann 2003; Ware 2003; Garner and Gillingham 1998; Harasim et al. 1995.

9   It is unclear what Rob is cautioning against in this comment. It is doubtful that he understood the irony implicit in Marie's reference to 'the former third empire'. By calling Germany 'the former third empire' she is using a phrase that has become taboo nowadays since it is the Nazi name (*das dritte Reich*) for what Americans call 'Nazi Germany'. She is, however, echoing Rob who right from the start highlighted the fact that she comes from 'the former German Democratic Republic', which for her seems to be as embarrassing a phrase as for someone to acknowledge his association with 'the third empire'. Rob might learn from this exchange the role that categorization plays in the writing of history.

10 Although written communication is characterized by the absence of reader and writer from each other, as is the telephone for speakers and listeners, the unalterable material base of the original ink and paper, or of the human voice in the case of the telephone, acts as a reminder or a representative of an autonomous original presence somewhere in the world. One could argue that through Skype technology, the two interlocutors can see and hear each other online, but nowadays digitized image and voice do not necessarily guarantee the authenticity of the speaker, or rather, they redefine the very notion of authenticity.

11 The term *warhawk* was a metaphor used during the Vietnam war mostly by the left-wing liberals who opposed the war, i.e. the 'doves'. Suggesting that George W. Bush might be a 'warhawk' is adopting a discourse of the left that many Republicans consider unpatriotic, or even un-American. When used by a foreigner, it may raise the suspicion of anti-Americanism. The phrase *die ehemalige DDR* (the

former GDR) is, like the phrase *die Ostzone* [the East German occupied zone] used by many West Germans after the war, an ideologically loaded phrase. On the one hand, it was the official term used in Germany after the 1989 reunification to denote the former territory of the German Democratic Republic. On the other hand, when used today, it is a not always welcome reminder for Germans from the eastern part of Germany that their nation-state no longer exists and therefore their history is no longer relevant.

12 A simulacrum is not a copy of the real but a truth in its own right, i.e. a hyperreality. It is a space that, as Murray (1997: 292) describes it, 'teeters on the border between a powerfully present illusion and a more authentic but flickeringly visible ordinary world'.

13 The term *hyperreality* was coined by Umberto Eco (1986), then used by the French postmodern theorist Baudrillard (1983) to refer to the substitution of a reproduction for the actual object. Bell (2001: 76) describes hyperreality thus: 'Instead of representation, we have simulation...First, signs straightforwardly represent reality; second, signs distort reality, or misrepresent it; third, the sign disguises the fact that there is no underlying corresponding reality—signs become representations of representations, and fourth, the sign no longer bears any relation to reality—images have replaced reality.' Murray (1997: 292) comments, '[Hyperreality] is a useful concept for thinking about the dizzying merger between the real and the simulated, as in events staged for the media, like a presidential inauguration; crimes committed in imitation of movies; and places like Disneyworld's Main Street, which is based on a combination of cultural fantasy and corporate merchandising rather than on social reality.'

14 'Cyberspace is the conceptual space where words and human relationships, data and wealth and power are manifested by people using CmC technology; virtual communities are cultural aggregations that emerge when people bump into each other often enough in cyberspace' (Rheingold 2000: 56).

15 In her famous *Cyborg Manifesto* Donna Haraway coined the term *cyborg*, or *cyber*netic *org*anism: 'A cyborg is a cybernetic organism, a hybrid of machine and organism, a creature of social reality as well as a creature of fiction...By the twentieth century, our time, mythic time, we are all chimeras, theorized and fabricated hybrids of machine and organism. In short, we are all cyborgs. The cyborg is our ontology; it gives us our politics' (Haraway 1991, reproduced in Bell and Kennedy 2000: 291–2). She claims that our consciousness of ourselves and others has so much been shaped by our technological artifacts (print, telephone, TV, computer) that the man–machine distinction of the eighteenth century no longer holds.

16 The concept of the networked self puts into question the autonomy of the body-in-the-mind organism that we discussed in Chapter 2. One of the first to voice concerns was an MIT computer scientist, Joseph Weizenbaum (1976). Since then several scholars (Siegel and Markoff 1985; Noble 1984; Dreyfus and Dreyfus 1986; Poster 1990; Hayles 1999; Rheingold 2000; Goldberg 2000; Canny and Paulos 2000; Taylor 2001; Dreyfus 2001) have cautioned against what Dreyfus called the 'disembodied telepresence' offered by the computer (Dreyfus 2001: Chapter 3) and educational researchers have urged caution as well (Hawisher and Selfe 1989).

7
Teaching the multilingual subject

If language is one symbolic system among many through which our bodies and minds apprehend themselves and the world around them, then speaking or writing another language means using an alternative signifying practice, that orients the body-in-the-mind to alternative ways of perceiving, thinking, remembering the past, and imagining the future. Each of the languages we speak adds its unique dimension to our signifying self that, in its efforts to maintain its autonomy, its continuity and coherence, struggles to become a multilingual subject. As we have seen throughout this book, the symbolic power that comes from being able to use several symbolic systems is not only a declarative power, that is, the power to represent the world in different linguistic codes, but a performative power that can create different symbolic realities in different languages and, by changing others' perceptions of social reality, can change that reality.

A multilingual perspective on foreign language education is different from the traditional monolingual perspective taken up to now. The growing presence of multilingual learners and language users around the world increases the need for language educators to take into consideration the three main dimensions of the multilingual subject: symbolic self, symbolic action, symbolic competence. In the remainder of this chapter, I examine what it means for language educators to take these three dimensions into consideration.

1 Expanding the symbolic self

I suggested in the Introduction that language use is symbolic in sense [1] because it mediates our existence through symbolic forms or signs that are conventional and represent objective realities; it is also symbolic in sense [2] because symbolic forms construct subjective realities such as perceptions, emotions, attitudes, and values. We saw in Chapter 1 (section 5) how the meaning of a word depends on what kind of semiotic reference the signifying self chooses to establish between a sign and its object. Speakers may interpret a word to be correlated with or resemble the form of some other word (iconic reference), or to index a given context (indexical reference), as when they produce correctly and appropriately formulaic phrases that help them get by, or they may refer to objects in the real world (symbolic reference). But while this symbolic activity is exercised by all language users, multilinguals might have various ways of both espousing and distancing themselves from the symbolic [1] system they are using and might not share the same symbolic realm [2] as monolinguals.

Traditionally, language education has emphasized the referential or instrumental uses of language and the way it expresses conventional meanings agreed upon or imposed by a community of monolingual native speakers. The self that traditional language teaching has imagined the learner to be is a monolingual self eager to abide by the symbolic order of an Other and its monolingual rules. It was the self that Hoffman strove to embrace in English in Canada and that Kaplan tried to become when she desired above all 'André's language'. It was the self that the Australian student John couldn't get himself to be when in France, and that the Salvadoran immigrant Camila decided to become in the United States. The self that gets constructed through learning the standard forms of grammar, vocabulary, or pragmatics is a symbolic self that agrees to subject him- or herself to the symbolic order of another language.

However, as we saw in all these cases, the symbolic self of a multilingual does not merely abide by the symbolic order of the Other. It retains an outsideness that enables it to play with various objective and subjective meanings. Despite her total infatuation with French, Kaplan retained a critical distance toward the French precisely because of her father's association with the Nuremberg trials; she replaced André with a critical scholarship on Céline. Hoffman, despite her efforts to imitate and adopt the American voices of her environment, retained her double sensibility and dual perspective as a multilingual. The outsider's perspective that she retained on her own development as a multilingual subject accounts for the success of her narrative as a language memoir. John's outrage at the rude manners of the French was made into a good story in which the narrator put his symbolic self theatrically on display and thus could observe almost tongue-in-cheek the subject-in-process he was becoming. Camila skillfully cast her story into a telenovela genre from which she claimed at the same time to distance herself, and she got admired and rewarded for it. In all four cases, the self that becomes aware of the subjective realities indexed by various languages, including his or her own, embraces another kind of symbolic realm and experiences another kind of symbolic power than that usually attributed to language learners who have successfully mastered another language. This symbolic self is less intent on decoding than on interpreting words and their indexicalities, less focused on the standard monolingual use of one language than on the ability to use one language or the other, less keen on explaining and judging one national culture versus another than on understanding their own and others' historical trajectories and values. The symbolic power exercised by a multilingual subject is less a communicative competence than a symbolic competence, as we shall see in the remainder of this chapter.

If communicative language teaching was anchored around the expression, interpretation, and negotiation of referential meanings from a monolingual perspective, a multilingual approach to language learning strives to help the multilingual subject express and interpret subject positions that are sometimes non-negotiable. For what gets expressed, interpreted, and negotiated, especially in multilingual encounters, is not so much information as emotions and memories, values and subject positions—the realm of the symbolic. There are two main reasons why the full symbolic dimension of language instruction should be given more attention.

The first is that the goals of traditional language teaching have been found wanting in this new era of globalization. Its main tenets (monolingual native speakers, homogeneous national cultures, pure standard national languages, instrumental goals of education, functional criteria of success) have all become problematic in a world that is increasingly multilingual and multicultural, even though for many language teachers they are still convenient fictions. An education based on the transmission of information or on communicative training does not prepare the new generations adequately for the complexities of a multilingual world. The competencies required to become a multilingual subject are of a much more symbolic nature than has been acknowledged up to now.

The second reason for paying attention to the symbolic self of language users is that, in most learning environments today, learners of a second, foreign, or heritage language are not the monolingual speakers that early SLA research had envisaged. Migrations and a global economy, as well as increased access to the Internet and to global means of communication have changed the symbolic landscape of language classrooms. What teachers are often faced with today are learners with embodied memories of various languages acquired in various circumstances and with varying degrees of proficiency. Even if these languages have not been learned in any formal manner, they are visible and audible in the streets, online, and in the many multilingual encounters of modern life. They affect the symbolic self we have identified in this book.

These changes call for an ecologically oriented pedagogy that approaches language learning and language use not just as an instrumental activity for getting things done but as a subjective experience, linked to a speaker's position in space and history, and to his or her struggle for the control of social power and cultural memory (Kramsch 2002b; Kramsch and Steffensen 2008; van Lier 2004). In the US, the Ad Hoc Committee on Foreign Languages of the North American Modern Language Association issued a report that paved the way for such a pedagogy.

The goal [of college and university foreign language majors] is translingual and transcultural competence. The idea of translingual and transcultural competence places value on the *multilingual ability to operate between languages*...In the course of acquiring functional language abilities, students are taught critical language awareness,

interpretation and translation, historical and political consciousness, social sensibility, and aesthetic perception.
(MLA Ad Hoc Committee 2007: 237, emphasis added)

In Europe, an international research group has published the result of a three-year research project on *Plurilinguisme et pluriculturalisme en didactique des langues* (Zarate, Lévy, and Kramsch 2008) that defines multilingualism thus:

> Linguistic and cultural pluralism is more than the mere coexistence of various languages. It is primarily about *the transcultural circulation of values across borders*, the negotiation of identities, the inversions, even inventions of meaning, often concealed by a common illusion of effective communication... The teacher trainers of tomorrow will need to operate in a globalized space where verbal exchanges will be increasingly plurilingual and pluricultural.
> (Kramsch, Lévy and Zarate, 2008: 15, my translation, emphasis added)

If we view language learning as expanding a learner's symbolic self by focusing on the 'multilingual ability to operate between languages' and on the 'transcultural circulation of values across borders', we are not talking here about training polyglot whizzes or just adding to a monolingual elite's well-rounded education. We are teaching the very core of what it means to become multilingual. Teaching the multilingual subject means teaching language as a living form, experienced and remembered bodily, with a relation to an Other that is mediated by symbolic forms—an experience that an increasing number of students nowadays have already had at home or by living in multilingual neighborhoods. Learning another language in an academic environment can give them words to understand that experience.

2 Modeling symbolic action

The fact that ideas do not act directly on people or events, but are mediated through symbolic forms that have different symbolic value for different people, means that language teachers have to prepare learners not only for physical but also for symbolic action in both senses of the term 'symbolic'. By contrast with physical acts such as opening a door, symbolic acts such as asking someone to open the door, or playing at doing so, or doing so ironically, citationally, ostensibly, or metaphorically, or engaging in the cultural rituals of open and closed doors, require a different pedagogy. They cannot be taught directly as so many facts of grammar or vocabulary. As historically and bodily contingent, symbolic action can only be modeled or examined critically and interpreted. This paradox is captured in a statement made recently by Candlin (2001: p. xiii):

> The foreignness of foreign language education is not merely a means by which the exotic can be paraded, external to the lived experience and consciousness of teachers and pupils seen as voyeurs, but as a means and method through which, interculturally, learners as selves and persons may

experience through their engagement with the Other, now intraculturally, the nature of their membership of their own society and may be enabled *to hold its practices and beliefs up to critical observation and evaluation*. Foreign language education, in this sense, is as much about own language education, and own social education, as it is about the foreign. At the same time, in an increasingly globalized, web-wired, multilingual and multicultural world, foreign language education is nonetheless the prime promoter of the foreign perspective, playing a key role in enabling learners *to accommodate to the social and cultural diversity of that world and to derive advantage from it.*
(emphases added)

This quote leads to two complementary pedagogical imperatives. The first is a critical one: 'to hold [one's] practices and beliefs up to critical observation and evaluation'. The second is a pragmatic one: 'to accommodate to the social and cultural diversity of the world and to derive advantage from it'. The first approach is a critical/reflexive approach, through which teachers and students discuss these paradoxes openly, point to their conditions of possibility, and place them into their larger historical and social context (Blommaert 2005). The second is a creative/narrative approach, where they can attempt to resignify the paradoxes by experiencing them in symbolic form (see Bruner 1986, 1991).

2.1 The critical/reflexive approach

There have been many calls recently for more reflective practice and awareness of the social, cultural, and political nature of language teaching (Schoen 1983; Kinginger 1995; Wallace 1992, 1997). In language teacher education, Freeman and Johnson (1998) have advocated shifting the focus of teacher education away from received content knowledge (i.e. grammar and vocabulary), and the received knowledge of SLA research, toward teaching itself, as an educational and institutional endeavor, in particular the social context of schools and schooling, and the socially negotiated, constructivist processes of the pedagogical activity.[1] In foreign language education in the United States, there is a call for a greater convergence between the goals of foreign language education and heritage language education. For example, Reagan (2002) and Reagan and Osborn (2002) argue that language classrooms provide the ideal space for explicitly discussing cultural, political, and ideological issues of language, power, and identity. They emphasize the need to base such discussions on the myths and ideologies that characterize the status quo, in particular the myth of monolingualism. But these proponents of a critical pedagogy remain within the bounds of national educational systems, teaching foreign and heritage languages for national needs.

In the teaching of English language and literacy, Luke (2005:16) sees the need for change on a more global scale. Language education, he argues, must develop strategies for taking up the 'challenges of globalization, geopolitical instability and multinational capitalism'. He makes an ardent plea to liberate language teachers from the myths of nationalism and to enable them to be the full educators they deserve to be, namely cosmopolitan, transcultural go-betweens, who can better respond to the new economic and political conditions of a globalized economy.[2] But he wants them to be critical educators, that is, to exercise a distantiation toward the world they live in.

> To be critical is to call up for scrutiny, whether through embodied action or discourse practice, the rules of exchange within a social field. To do so requires an analytic move to self-position oneself as 'other' even in a market or field that might not necessarily construe or structurally position one as other (that is, on the basis of colour, gender, class etc.)....Having access to multiple discourses, competing discourses, contending and abrading discourses *may* but *will not necessarily* set the generative grounds for the critical...For the critical to happen, there must be some actual dissociation from one's available explanatory texts and discourses, a denaturalization and discomfort and 'making the familiar strange', as the classic ethnographic axiom suggests.
> (Luke 2003: 11–12, emphasis added)

Several obstacles to this critical approach must be acknowledged here. First, the backlash of a critical/reflexive pedagogy has already been felt in foreign language teaching at US institutions. At the University of North Carolina, Kubota, Austin, and Saito-Abbott (2003) responded to calls by researchers such as Osborn (2000) and Valdes (1997) to pay closer attention to the sociopolitical and ideological nature of language in language classes. They surveyed a total of 244 beginning learners of Japanese, Spanish, and Swahili, as well as advanced learners of Spanish, with the question: 'Does FL learning invite you to reflect on issues of race, gender, class, and social justice? Why or why not?' While advanced students definitely made the link more readily than beginning students, the results showed that some, particularly male students, resist engaging in sociopolitical issues in language classes. Kubota, Austin, and Saito-Abbott (2003: 21–2) write:

> Further research is needed to find out if the resistance is related to resentment toward multiculturalism in general or a desire for detachment from one's own marginalized racial/ethnic background. This desire for detachment suggests the need for further investigation into culturally responsive pedagogy...[In particular], some minority students in this study did not think that foreign language learning should be made relevant to their ethnic background...Incorporating a sociopolitical aspect of culture is often challenging, as expressed by Tedick and Walker 1994: 'It is easier to deal with Oktoberfest in the German classroom than to explore the emergence of xenophobia among youth in Germany and to contrast and compare their emergence to parallel patterns in the United States (p. 308).

Nevertheless, and because students fresh out of high school are less likely to be as politically aware as they are once in college, Kubota, Austin, and

Saito-Abbott (ibid. 22) conclude their article with a plea for more critical reflection in college language classes.

> Foreign language education will continue to be viewed as a major educational agenda in the age of globalization. At the same time, it inevitably will be situated in an increasingly more diverse society. Researchers and practitioners must shift their attention beyond apolitical appreciation and celebration of foreign culture, to critically explore issues of diversity and sociopolitical aspects of human communication, and to make foreign language education instrumental in creating greater equality.

Second, even if critical reflection is integrated into the foreign language curriculum, should it be carried out in the L2 or the L1? Without undoing the advances made by L2 immersion in communicative language teaching over the last forty years, there should be space for the critical awareness of language use in the foreign language classroom. In the same manner as grammar and lexical structures are taught with simple L2 metalinguistic vocabulary, and the motives, intentions, and actions of characters in stories are discussed in simple L2 stylistic language, so can live conversations, blog postings, email exchanges, websites, students' autobiographical essays and stories be critically discussed and reflected upon in the L2. Such an analysis would bring to the fore the indexicalities, stances, and subject-positions used by speakers and writers to construct the symbolic realities we call culture (see as examples the analysis of Camila's story in Chapter 4, or of Jocelyn's and Zoe's essays in Chapter 5).

Third, there is a danger that the development of the cosmopolitan jetsetting multilingual speaker might be incompatible with the development of the local citizen within the boundaries of a nation-state. There is currently a great deal of enthusiasm for the ability of the Internet to provide a supranational, global home for precisely the kind of transcultural teacher and student Luke advocates (Lam 2003), but it is not clear how national educational systems can cope with this global competition. And those sociolinguists (such as Scollon 2004; Makoni et al. 2003) who, like Luke, rightly put into question the hegemony of standard national languages and advocate doing away with the tripartite equation 'one language = one culture = one nation', are the first to be concerned about the dangers of deinstitutionalizing education in a world of global, market-driven, English-speaking capitalism (see Touraine 1992, 1995; Florio-Hansen and Hu 2003; Phillipson 2003). It might be that the more real-world communication takes place in the virtual world of networked computers, the more crucial it becomes for instructional environments not to emulate the computer, but to offer precisely what the computer cannot do, namely, reflect critically on its own symbolic and virtual realities.

Thus we find foreign language education at the intersection of some of the major educational issues of our times. There is a growing demand for greater critical awareness of the international and global dimensions of language teaching, and of the domestic social justice agenda at home, but many students just want to play it safe, pass the test, and maintain their grade point average.

They do not wish to have their thinking changed (see Atkinson 1999, 2002: 748; Kubota 2001 for a debate around this issue). For language teachers who want to teach to their students' multilingual symbolic self and show them that there is more to life than grades on a test, is there another point of leverage?

2.2 The creative/narrative approach

In the previous chapters we saw how some multilingual subjects, whether they are students or published writers, construct through language symbolic spaces that enable them to 'indulge, cultivate and ultimately valorize [their] experience of otherness and difference' (Luke 2003: 12). Their deep understanding that languages are fundamentally non-interchangeable has made them cautious of words, but at the same time it has given them a rich repertoire of linguistic means to express irreconcilable paradoxes, and a penchant for language creativity, play, and authorial maneuvering between distance and closeness. It is as if multilingual subjects, rather than being condemned to some original division against themselves, can draw strength from the flexibility and versatility afforded by their various languages.

This flexibility can be encouraged by making space for language play and for the emotional identification with the worlds of fiction created by multilingual writers. It can also be fostered through creative writing exercises in several languages. As I have suggested in Chapter 5, multilingual writers' positionings as linguistic subjects—as authorial and narratorial selves—may prefigure their positionings as social subjects (see also Kramsch 1999, 2009a). Indeed, it is through the aesthetic experience of writing and other forms of artistic expression that they can act out the social subjects they might want to become. A beautiful example is to be found in the creative writings of primary school children in both their mother tongues and in English, as documented in Datta (2000).

Narrative, that Barthes (1977: 79) saw as an 'international, transhistorical, transcultural' genre, has become a favorite practice of language teachers who have students create autobiographical narratives of the written or digital kind (Hinton 2001; Hull and Katz 2006), diaries, poems, and personal journals as reflexive practice (Hinton 2001; Belz 2002b; de Courcy 2002; Norton 2000). However, in school settings, many of these efforts have been supported, not by the desire to help youngsters 'construct new meanings', but by the hope that the narrative genre will enable them to master the academic genres of literacy necessary for school success (for example, critical text analysis, book report, argumentative essay). This practice has neither led to greater academic literacy in these genres nor fostered the students' personal growth as multilinguals, even though it has given a voice to their individual experience.

Shirley Brice Heath, who has worked over the last fifteen years with groups of adolescents and young adults from various countries, makes the distinction in this regard between narratives of the past and narratives of possibility (or 'future scenarios of possibility' Heath 2000: 126). The first are '*What happened*' narratives, the second are '*What would happen if…*' narratives.

In an interview with Claire Kramsch at UC Berkeley on 29 September 2003, she explains:

> I think in the last ten years we've come to romanticize narratives of the past. So, whether it's from psychotherapy to self-esteem after school classes, we've talked about the importance of telling your own story, the importance of getting your story out there ... Somehow through all of the promotion of narrative has run the unspoken expectation that the writing of that narrative was going to launch them into academic genres. Sadly, such a transfer rarely happens.

> One of the strongest predictors for academic success, I would argue, is the ability of young people to do scenario planning and to look at the number of variables and the ways in which they set those variables up as they relate to consequence and cause. Because of the changing nature of language socialization over the last twenty years in particular, young people have very little experience in narratives of possibility and probability. They tend to come through joint experience with an expert. Someone has to be saying, 'Hang on, you're not going to be able to do that! If you mix those two elements together, you know what you're gonna get?' Or, 'Hang on, you can't put that many people in [the boat] because you're never going to make it to the other side in time. Do you realize that this is only a 15-horse power motor and you know how much weight's in there?' Learning from such questions enables one to envision and to articulate the possibilities and the probabilities against your scenario. That kind of modeling, as well as co-engagement with a project or extended task, strengthens capacity for effective future scenario building. I have argued for years that if students have never spoken the kinds of arguments that go into an academic essay, we will have very little success having them write this or any other genre that has never been shaped orally ... Young people don't have enough experience and enough expert support for building future scenarios, narratives of hypotheticals.
> (Heath and Kramsch 2004: 87–8).

Real power, she argues, comes not from solving problems formulated by others or by the teacher, but from framing problems, figuring out what the problems are or will be. We could call it a 'symbolic competence' that combines symbolic power [1] and [2].[3] To be symbolically competent, students must master the grammar, the spelling, the conventions of the genre—in short, the technologies of representation or symbolic power [1], otherwise, they just tell their past stories in the established genres. But in addition they have to be in touch with the symbolic value of words and their subjective resonances. For instance, many of the narratives written by Korean-Americans in Hinton's corpus (see Chapter 3) are narratives of the past. They replicate the dominant story of fall and redemption, of victory over adverse circumstances, of making it against all odds—a genre that is often expected of students at American schools. By contrast, the Vietnamese student in Excerpt 3.13 takes a different tack. 'What if there were a difference between *speaking* English and *talking* English?' he asks. The narrative that ensues delineates a space of future possibilities that feels quite different from the others. Similarly, the multilingual narratives elicited by Belz in Chapter 1 (Belz 2002b), and others expressed in different genres in this book (cf. Valerie's poem in Chapter 3, students' essays in Chapter 5), are attempts to imagine alternative future scenarios of what it means to be multilingual. They capitalize on the aesthetic, that is, the formal aspects of language as symbolic system combined with the subjective resonances of these forms in the emotions, memories, and fantasies of their users.

Both critical thought and narrative experience reveal the paradoxes of social reality, the incompatibility of the individual and the social, of one language or worldview and the other. But while critical thought *points to* these paradoxes, the narrative/creative experience *reconciles* them by inserting a space that opens up new possibilities or, at least, the hope of a better future (Rorty 1998). This reconciliation requires concentration and a particular openness to the potentiality of the Self and the Other. In narrative, this openness takes the form of various *what...if* scenarios—the essence of the aesthetic experience. A passage from Salman Rushdie's 1999 novel, *The Ground Beneath Her Feet,* highlights this double aspect of the aesthetic experience. In the culturally multiple and mixed urban context of India, two adolescents, Vina and Ormus, 'tailor' their own culture, making what society, history, and tradition supply 'fit' into a kind of *autocouture*, that combines creativity and adaptation to the demands of the market.

> What's a culture, look it up, a group of microorganisms grown in a nutrient substance under controlled conditions. A squirm of germs on a glass slide is all, a laboratory experiment calling itself a society. Most of us wrigglers make do with life on that slide; we even agree to feel proud of that 'culture'. Like slaves voting for slavery or brains for lobotomy, we kneel down before the god of all moronic microorganisms and pray to be homogenized or killed or engineered. We promise to obey. But if Vina and Ormus were bacteria too, they were a pair of bugs who wouldn't take life lying down. One way of understanding their story is to think of it as an account of the creation of two bespoke identities tailored for the wearers by themselves. The rest of us get our personae off the peg, our religion, language, prejudices, demeanor, the works. But Vina and Ormus insisted on what one might call *autocouture* and music was the key that unlocked the door for them, the door to magic lands.
> (ibid. 95)

On the one hand, this passage can be seen as rejecting the idea of a personal development that would be mandated by academic institutions. Nowadays there are plenty of multilingual subjects such as Vina and Ormus around the world, who move into adult roles on the margins of institutional constraints. Art, for example, music, is often the key that unlocks for them 'the door to magic lands'. As Heath noticed in the international young people she studied, art has a symbolic value that seems to transcend both institutions and market forces. In a statement reminiscent of Lévi-Strauss's *bricolage* and de Certeau's tactics, she comments:

> With a young Pakistani or with a young Middle Eastern drummer, that is a fascinating thing to watch, when you have two people learning a language around a common interest ... They're certainly using English, but they're not using it as the standard; the standard may be Taiwanese, it may well be Spanish, it's moving, depending on the arena of difficulty if you will, of the particular problem or the agreed upon hierarchy of experts and their language. Then that's the way it goes. So there are those who are multilingual who can move across them, and so therefore your position in a hierarchy comes in connection with the number of languages and your competence in recognizing when and how you need these languages. I see the same thing happening with young people, as they figure this out. I don't need to learn to speak German the way you, in the teaching of German in your class, necessarily want me to speak it. I want to speak it the way I want to speak it, which is to be able to hang out with a graffiti artist in Munich. And if we know what we're talking about we can get along fine. Never mind that I'm a kid who immigrated to Sweden from Ethiopia. Young people cross into these hybrid forms all the time and also cross languages much more competently than we might expect, if they are crossing in the pursuit of a common interest.
> (Heath 2003, personal communication)

Such multilingual tactics are sure to make language teachers, the gatekeepers of standard languages, wonder what their role should be, but the need for transgression doesn't invalidate the need for boundaries, as we saw in the last chapter. Even in the multimodal approach to language education mentioned above, Heath and Roach (1999) build on traditional monolingual scenarios to propose future multilingual scenarios in various forms of expression. Film animation, painting, theater, can help imagine a future that is not restricted to one language or one semiotic modality. The transformation that, according to Vygotsky (1971), occurs at the boundary of art and life, in this aesthetic zone of proximal development between the actual child and the imagined child, is not only an emotional one, but also a cognitive one. As Heath and Roach have documented, the multilingual and transnational artistic creativity they observed in its various forms—narrative, poetry performance, theater, painting, or music—brings about cognitive benefits (such as hypothesizing, problem-solving, evaluating cause–effect) that are similar to those gained through scientific thought.

So on the one hand, we have the enormous resourcefulness of multilingual subjects, living at the intersection of multiple linguistic codes, modalities of expression, personal memories, and cultural backgrounds finding fulfillment in joint artistic endeavors. These endeavors enable them to envisage and give expression to hybrid, cosmopolitan worlds, on the margins of established genres, styles, and canons of beauty. Art gives them the cognitive and emotional maturity to imagine future scenarios of possibility that might, eventually, change the social order.

On the other hand, Rushdie's striking use of the hybrid coinage, *autocouture*, that combines the Greek *auto-* for self, and the French *couture* for fashion, should make us pause. To what extent are these youngsters not being coopted by a popculture fashion industry that is all too eager to recuperate as an artistic event any attempt to subvert existing forms of consecrated art? Youth is particularly vulnerable to this form of recuperation, especially if it is linked to popularity and commercial benefits. Thus one could interpret this passage as highlighting the tension between the concept of autonomy, displayed by Vina and Ormus, and the market forces that cannot but shape their choices, not to mention the threats to their autonomy posed by a networked culture, as we saw in Chapter 6. Similarly, multilingual subjects can be recuperated as global polyglot jetsetters, and foreign language learners can be enlisted as linguistic resources for the intelligence community. In both cases, their autonomy is vulnerable to what Touraine (1992) has called 'the tyranny of the community' and the 'domination of the markets', not to speak of the pressures of what Eisenhower had called the industrial–military complex. All the more reason for language teachers to use both a creative/narrative and a critical/reflexive approach to the development of their students' symbolic competence.

3 Developing symbolic competence

For the growth of a multilingual's sense of symbolic self, the development of his or her ability to take symbolic action and to exercise symbolic power, I have suggested the term 'symbolic competence' (Kramsch 2006; Kramsch and Whiteside 2008). By using the term 'symbolic competence' in language education, I wish to resignify the notion of communicative or intercultural competence and place it within the multilingual perspective adopted in this book. Symbolic competence does not replace (intercultural) communicative competence, but gives it meaning within a symbolic frame that I had earlier called 'third place' (Kramsch 1993) and that I propose to view now as a more dynamic, flexible, and locally contingent competence. Multilingualism, always the norm in many regions of the globe but occulted by the monolingual policies of powerful nation-states, prompts us to rethink the notion of 'third place' proposed in the 1990s under various names in applied linguistics.

The concept of *third place* (ibid.) or *third culture* (Kramsch 2009a) was proposed as a metaphor for eschewing the traditional dualities on which language education is based: L1/L2, C1/C2, NS/NNS, Us/Them, Self/Other. Third place did not propose to eliminate these dichotomies, but suggested focusing on the relation itself and on the heteroglossia within each of the poles. It was conceived as a symbolic place that is by no means unitary, stable, permanent, or homogeneous. Rather it was seen, like all subject positions, as multiple, always subject to change and to the tensions and even conflicts that come from being 'in between' (Weedon 1987). These tensions can be painful, but they can also be fruitful in the same manner as unsuccessful socialization can be the mother of invention. In the way I described it in 1993, the third culture or third place of the language learner had a subversive, carnivalesque character. It evoked a bilingual, oppositional culture that, like popular culture, thrives in the interstices of dominant monolingual cultures, whether they be C1 or C2. It encouraged reading against the grain, questioning social characterizations of experience and their framing, and seeing people and events in their larger historical context.

In 1993, the concept of third place was meant to capture the experience of the symbolic boundary between NS and NNS. Since then, the concept has been applied to the experience of immigrants and minorities in the US, especially Hispanic minorities, who crossed physical boundaries at a lot of human cost and suffering. Their experience inspired language teachers to have their students read published language memoirs such as those of Gloria Anzaldua, Richard Rodriguez, Eva Hoffman, Alice Kaplan or Nancy Huston and prompted researchers such as Hinton (1999), Norton (2000), Pavlenko (2001b), Pavlenko and Lantolf (2000), Kinginger (2004a), Coffey and Street (2008) to elicit students' narratives of their experience with linguistic and cultural borders. But fifteen years later, in a globalized economy where computer-mediated communication seems to have done away with borders, and the spread of a common world language fosters the illusion that we all think the same, the notion of third place needs to be revisited.

The spatial metaphor of third place now seems too static for a relational state of mind that, as the Report of the Ad Hoc Committee on Foreign Languages of the Modern Language Association has suggested, should enable multilingual speakers to 'operate between languages' (MLA 2007, see below). It seems too smug for a decentered subject that has to navigate several symbolic systems and their cultural and historical boundaries. Predicated on the existence of a first and a second place that are all too often reified in 'country of origin' and 'host country', third place can be easily romanticized as some hybrid position that contributes to the host country's ideology of cultural diversity. Finally, the term 'third place' or 'third culture' too often ignores the symbolic nature of the multilingual subject—both as a signifying self and as a social actor who has the power to change social reality through the use of multiple symbolic systems.

For all these reasons, I propose reframing the notion of third place as symbolic competence, an ability that is both theoretical and practical, and that emerges from the need to find appropriate subject positions within and across the languages at hand. The multilingual subject is defined by his or her growing symbolic competence. As we have seen in the many language memoirs and learners' testimonies, personal essays, and other verbal productions we have examined in this book, the symbolic competence necessary to become a multilingual subject includes:

- an ability to understand the symbolic value of symbolic forms and the different cultural memories evoked by different symbolic systems.
- an ability to draw on the semiotic diversity afforded by multiple languages to reframe ways of seeing familiar events, create alternative realities, and find an appropriate subject position 'between languages', so to speak.
- an ability to look both *at* and *through* language and to understand the challenges to the autonomy and integrity of the subject that come from unitary ideologies and a totalizing networked culture.

If being a multilingual subject means having the choice of belonging to different communities of sign users, resonating to events differently when expressed through different semiotic systems, positioning oneself differently in different languages, and ultimately having the words to reflect upon this experience and to cast it into an appropriate symbolic form, then we need to revisit the notion of imagination and its link to language. For teachers, learners, and language users of all kinds, a multilingual imagination is the capacity to envision alternative ways of remembering an event, of telling a story, of participating in a discussion, of empathizing with others, of imagining their future and ours, and ultimately of defining and measuring success and failure. A multilingual imagination opens up spaces of possibility not in abstract theories or in random flights of fancy, but in the particularity of day-to-day language practices, in, through, and across various languages.

Through critical reflection, language play, and narrative/creative writing, the multilingual experience can be given form, its pleasures and paradoxes can be shared with others. What was experienced in fragmentary form—a language spoken with a grandmother here, another language spoken with one's parents there, a new language learned in adolescence or adulthood, a few words of another gathered along the way, another one forgotten or lost— all these linguistic experiences are given meaning, coherence, and a sense of purpose when represented symbolically in the form of an analytic argument, mischievous code-switching and punning, or a well-told story. The symbolic form not only assembles the randomness of experience into a coherent whole, but makes it comprehensible to others, despite the autobiographical and cultural differences, because of common emotional resonances. The traces left in our bodies by the dispositional representations and image schemas called forth by various languages orient our desires in multifarious ways.

Ultimately, the ability to wield several symbolic systems, each with a different social and historical ecology and different subjective resonances holds political promise both for language learners and applied linguists. For language learners, symbolic competence can open up multiple perspectives on historical and social realities and appropriately prepare them for today's multilingual world. For applied linguists, a focus on the symbolic and subjective aspects of language can close the gap between the social sciences and the humanities and make the field of applied linguistics central to the teaching of foreign languages, literatures, and cultures.

4 Teaching the multilingual subject

If, then, speaking in a foreign language means not just activating a standard national linguistic system but experiencing a new way of seeing themselves as symbolic selves, language teachers might want to develop a pedagogy that addresses students' subjectivity, not just the effectiveness of their information exchanges or their ability to satisfy the rules of grammar, play predetermined roles, or accomplish predesigned tasks. Such a pedagogy might not be characterized by any new kinds of tasks or activities, but it would be guided by special attention paid to crucial aspects of language learning as symbolic activity. The first four sections below pertain to the lesson, the next four to the student, the last four to the teacher.

4.1 Pace

As language teachers, we have usually been trained to keep our lessons going at a brisk pace. We are pressured to cover the syllabus, do the grammar in two semesters, move on to the next chapter, and test at predetermined intervals how successful our instruction has been. This quantitative approach perhaps satisfies our students' minds, but it does not take their bodies into consideration. As we saw in the first half of this book, the symbolic self is grounded in the perceptions, memories, and projections of the body-in-the-mind. We have seen that the time of the body is different from the time of the mind. It is characterized by slow maturation, repetitive retracing of paths, rhythms, rituals, each new reenactment being another experience, eliciting different emotions. The body likes to re-member, re-thread, re-cognize. The time of the body is conservative.

Rather than rush to the next point of grammar, we might want to spend more time on the contextual variations of the previous point. Rather than be hostage to the linear progression of the textbook, we might want to think of ever-widening circles of understanding. Extensive reading should leave space for intensive reading; one sentence or one paragraph discussed slowly and in depth can serve as a metonymy for the whole work. It can be more memorable and a more fruitful learning experience in the long run than fifty pages skimmed over and half understood. Moreover, because it will be so memorable, it can be quoted in subsequent lessons, returned to as a point of reference or contrast, used as an illustration of a new grammatical or lexical point, and it will forge bonds of collective memory that will weld the class together (see section 4.2).

4.2 Rhythm

Anxious lest our students become bored, we tend to change activities and participation structure (whole class, pairwork, groupwork) every ten minutes, keeping students alert through busy work, and reading a new text every day. Once the chapter quiz is over, we pass on to the next chapter. The lesson thus becomes a juxtaposition of various activities and exercises, that don't necessarily foster sustained thinking or personal insights. Good teaching is all a question of rhythm and timing. Good teachers watch out for the intervals between lessons, the transitions between one activity and the next, one utterance and the next. They use these intervals to move in and out from 'doing' language to reflecting on oneself doing language. Thus they model the communicative/reflective stance that they want their students to adopt.

A good lesson plan has an organic rhythm, it is both ritualistic and spontaneous; it has no more than one or two themes with multiple variations. It has enough predictability to keep the theme going, and enough unpredictability to make the students curious about the next variation—a kind of (un)predictability by design, that both calms the body and stimulates the mind. Teaching a language class means building a pool of common memories, common recognitions, reference points, and anticipations over the course of a semester or a year, as well as providing opportunities to disrupt or subvert expectations (see section 4.7).

4.3 Multimodality, multiple perspectives

If we teach language not just as linguistic forms but as meaning-bearing signs, then we have to remember that signs are realized not only in different codes (linguistic or digital symbols), but also in different physical materials or modes (vocal, graphic, acoustic, visual, gestural), disseminated by different media (speech, writing or print, television or computer). The sign for JOY, for example, can be expressed by the exclamation 'wonderful!' (spoken medium), or by Schiller's *Ode to Joy* (written medium), by Beethoven's Ninth Symphony (musical medium), or by a picture of cheering crowds (visual medium), even though each mode represents joy from a different perspective and expresses different aspects of the feeling of joy. All signs and messages are always multimodal, and this multimodality permeates any given medium. Writing can display features of the spoken mode, and all modes coexist in the electronic medium. And, as we saw in Chapter 1, the meaning of a written word can be decoded not only as semantic reference, but also as sound, as shape, as rhythm, as semiotic gesture to other words.

Foreign language pedagogy usually gives precedence to the linguistic code and to the verbal mode over other semiotic modes. And yet, as we saw in this book, language learners apprehend the foreign language with all their senses: the sounds, the shapes, the tastes of words and other symbolic forms, and the meanings that each mode makes available. The development of visual literacy can be a pathway into verbal literacy (Kress and van Leeuwen 1996; Kress 2000; Kern 2000), especially for learners who have grown up in a televisual environment. For example, the students' ability to analyze a poster or a painting can be put to use when they have to analyze a text (Kramsch 2001). In addition to the traditional academic essay, other modes of expression such as drama, reader's theater, drawing, painting, or playing music can be incorporated into regular activities, as alternative ways in which students may display their understanding of a poem, a short story, an idiom, or a theme (Kramsch 1993: Chapter 5; Portmann-Tselikas 1999; Kramsch and Mueller 1991). What meanings can the film express one way, the book another? How is point of view realized filmically, rhetorically, in painting? How is the meaning of a poem conditioned by its shape, its rhymes, assonances, and alliterations? How is the same historical event represented in history textbooks or in the press in the US, in France, in Germany, in Russia (Kramsch 2008, 2009b)? We may want to apply the principle of 'intertextuality', that is, the transposition of various signifying systems (see Chapter 3 section 3.4), and of 'reaccentuation' (Chapter 4 section 2.4) to engage the students in semiotic transpositions of all kinds.[4]

4.4 Translation

Responding to the built-in structure of syllabi and textbooks and the coverage syndrome they tend to foster, we often focus on the various parts of the language as on so many pieces of a puzzle spread across the chapters of the textbook. As the puzzle gets assembled, the picture of an autumn forest emerges: this piece shows the end of a branch, that piece a red leaf, that piece the tip of a root. Most of us remind our students of the larger picture, we show the place of the branch in the context of the forest. But what we don't show is how the branch is, in fact, from a mythical and ecological perspective, just a translation or other manifestation of a leaf or a root. In the general ecology of growth and survival, a *branch* is a kind of *leaf*, which is, in turn, a *root* in another form. The root is but a downward branch, the branch is but a bigger leaf; they live on different time scales, they are each a metonymy for the whole tree (Bateson 1979; Lemke 2002). The tree itself is another manifestation of the forest, and the tree and the forest are just different manifestations of the world's ecology.[5]

Applied to the teaching of grammar, the concept of translation means that a noun versus its dictionary definition, an active voice versus a passive voice, a dependent clause versus two main clauses, are but different ways of constructing the same event but through different lenses, and thus construct two different realities. It is according to these constructed realities that we feel, act, and lead our daily lives. If meaning is relational, then what we are teaching are not linguistic facts, but semiotic relations between words, between linguistic codes, between texts, and between the associations they evoke in the minds of hearers and readers. In this regard, it is time to rehabilitate translation and the study of style and voice at advanced levels of language instruction.[6]

Applied to our students' subjectivities, the notion of translation suggests that learners are what Lemke calls 'heterochronous' subjects. In an ecological perspective, the adolescent we teach today contains the child that he or she was and the adult that he or she will become.

He may be 12 by the calibrations of calendars, but as a member of the community he is dynamically heterochronous, some mix of every age he's already been, and every age he's learned to cope with, and many ages he's begun to understand and imagine and model. The age we see is to a large degree the age-identity we know how to call forth; it is itself always an age-identity mix, with which he responds to us and to this situation. (Lemke 2003: 81)

The challenge for teachers, as Vygotsky repeatedly stressed, is to teach to the potential adult, not just to the past or even the actual adolescent. This means giving the students space to engage both the teenagers that they are and the adults they might become. The language classroom is precisely the place to explore with our students alternative ways of representing themselves and the preconceived notions they bring with them to the study of the foreign language. Examples can be found in Krumm and Jenkins (2001) who report interesting attempts to have students paint a visual objectification of their multilingual selves by filling in a penciled outline of their body with the various languages they know or wish to learn. Attempts to use critical incidents in the classroom to question dominant views of history are described in Byram and Kramsch 2008, as well as in Kramsch 2008b and 2009b.

4.5 Engagement

The interest in student motivation has a long tradition in SLA research. It has usually focused on what incites the student to learn the foreign language, in the hope of finding out how to make the learning outcome successful. But little attention has been paid to what makes students desire to escape the constraints of their native language, the boundaries of their native culture, and to develop an entirely different habitus. The term 'motivation' is too weak to cover the strong feelings of attraction and rejection that we found in learners such as Kaplan, Esteban, or Makine, or in students such as Valerie and Nathalie (Chapter 3), Estella and Zoe (Chapter 5). It does not help us understand why Rob dropped out of the telecollaborative exchanges with his German peers (Chapter 6). Some educators have started using another concept, namely, 'engagement'.

On the one hand, 'engagement' is a term used by researchers in the socio-cognitive or even sociocultural strand of SLA research. For example, van Lier (1996: 53, 66) tells us that language education is 'enhanced by such things as *engagement*, intrinsic motivation, and self-determination' (ibid.193, emphasis added). Engagement here has to do with intentionality, rational choice (p. 102), practical and cognitive demands in conversational interaction (p. 146), and affordances in the environment (p. 171). The argument has been made (Ware 2003) that in the exchange between Rob and Marie (Chapter 6), neither interlocutor was 'engaged' enough to follow up on what the other was trying to say, and Rob preferred to opt out rather than 'engage' Marie in negotiation of meaning across cultural boundaries.

On the other hand, 'engagement' is a term used by applied linguists interested in issues of race, class, gender, and sexual identity in SLA. For example, Pennycook (1999, 2001) proposes a *pedagogy of engagement* which, he says, is 'more than arranging the chairs in a circle and discussing social issues' (1999: 338). Rather than simply including multicultural topics (such as food, customs, religions, etc.) to broaden the representation of people from different backgrounds in the curriculum, or promoting rational discussion and debate of social issues on a general level, a pedagogy of engagement, he argues, focuses on how students are invested in particular discourses and how these discourses structure their identities and pathways in life. It links teaching with the lives and concerns of students and requires any educator of second language learners to consider the question: 'What identities or subject positions do we make available in our classes? And how might we both create more possibilities and find ways of working with students' identity formation?' (Pennycook 2001: 157). Ibrahim, studying francophone African learners of English in Britain, uses the concept of engagement in the same way: 'we as teachers must, first, identify the different sites in which our students invest their identities and desires and, second, develop materials that *engage* our students' raced, classed, gendered, sexualized, and abled identities' (1999: 366, italics added). Norton's concept of investment (2000; Peirce 1995) is synonymous with engagement in Pennycook's and Ibrahim's sense. Byram and Zarate's (1994) fourth aspect of intercultural competence, *savoir s'engager*, points to the political responsibility implied by the term.

These definitions of engagement remind us that learning is a participatory activity, that is very much affected by how the participants perceive each other, based on their visible and audible identity characteristics. In turn, other-perception affects self-perception and the way learners invest emotionally in particular identities and roles (see Chapter 5).

4.6 Desire

In the perspective adopted in this book, motivation, engagement, and investment in language learning are all manifestations of a more potent drive that Kristeva calls *desire in language* and that we discussed in Chapter 3. It has to do with symbolic identification with the Other, but not necessarily a racially, ethnically, or sexually defined other. Many language learners, anxious to liberate themselves from the constraints of the one (monolingual) mOther tongue[7] and its associated habitus, seek emotional, cognitive, social fulfillment in a multilingual subjectivity. The power of that desire and the disillusion that arises when it is thwarted became apparent in the story of Alice and André in Chapter 3, and in the exchange between Rob and Marie in Chapter 6. How can we, as language teachers, appeal to our students' desire?

One way is to leave space for an aspect of the language that has been virtually dropped from communicative language teaching, namely the aesthetic appeal of the language itself. What people find beautiful or moving often responds to their desires and stills their fears. These desires and fears should not necessarily be explicitly and publicly discussed as such, but space should be made for their artistic expression. We may want to encourage students to find beauty in a grammatical paradigm, a line of verse, a well-wrought sentence, and to express that beauty in visual form; encourage them to read texts metaphorically (Kramsch 2003a); recapture the oral tradition and the beauty of the spoken word by telling them stories, reading texts aloud for them, reciting poems that we have memorized and cherished over the years—and have our students do the same. Too often, we forget that the most precious gift we can give our students is to explore with them (not for them) the immense wealth of meanings opened up by the language we teach. Like actors, who at their nth representation of Macbeth still find unexpected meanings in their lines, so can we find new meanings in a poem that we have taught for twenty years—in part because of the new personal experiences we are able to connect with the text, in part because of our ever renewed audiences.

4.7 Transgression

As representatives of an institution, we are expected to be in control of the syllabus, the lesson plan, the activities, and the rules of behavior of the students in our classes. But as multilingual subjects, we know the pleasure that comes from transgressing the rules, from discovering unexpected meanings in a text, from testing how much the language will allow us to get away with. If the subject grows at the thetic juncture of the semiotic and the symbolic, on the border between the individual and the social, then we might want to provide space for breaking the rules, such as subverting situational role-plays (Bannink 2002), building 'ludicrous invented sentences' (Cook 2001), creating imagined autobiographies, constructing absurd dialogues with grammatical paradigms from the textbook, writing parodies of the reading selections or anti-fairy tales (Kramsch 2002a, 2003), writing multilingual journals (Chapter 3). The better prepared our lesson plan is, the freer we are for improvisation and the more space we are able to leave our students for transgressing our boundaries.

The spirit of transgression may be extended to the institutional rules of the classroom. We may want to let the students decide which ten words of vocabulary they want to learn each day, which topics they want to write about, in which genre. We may let them compose the final exam themselves, decide which items to test, how much each item should be scored. This does not let us off the hook, on the contrary. For instance, in order to guide the students into writing a final, we have to know how we would write it.

4.8 Pleasure

As teachers, we tend to keep students' attention by appealing to their pride (through praise and rewards), their interest (through a varied, new, and relevant syllabus), or their fear (through threats and guilt trips). Too often we forget to appeal to their pleasure (see, however, Schwerdtfeger 1997a, b). Pleasure is not 'fun' in the sense of 'Is language learning fun?' (Broner and Tarone 2001). Rather, as in Barthes's *The Pleasure of the Text* (1975), pleasure is an aesthetic concept that has to do with the perceived match between form and content, between what you wanted to say and the way you said it, between a word and the resonances it has for you (for example, 'What is your favorite word?'). Unlike fun, pleasure is an embodied sense of calm and serenity that comes from a lesson well run, a word said just at the right moment to the right person, a sentence written just as you think it should be written. With respect to reading, Barthes locates the source of pleasure not in the narrative suspense or in the informative content of a text, but in the way it is written—'in the uttering, not in the sequence of utterances: not to devour, to gobble, but to graze, to browse scrupulously, to rediscover...the leisure of bygone readings: to be *aristocratic* readers' (1975: 13, Barthes's emphasis). It is the sense of fulfillment, of being in sync with the language of the text, that Rosenblatt (1978) called 'aesthetic reading'. In this respect, pleasure is not an expendable luxury, or a random by-product of the language-learning experience. It is the crucial experience of the gap between form and meaning, between signifier and signified that, as we have seen throughout this book, is essential to the formation of the multilingual subject.

4.9 Teacher subjectivity

No teaching can be meaningful if it doesn't enlist, beyond rational and well-thought-out lesson plans, also emotions and feelings, that is, teacher subjectivity. Language teachers themselves are multilingual subjects, with memories, passions, interests, and ways of making sense of their own and their students' lives. We have our own reasons for having desired the language strongly enough to go on teaching it for many years. The pressure to be professionals, that is, to apply the latest research findings, adopt the latest methodology, use the latest technology, often makes us forget that we too are vulnerable to pleasure, sadness, and disappointment. What do we like/hate in the language we teach? What did we project into it, what were we trying to escape when we first learned it? Awareness of the subjective aspects of our trade can make us better able to help adolescents deal with the conflicts that come from learning to speak in a language that is different from that of their family, their friends, and their neighbors, and that often leads them to think differently from them. The student as a multilingual subject can be engaged only by a teacher who has recognized herself, too, as a subject, and who can let herself be affected by a word, a poem, or a short story in the foreign language. Even if we teach a syllabus that is not of our choice and texts we have not selected, we need to find something about them that we either love or hate, but that we are not indifferent to. If we are, our indifference will become our students' boredom.

4.10 Teaching as modeling

As teachers we transmit what we know in two ways: through direct teaching and indirect modeling. Much of what we teach can only be modeled: how *we* deal with being multilingual, how we ourselves have dealt with culture shock, identity crises, wondering where we belong and what it means to learn or use a language other than our own. Like Canetti, Hoffman, Kafka, Kaplan, Makine, Sarraute, we have experienced rejection and inadequacy, but also the pleasure and the thrill of using multiple languages, dialects, and registers, even if we teach only our native tongue and have never left our country. We may not forget that our students learn as much from who we show ourselves to be and what we do, as from what we say in class. Teaching is modeling for our students how we have dealt with these experiences—not necessarily in a confessional mode, but through a willingness to recognize the feelings they elicit in our students.

4.11 The value of repetition

In an effort to make language use more authentic and spontaneous, communicative language teaching has moved away from memorization, recitation, and choral responses. It has put a premium on the unique, individual, unrepeatable utterance in unpredictable conversational situations. And yet, there is value in repetition as an educational device: utterances repeated are also resignified. We may want to put the principle of iterability at work (see Introduction Note 5): The same text, reread silently or aloud, can yield new meanings. The same utterance, repeated in various contexts, with different inflections, can index different emotions, evoke different associations. The same poem, memorized and performed two or three times in front of the same class, yields each time new pleasures of recognition and anticipation. The same story, told to three different interlocutors, can enable the storyteller to put different emphases on the same general theme depending on the listener (see Kramsch 1993).

4.12 The value of silences

As teachers of language we have been trained to hate silences. We like lively classes, we want to see the students participate, speak up, take the floor, contribute actively to class discussion. Communicative language teaching puts a premium on talk and thus often rewards students who 'do' conversation and self-expression rather than those who reflect and understand in silence. But words have no meaning without the silences that surround them and silences have different meanings across cultures. We may want to leave time in class for students to write in silence, to have a silent, private contact with the shape of a poem and its silent sounds, to listen in silence to the cadences of a student or to our own voice reading aloud, to follow silently the rhythm of a conversation played on tape, the episodic structure of a story well told. We may want to even foster silence as a way of letting the students reflect on what they are right now experiencing.

To view the foreign language classroom as a deficient, less than authentic instructional setting is to ignore its potential as a symbolic multilingual environment, where alternative realities can be explored and reflected upon. Language teaching is not just a question of devising the right activities. It has to do with the economy of embodied time—the institutional time of the lesson, the biological, psychological, and emotional time of the participants, the sedimented time of pleasant and unpleasant memories. Beneath the homogeneous time of academic calendar and official curriculum, time is experienced according to the heterochronous rhythms of memories, perceptions, and anticipations. In this hidden curriculum, the adolescent can indulge in the fantasies of the child without losing face, can live various personae vicariously, can play at being someone else and reshape the world in unanticipated ways. While other classes in the curriculum activate mostly the brain, the language class engages the whole body, its emotions, feelings, desires, and projections. The conservative rhythm of the body anchors the mind in personal authenticity and truthfulness, even if institutional pressure often obliges the mind to bluff and 'do' learning instead of really learn. The acquisition and practice of another language can put one in touch with the deep desires of escape, adventure, and fulfillment that we find in fairy tales. Ultimately, the multilingual imagination is a mythic imagination, that can bring about an 'uncoercive rearrangement of desires' (Spivak 2002) by offering a symbolic alternative to the traditional time–space axes of our students' existence.[8]

Notes

1 Freeman and Johnson (1998: 412) write:
   We believe that teachers must understand their own beliefs and knowledge about learning and teaching and be thoroughly aware of the certain impact of such knowledge and beliefs on their classrooms and the language learners in them. We believe that teachers must be fully aware of and develop a questioning stance toward the *complex social, cultural, and institutional structures* that pervade the professional landscapes where they work … This drive to understand oneself and the impact of one's work on others lies at the core of the activity of teaching; it is the wellspring of *reflective practice, classroom inquiry, and ongoing professional development.* (emphasis added)

2 Allan Luke (2003: 14) writes:
   What is needed is nothing short of the reenvisioning of a transcultural and cosmopolitan teacher; a teacher with the capacity to 'shunt' between the local and global, to explicate and engage with the broad flows of knowledge and information, technologies and populations, artifacts and practices that characterize the present moment. What is needed is a new community of teachers that could and would work, communicate and exchange—physically and virtually—across national and regional boundaries.

3 Heath argues that this symbolic power is related to the skills needed for effective organizational management and financial planning. She comments on her study: 'The only criterion for success that we've used in this study...has been whether or not the young people involved in it have the view that they learned anything that is portable for them, that they want to put in their suitcase and carry with them. We look for ways to determine whether or not their youth organization experiences are ones they wish to return to...It may be that what they did on occasion turned out to be an aesthetic failure, but they learned a great deal from the experience...A large part of success comes from a willingness to undertake self-critique.' (Heath and Kramsch 2004: 86)

4 Gunther Kress gives an example of the different meanings expressed in different modes. For example, in verbal communication, the meaning 'social distance' is expressed through the use of pronouns: French *tu/vous*, German *Du/Sie*, English 'we' rather than 'I' (as in '*we* regret to inform you' rather than '*I* regret') or the use of the past tense (as in ' *I wanted* to ask you for a loan') rather than the present tense ('*I want* to ask you for a loan'). In visual communication, this meaning is expressed through the distance of viewer from object or by vertical camera angles (for example, looking up to an object or person of power or looking down on a person or object of lesser power) (Kress 2000: 154).

5 René Magritte's paintings are beautiful illustrations of this principle.

6 Translation as a way of exploring the relation between different sign systems has an important role to play in language pedagogy. Unfortunately the use of translation has been associated with a philological method of teaching foreign languages, the grammar/translation method, that has fallen out of favor. But as a practice that brings out the cultural differences in the relation of language and thought, translation should be rehabilitated, not only from L1 to L2 or L2 to L1, but across the languages shared by students in the class, or across modalities, textual, visual, musical (see MLA AdHoc Committee 2007).

7 Spelling 'mother tongue' as 'mOther tongue' emphasizes the deep psychological tension between the child and the first Other he/she ever encounters.

8 'Education in the humanities attempts to be an *uncoercive* rearrangement of desires' (Spivak 2002: 173). For an application to the training of teachers, see von Hoene 1995.

Bibliography

Abelson, H. and G. J. Sussman with J. Sussman. 1985. *Structure and Interpretation of Computer Programs*. Cambridge, Mass.: MIT.

Anderson, B. 1983. *Imagined Communities*. London: Verso.

Arceneaux, J., D. Clifton, E. Desmarais, K. Guillory, F. Leblanc, I. Le Jeune, K. Richard, and Z. Richard. 1980. *Cris sur le bayou: Naissance d'une poésie acadienne en Louisiane*. Montréal: Éditions Intermède.

Atkinson, D. 1999. Comments on Ryuko Kubota's 'Japanese culture constructed by discourses: implications for applied linguistics research and ELT'. *TESOL Quarterly* 33/4: 745–8.

——2002. Comments on Ryuko Kubota's 'Discursive construction of the images of U.S. classrooms'. *TESOL Quarterly* 36/1: 79–83.

Austin, J. 1962. *How To Do Things with Words*. 2nd edn. Oxford: Oxford University Press.

Baker, C. 1993. *Foundations of Bilingual Education and Bilingualism*. Clevedon: Multilingual Matters.

Bakhtin, M. 1981. 'Discourse in the novel' in *The Dialogic Imagination*. Austin: University of Texas Press.

——1986. 'The problem of speech genres' in *Speech Genres and Other Late Essays*, C. Emerson and M. Holquist (eds.), trans. Vern McGee. Austin: University of Texas Press.

Bannink, A. 2002. 'Negotiating the paradoxes of spontaneous talk in advanced L2 classes' in Kramsch (2002c: 237–65).

Barthes, R. 1957. 'Myth today' in *Mythologies*, trans. Annette Lavers. New York: Hill & Wang, 109–58.

——1975. *The Pleasure of the Text*, trans. Richard Miller. New York: Hill & Wang.

——1977. 'Introduction to the structural analysis of narratives' in *Image, Music, Text*, trans. Stephen Heath. New York: Noonday.

Basso, E. B. 1990. 'The trickster's scattered self'. *Anthropological Linguistics* 303/4: 292–318.

Bateson, G. 1979. *Mind and Nature: A Necessary Unity*. New York: Bantam.

Baudrillard, J. 1983. *Simulations*. New York: Semiotext(e).

——1995. *Simulacra and Simulation*, trans. S. F. Glaser. Ann Arbor: University of Michigan Press.

Becker, A. L. 2000. *Beyond Translation: Essays toward a Modern Philology*. Ann Arbor: University of Michigan Press.

Beckerman, H. S. 1989. *Heartworks: Inspirations for English as a Second Language*. Englewood Cliffs, NJ: Prentice Hall.

Bell, D. 2001. *An Introduction to Cybercultures*. London: Routledge.

——and B. M. Kennedy (eds.) 2000. *The Cybercultures Reader*. London: Routledge.

Bell, J. S. 1995. 'The relationship between L1 and L2 literacy: some complicating factors'. *TESOL Quarterly* 29/4: 687–704.

Bellah, R., R. Madsen, W. Sullivan, A. Swidler, and S. Tipton. 1985. *Habits of the Heart: Individualism and Commitment in American Life*. Berkeley: University of California Press.

Belz, J. A. 1997. 'Language use as an index of the self-in-transition: evidence from written multilingual texts'. Paper presented at the Annual Meeting of the American Association for Applied Linguistics, March. Orlando, Florida.

——2002a. 'The myth of the deficient communicator'. *Language Teaching Research* 6/1: 59–82.

——2002b. 'Social dimensions of telecollaborative foreign language study'. *Language Learning & Technology* 6/1: 60–81. Available online at: <http://llt.msu.edu/vol6num1/default.html>, accessed 29 June 2009.

——2002c. 'Second language play as a representation of the multicompetent self in foreign language study'. *Journal of Language, Identity, and Education* 1/1: 13–39.

——2003. 'Linguistic perspectives on the development of intercultural competence in telecollaboration'. *Language Learning & Technology* 7/3.

——and **Muller-Hartmann**, A. 2003. 'Teachers as intercultural learners negotiating German-American telecollaboration along the institutional fault line'. *The Modern Language Journal* 87.

Benson, P., and D. Nunan (eds.). 2004. *Learner's Stories: Difference and Diversity in Language Learning*. Cambridge: Cambridge University Press.

Benveniste, E. 1966. 'L'homme dans la langue'. *Problèmes de linguistique générale*. Paris: Gallimard.

Bernstein, B. 1996. *Pedagogy, Symbolic Control and Identity*. London: Taylor & Francis.

Besemeres, M. 2002. *Translating One's Self*. Bern: Peter Lang.

Bialystok, E. (ed.). 1991. *Language Processing in Bilingual Children*. Cambridge: Cambridge University Press.

——**F. I. M.,** Craik, C. Grady, W. Chau, R. Ishii, A. Gunji, and C. Pantev. 2005. 'Effect of bilingualism on cognitive control in the Simon task: evidence from MEG'. *NeuroImage* 24: 40–9.

Bichsel, P. 1969. 'Ein Tisch ist ein Tisch' in *Kindergeschichten*. Darmstadt: Hermann Luchterhand (repr. in J. Moeller, H. Liedloff, W. Adolph, and B. Mabee, *Kaleidoskop: Kultur, Literatur und Grammatik*. 4th edn. Boston: Houghton Mifflin, 47–50).

Block, D. 2007. *Second Language Identities*. London: Continuum.

Blommaert, J. 2005. *Discourse*. Cambridge: Cambridge University Press.

Blum-Kulka, S., J. House, and G. Kasper (eds.). 1989. *Cross-cultural Pragmatics: Request and Apologies*. Advances in Discourse Processes 31, ed. R. O. Freedle. Norwood, NJ: Ablex.

Borges, J. L. 1964. 'The analytical language of John Wilkins' in *Other Inquisitions 1937–1952*, trans. R. L. C. Sims. New York: University of Texas Press, 101–5.

Bourdieu, P. 1991. *Language and Symbolic Power*. Cambridge, Mass.: Harvard University Press.

——1997. *Pascalian Meditations*, trans. Richard Nice. Stanford: Stanford University Press.

——and J. C. Passeron. 1977. *Reproduction in Education, Society and Culture*, trans. Richard Nice. London: Sage.

Braudel, F. 1969. 'Histoire et sciences sociales: la longue durée' in *Écrits sur l'Histoire*. Paris: Flammarion, 41–83.

Brod, M. F. Kafka, M. Pasley, and H. Rodlauer. 1989. *Max Brod, Franz Kafka. Eine Freundschaft*. Franfurt am Main: S. Fischer.

Broner, M. and E. Tarone. 2001. 'Is it fun? Language play in a fifth-grade Spanish immersion classroom'. *The Modern Language Journal* 85/3: 363–79.

Brooke-Rose, C. 1968. *Between*. London: Michael Joseph.

Bruner, J. 1986. 'Two modes of thought' in *Actual Minds, Possible Worlds*. Cambridge, Mass.: Harvard University Press, 11–43.

——1991. 'The narrative construction of reality'. *Critical Inquiry* 18: 1–21.

——1994. 'The "remembered" self' in Neisser and Fivush (1994: 41–54).

——2001. 'Self-making and world-making' in J. Brockmeier and D. Carbaugh (eds.): *Narrative and Identity: Studies in Autobiography, Self and Culture*. Amsterdam: John Benjamins, 25–38.

——and S. Weisser. 1991. 'The invention of self: autobiography and its form' in D. R. Olson and N. Torrance (eds.): *Literacy and Orality*. Cambridge: Cambridge University Press, 129–47.

Bunyan, J. 1678/2003. *The Pilgrim's Progress*, ed. W. R. Owens. Oxford World's Classics. Oxford: Oxford University Press.

Burck, C. 2005. *Multilingual Living: Explorations of Language and Subjectivity*. New York: Palgrave.

Butler, J. 1997. *Excitable Speech: The Political Promise of the Performative*. New York: Routledge.

——1999. 'Performativity's social magic' in Richard Shusterman (ed.) *Bourdieu: A Critical Reader*. Oxford: Blackwell, 113–28.

Byram, K. and C. Kramsch. 2008. 'Why is it so difficult to teach language as culture?' *The German Quarterly* 81/1: 20–34.

Byram, M. and G. Zarate. 1994. *Definitions, Objectives and Assessment of Socio-cultural Objectives*. Strasbourg: Council of Europe.

Cameron, D. 2000. *Good to Talk? Life and Work in a Communication Culture*. London: Routledge.

Campbell, R. and D. Christian. 2003. 'Directions in research: intergenerational transmission of heritage languages'. *Heritage Language Journal* 1/11–14.

Canagarajah, A. S. 1999. *Resisting Linguistic Imperialism in English Teaching*. Oxford: Oxford University Press.

Candlin, C. 2001. Introduction in V. Kohonen, R. Jaatinen, P. Kaikkonen, and J. Lehtovaara. *Experiential Learning in Foreign Language Education*. London: Pearson Education.

Canetti, E. [1977]1979. *The Tongue Set Free*. [*Die gerettete Zunge. Geschichte einer Jugend*], trans. J. Neugroschel. New York: Farrar, Straus & Giroux.

Canny, J. and E. Paulos. 2000. 'Tele-embodiment and shattered presence: reconstructing the body for online interaction' in Goldberg (2000).

Carrier, M. 1997. 'ELT online: The rise of the Internet'. *ELT Journal* 51:3, 279–309.

Carroll, J. B. 1962. 'The prediction of success in intensive foreign language training' in R. Glaser (ed.). *Training Research and Education*. Pittsburgh: University of Pittsburgh Press, 87–136.

Carroll, R. 1988. *Cultural Misunderstandings: The French-American Experience*. Chicago: University of Chicago Press.

Chen, D. W. 2003. 'In China, it's easier to get lost in the crowd'. *New York Times* 16 Nov. 2003, Week in Review, 14.

Chiellino, G. 1992. *Sich die Fremde nehmen: Gedichte 1986–1990*. Kiel: Klener Malik.

——1995. *Fremde: Discourse on the Foreign*, trans. L. von Flotow. Toronto: Guernica.

Clark, H. 1996. *Using Language*. Cambridge: Cambridge University Press.

Coffey, S. and B. Street. 2008. 'Narrative and identity in the "language learning project"'. *Modern Language Journal* 92/3: 452–64.

Cook, G. 1994. 'A basis for analysis: schema theory, its general principles, history, and terminology' in *Discourse and Literature*. Oxford: Oxford University Press, 9–22.

——1997. 'Language play, language learning'. *ELT Journal* 51/3: 224–31.

——2000. *Language Play, Language Learning*. Oxford: Oxford University Press.

Crystal, D. 1998. *Language Play*. London: Penguin.

——2008. *txtng: the gr8 db8*. Oxford: Oxford University Press.

Damasio, A. 1994. *Descartes' Error: Emotion, Reason, and the Human Brain*. New York: Putnam Books.

——1999. *The Feeling of What Happens: Body and Emotion in the Making of Consciousness*. New York: Harcourt.

——2003. *Looking for Spinoza: Joy, Sorrow, and the Feeling Brain*. New York: Harcourt.

Danquah, m. n.-a. (ed.). 2000. *Becoming American: Personal Essays by First Generation Immigrant Women*. New York: Hyperion.

Datta, M. (ed.) 2000. *Bilinguality and Literacy: Principle and Practice*. London: Continuum.

Deacon, T. 1997. *The Symbolic Species*. New York: W. W. Norton.

De Certeau, M. 1984. *The Practice of Everyday Life*, trans. Steven Rendall. Berkeley, Calif.: University of California Press.

De Courcy, M. 2002. *Learners' Experiences of Immersion Education: Case Studies of French and Chinese*. Clevedon: Multilingual Matters.

de Courtivron, I. (ed.) 2003. *Lives in Translation: Bilingual Writers on Identity and Creativity*. New York: Palgrave Macmillan.

Derrida, J. 1971/88. 'Signature, event, context' in *Limited, Inc.* Gerald Graff (ed.). Chicago: University of Chicago Press, 1–23.

—— 1972. 'La Différance' in *Marges*. Paris: Minuit.

—— 1998. *Monolingualism of the Other, or The Prosthesis of Origin*, trans. Patrick Mensah. Stanford, Calif.: Stanford University Press.

Dorfman, A. 1998. *Heading South, Looking North: A Bilingual Journey*. New York: Farrar, Straus, & Giroux.

Dornyei, Z. 2001. *Teaching and Researching Motivation*. Harlow: Longman.

Dreyfus, H. L. 2001. *On the Internet*. London: Routledge.

—— and S. E. Dreyfus with T. Athanasiou. 1986. *Mind over Machine: The Power of Human Intuition and Expertise in the Era of the Computer*. New York: The Free Press.

Duranti, A. and C. Goodwin (eds.). 1992. *Rethinking Context. Language as an Interactive Phenomenon*. Cambridge: Cambridge University Press.

Eco, U. 1986. *Travels in Hyperreality*. Orlando: Harcourt Brace Jovanovich.

Ellis, R. 1997. *Second Language Acquisition*. Oxford: Oxford University Press.

Ellison, N., C. Steinfield, and C. Lampe. 2007. 'The benefits of Facebook "friends": Social capital and college students' use of online social network sites'. *Journal of Computer-Mediated Communication*, 12/4, article 1. <http://jcmc.indiana.edu/vol12/issue4/ellison.html>, accessed 29 June 2009.

Elmarsafy, Z. 1994. 'Translator's introduction to *Dog Words* by Abdelfattah Kilito' in Angelika Bammer (ed.): *Dis-placements: Cultural Identities in Question*. Bloomington: Indiana University Press, xxi.

Engeström, Y., R. Miettinen, and R. L. Punamaki (eds.). 1999. *Perspectives on Activity Theory*. Cambridge: Cambridge University Press.

Esteban, C. 1990. *Le Partage des mots*. Paris: Gallimard.

Fairclough, N. 1992. *Discourse and Social Change*. Cambridge: Polity.

Fauconnier, G. and M. Turner. 2002. *The Way We Think*. New York: Basic Books.

Florio-Hansen, I. de and Adelheid Hu (eds.). 2003. *Plurilingualität und Identität. Zur Selbst- und Fremdwahrnehmung mehrsprachiger Menschen*. Tübingen: Stauffenburg.

Foley, W. A. 1997. *Anthropological Linguistics: An Introduction*. Oxford: Blackwell.

Foucault, M. 2003. *Society Must be Defended: Lectures at the Collège de France, 1975–1976*, trans. David Macey. New York: Picador.

Franceschini, R. and J. Miecznikowski (eds.). 2004. *Leben mit mehreren Sprachen / Vivre avec plusieurs langues*. Bern: Peter Lang.

Freeman, D. and K. Johnson. 1998. 'Reconceptualizing the knowledge-base of language teacher education'. *Research and Practice in English Language Teacher Education, TESOL Quarterly* Special Issue.

Gardner, R. C. and W. E. Lambert. 1972. *Attitudes and Motivation in Second Language Learning*. Rowley, Mass.: Newbury House.

Garfinkel, H. 1967. *Studies in Ethnomethodology*. Englewood Cliffs, NJ: Prentice Hall.

Garner, R. and M. G. Gillingham. 1998. 'The internet in the classroom: is it the end of transmission-oriented pedagogy?' in Reinking et al., 1998: 221–31.

Genesee, F., R. Tucker, and W. E. Lambert. 1975. 'Communication skills of bilingual children'. *Child Development* 46: 1010–14.

Goffman, E. 1981. *Forms of Talk*. Cambridge, Mass.: Harvard University Press.

Goldberg, K. (ed.). 2000. *The Robot in the Garden: Telerobotics and Telepistemology in the Age of the Internet*. Cambridge, Mass.: MIT.

Graddol, D. 1994. 'Three models of language description' in D.Graddol and O. Boyd-Barrett (eds.): *Media Texts: Authors and Readers*. Clevedon: Multilingual Matters, 1–21.

Grimm Brothers. 1993. *Grimm's Complete Fairy Tales*. New York: Barnes & Noble.

Grossberg, L. 1997. 'Globalization, media and agency'. Paper presented at the The Relocation of Languages and Cultures: a transnational and transdisciplinary workshop. Duke University, 5–10 May.

—— 2000. 'History, imagination and the politics of belonging: Between the death and the fear of history', in P. Gilroy, L. Grossberg, and A. McRobbie (eds.): *Without Guarantees: In Honour of Stuart Hall*. London: Verso, 148–64.

Gumperz, J. J. 1996. 'Introduction to Part IV' in Gumperz and Levinson 1996.

—— and **Steven Levinson** (eds.): *Rethinking Linguistic Relativity*. Cambridge: Cambridge University Press, 359–74.

Hacking, I. 1999. *The Social Construction of What?* Cambridge, Mass.: Harvard University Press.

Halliday, M. A. K. 2002. 'Applied linguistics as an evolving theme'. Keynote address presented at the 13th World Congress of Applied Linguistics, Singapore.

Hanks, W. 1996. *Language and Communicative Practices*. Boulder: Westview Press.

Hanna, B. E. and J. de Nooy. 2003. 'A funny thing happened on the way to the forum: electronic discussion and foreign language learning'. *Language Learning & Technology* 7/1: 71–85.

—————— 2009. *Learning Language and Culture via Public Internet Discussion Forums*. New York: Palgrave Macmillan.

Harasim, L., S. R. Hitz, L. Teles, and M. Turoff. 1995. *Learning Networks: A Field Guide to Teaching and Learning Online*. Cambridge, Mass.: MIT.

Haraway, D. 1991. *Simians, Cyborgs, and Women: The Reinvention of Nature*. London: Free Association Books.

—— 2000. 'A cyborg manifesto: science, technology and socialist-feminism in the late twentieth century' in Bell and Kennedy (2000: 291–324).

Hawisher, G. E. and C. L. Selfe, (eds.). 1989. *Critical Perspectives on Computers and Composition Instruction*. New York: Teachers College Press.

Hayles, K. 1999. *How We Became Posthuman: Virtual Bodies in Cybernetics, Literature and Informatics*. Chicago: University of Chicago Press.

Heath, S. B. 2000. 'Seeing our way into learning'. *Cambridge Journal of Education* 30/1: 121–32.

—— and C. Kramsch. 2004. 'Shirley Brice Heath and Claire Kramsch in conversation: individuals, institutions and the uses of literacy'. *Journal of Applied Linguistics* 1/1: 75–91.

—— and A. Roach. 1999. 'Imaginative actuality: learning in the arts during the nonschool hours' in *Champions of Change: The Impact of the Arts on Learning*. Washington, DC: President's Committee on the Arts and Humanities.

Hinton, L. 2001. 'Involuntary language loss among immigrants: Asian-American linguistic autobiographies' in J. Alatis and Ai-Hui Tan (eds.): *Language in our Time. Georgetown University Roundtable on Languages and Linguistics* GURT '99. Washington, DC: Georgetown University Press, 203–52.

Hoffman, E. 1989. *Lost in Translation: A Life in a New Language*. New York: Penguin.

Hull, G. and M. Katz. 2006. 'Crafting an agentive self: case studies of digital storytelling'. *Research in the Teaching of English* 41: 1, 43–81.

Huston, N. 1999. *Nord perdu*. Paris: Actes Sud; Québec: Leméac.

—— and L. Sebbar. 1986. *Lettres parisiennes: Autopsie de l'exil*. Paris: Barrault.

Hyde, Lewis. 1998. *Trickster Makes this World: Mischief, Myth, and Art*. New York: Farrar, Straus, & Giroux.

Ianco-Worrall, A. 1972. 'Bilingualism and cognitive development'. *Child Development* 43: 4, 1390–1400.

Ibrahim, A. K. M. 1999. 'Becoming Black: Rap and hip-hop, age, gender, identity, and the politics of ESL learning'. *TESOL Quarterly* 33/3: 349–370.

Ivanic, R. 1998. *Writing and Identity*. Amsterdam: John Benjamins.

Jakobson, R. and L. Waugh. 1987. *The Sound Shape of Language* (2nd edn.). Bloomington: Indiana University Press.

Jameson, F. 1984. 'Post-modernism, or the cultural logic of late capitalism'. *New Left Review* 146: 53–92.

Jenkins, J. 1973. 'Language and memory' in George A. Miller (ed.): *Communication, Language, and Meaning. Psychological Perspectives*. New York: Basic Books, 159–71.

Johnson, M. 1987. *The Body in the Mind: The Bodily Basis of Meaning, Imagination, and Reason.* Chicago: University of Chicago Press.

—— 1993. *Moral Imagination. Implications of Cognitive Science for Ethics.* Chicago: University of Chicago Press.

Kafka, F. 2002. *Drucke zu Lebzeiten: Kritische Ausgabe.* W. Kittler, H. G. Koch, and G. Neumann (eds.) Frankfurt am Main: Fischer Taschenbuch.

—— 1971. *A Report for an Academy* in *Kafka: The Complete Stories* (ed.). Nahum N. Glatzer. New York: Schocken Books, 250–9.

Kaplan, A. 1993. *French Lessons: A Memoir.* Chicago: University of Chicago Press.

Kellman, S. 2000. *The Translingual Imagination.* Lincoln: University of Nebraska Press.

Kern, R. 2000. 'Computers, language, literacy' in *Literacy and Language Teaching.* Oxford: Oxford University Press, ch. 8.

—— and O. McGrath. 2008. 'Literacy and technology in French language teaching: issues and prospects' in D. Ayoun (ed.): *French Applied Linguistics.* Amsterdam: Benjamins, ii. 255–94.

Kilito, A. 1994. *Dog Words* [*Les Mots canins*] in A. Bammer (ed.): *Displacements: Cultural Identities in Question.* Bloomington: Indiana University Press, pp. xxi–xxxi.

King, S. A. 1996. 'Is the internet addictive, or are addicts using the internet?' <http://webpages. charter.net/stormking/iad.html>, accessed 29 June 2009.

Kinginger, C. 1995. 'Toward a reflective practice of TA education' in C. Kramsch (ed.): *Redefining the Boundaries of Language Study.* Boston: Heinle, 123–41.

—— 2004a. 'Alice doesn't live here any more. Foreign language learning and identity reconstruction' in A. Pavlenko and A. Blackledge (eds.): *Negotiation of Identities in Multilingual Contexts.* Clevedon: Multilingual Matters, 219–42.

—— 2004b. 'Bilingualism and emotion in the autobiographical works of Nancy Huston'. *Journal of Multilingual and Multicultural Development* 25/2–3: 159–78.

Koven, M. 2007. *Selves in Two Languages: Bilinguals' Verbal Enactments of Identity in French and Portuguese.* Amsterdam: John Benjamins.

Kramsch, C. 1993. *Context and Culture in Language Teaching.* Oxford: Oxford University Press.

—— 1997. 'Language teaching in an electronic age' in G. M. Jacobs (ed.): *Language Classrooms of Tomorrow: Issues and Responses.* Singapore: SEAMEO Regional Language Centre, 105–17.

—— 1999. 'Thirdness: The intercultural stance' in T. Vestergaard (ed.): *Language, Culture and Identity.* Aalborg: Aalborg University Press, 41–58.

—— 2001. 'Language, culture, and voice in the teaching of English as a foreign language'. *NovELTy: A Journal of English Language Teaching and Cultural Studies in Hungary* 8/1: 4–20.

—— 2002a. 'Language thieves' in H. Barkowski and R. Faistauer (eds.): *Sachen Deutsch als Fremdsprache.* Hohengehren: Schneider, 91–103.

—— 2002b. 'Introduction. How can we tell the dancer from the dance?' in Kramsch (2002c).

—— (ed.). 2002c. *Language and Language Socialization Acquisition.* London: Continuum.

—— 2003a. 'Metaphor and the subjective construction of beliefs' in P. Kalaja and A. M. Ferreira Barcelos (eds.): *Beliefs about SLA: New Research Approaches.* Dordrecht: Kluwer, 109–28.

—— 2003b. 'The multilingual subject', in Florio-Hansen and Hu (2003: 107–25).

—— 2004. 'Language, thought, and culture' in A. Davies and C. Elder (eds.) *Handbook of Applied Linguistics.* Oxford: Oxford University Press, 235–61.

—— 2005. 'Post 9/11. Foreign languages between knowledge and power'. *Applied Linguistics* 26/4: 545–67.

—— 2006. 'From communicative competence to symbolic competence'. *Modern Language Journal* 90/2: 249–51.

—— 2008a. 'Multilingual, like Franz Kafka'. *International Journal of Multilingualism* 5/4: 316–32.

—— 2008b. 'The intercultural yesterday and today: political perspectives' in R. Schulz and
E. Tschirner (eds.): *Crossing Borders: Developing Intercultural Competence in German as
a Foreign Language*. Munich: iudicium, 5–27.

—— 2009a. 'Third culture and language education' in V. Cook (ed.): *Contemporary Applied
Linguistics*, i. *Language Teaching and Learning*. London: Continuum, pp. 233–55.

—— 2009b. 'Discourse, the symbolic dimension of intercultural competence' in Adelheid Hu
and M. Byram (eds.): *Intercultural Competence and Foreign Language Learning: Models,
Empiricism, Assessment*. Tübingen: Narr Francke Attempto.

—— and **M. Mueller.** 1991. *Celebrating, Understanding, Creating Poetry in the Foreign
Language Class*. Videocassette. Lincolnwood, Ill.: National Textbook Co.

—— and **S. V. Steffensen.** 2008. 'Ecological perspectives on second language acquisition and
socialization' in N. H. Hornberger (ed.): *Encyclopedia of Language and Education*, viii.
Language Socialization (2nd edn.). New York: Springer, 17–28.

—— and **P. Sullivan.** 1996. 'Appropriate pedagogy'. *ELT* 50/3: 199–212.

—— and **S. Thorne.** 2002. 'Foreign language learning as global communicative practice' in
D. Block and D. Cameron (eds.): *Globalization and Language Teaching*. London: Routledge,
83–100.

—— and **A. Whiteside.** 2008. 'Language ecology in multilingual settings: towards a theory of
symbolic competence'. *Applied Linguistics* 29/4: 645–71.

——, **F. A'Ness,** and **E. Lam.** 2000. 'Authenticity and authorship in the computer-mediated
acquisition of L2 literacy'. *Language Learning & Technology* 4/2: 78–104.

——, **D. Lévy,** and **G. Zarate.** 2008. 'Introduction générale' in Zarate, Lévy, and Kramsch
(2008 :15–23).

Kress, G. 2000. 'Design and transformation: new theories of meaning' in B. Cope and
M. Kalantzis (eds.): *Multiliteracies. Literacy Learning and the Design of Social Futures*.
London: Routledge, pp. 53–161.

—— and **T. van Leeuwen.** 1996. *Reading Images: The Grammar of Visual Design*. London:
Routledge.

Kristeva, J. 1980. *Desire in Language: A Semiotic Approach to Literature and Art* (eds.)
L. S. Roudiez; trans.T. Gora, A. Jardine, and L. S. Roudiez. New York: Columbia
University Press.

—— 1986. 'Revolution in poetic language' in T. Moi (ed.): *The Kristeva Reader*. New York:
Columbia University Press, 89–136.

—— 1991. *Strangers to Ourselves*, trans. L. S. Roudiez. New York: Columbia University Press.

Krumm, H.J. and **E.M. Jenkins** (eds.). 2001. *Kinder und ihre Sprachen—lebendige
Mehrsprachigkeit*. Vienna: Eviva.

Kubota, R. 2001. 'Discursive construction of the images of U.S. classrooms'. *TESOL
Quarterly* 35/1: 9–38.

——, **T. Austin,** and **Y. Saito-Abbott.** 2003. 'Diversity and inclusion of sociopolitical issues in
foreign language classrooms: An exploratory survey'. *Foreign Language Annals* 36/1: 12–24.

Labov, W. 1972. *Language in the Inner City: Studies in the Black English Vernacular*.
Philadelphia: University of Pennsylvania Press.

Lacan, J. 1977. *Écrits: A Selection*, trans. Alan Sheridan. New York: Norton.

Lakoff, G. 1987. *Women, Fire, and Dangerous Things: What Categories Reveal about the
Mind*. Chicago: Chicago University Press.

—— 1993. 'The contemporary theory of metaphor' in Andrew Ortony (ed.): *Metaphor and
Thought* (2nd edn.). Cambridge: Cambridge University Press.

—— and **M. Johnson.** 1980. *Metaphors We Live By*. Chicago: Chicago University Press.

—— and **M. Johnson.** 1999. *Philosophy in the Flesh: The Embodied Mind and its Challenge to
Western Thought*. New York: Basic Books.

—— and **M. Turner.** 1989. *More than Cool Reason: A Field Guide to Poetic Metaphor*.
Chicago: University of Chicago Press.

Lam, W. S. E. 2000. 'L2 literacy and the design of the self: a case study of a teenager writing on
the Internet'. *TESOL Quarterly* 34/3: 457–82.

—— 2003. 'Second Language Literacy and Identity Formation on the Internet: The Case of Chinese Immigrant Youth in the U.S'. Unpub. Ph.D. dissertation, UC Berkeley.

—— Forthcoming. 'Immigrant youths' digital practices in negotiating local and translocal affiliations' *Reading Research Quarterly*.

Lanham, R. 1993. *The Electronic Word*. Chicago: University of Chicago Press.

Lantolf, J. 1997. 'The function of language play in the acquisition of L2 Spanish' in W. R. Glass and A. T. Perez-Leroux (eds.): *Contemporary Perspectives on the Acquisition of Spanish*. Somerville, Mass.: Cascadilla, 3–24.

—— 2000. 'Introducing sociocultural theory' in *Sociocultural Theory and Second Language Learning*. Oxford: Oxford University Press.

Latour, B. 1999. *Pandora's Box*. Cambridge: Harvard University Press.

Leather, J. and J. van Dam (eds.). 2003. *Ecology of Language Acquisition*. Dordrecht: Kluwer Academic.

Lee, C.R. 1995. *Native Speaker*. New York: Riverhead Books.

Leith, S. 2007. 'Facebook—a thoroughly modern addiction' <http://www.telegraph.co.uk/comment/personal-view/3640672/Facebook—a-thoroughly-modern-addiction.html>, accessed 25 July 2008.

Lemke, J. L. 1998. 'Metamedia literacy: transforming meanings and media' in D. Reinking, M. McKenna, L. Labbo, and R. Kieffer (eds.) 283–302.

—— 2000. 'Across the scales of time: Artifacts, activities, and meanings in ecosocial systems'. *Mind, Culture, and Activity: An International Journal* 7/4: 273–90.

—— 2002. 'Language development and identity: multiple timescales in the social ecology of learning' in Kramsch (2002c), 68–87.

Leontiev, A. N. 1978. *Activity, Consciousness and Personality*. Englewood Cliffs, NJ: Prentice Hall.

LePage, R. B. and A. Tabouret-Keller. 1985. *Acts of Identity*. Cambridge: Cambridge University Press.

Lévi-Strauss, C. 1962. *La Pensée sauvage*. Paris: Plon.

Liddicoat, A. 2003. 'Teaching language for intercultural communication'. Paper presented at the UCCLLT Summer Seminar on 'Discourse and Culture', June. University of California at Berkeley.

Lim, S. G. -L. 1994. *Monsoon History: Selected Poems*. London: Skoob.

—— 2003. 'The Im/Possibility of Life-Writing in Two Languages' in Isabelle de Courtivron (ed.): *Lives in Translation*. New York: Palgrave Macmillan.

Lucy, J. 1992. *Language Diversity and Thought: A Reformulation of the Linguistic Relativity Hypothesis*. Cambridge: Cambridge University Press.

Luke, A. 2003. 'Two takes on the critical: a foreword' in B. Norton and K. Toohey (eds.): *Critical Pedagogies and Language Learning*. Cambridge: Cambridge University Press.

—— 2005. 'Curriculum, ethics, metanarrative: teaching and learning beyond the nation' in Y. Nozaki, R. Openshaw, and A. Luke (eds.): *Struggles Over Difference: Curriculum, Texts, and Pedagogy in the Asia-Pacific*. New York: SUNY, 11–24.

Lvovich, N. 1997. *The Multilingual Self: An Inquiry into Language Learning*. Mahwah, NJ: Lawrence Erlbaum.

Makine, A. 1997. *Dreams of my Russian Summers*, trans. G. Strachan (*Le Testament français*). Paris: Mercure de France, 1995.

Makoni, S., G. Smitherman, A. F. Ball, and A. K. Spears 2003 (eds.): *Black Linguistics*. London: Routledge.

Menard-Warwick, J. 2004a. 'Identity Narratives of Latino/a Immigrant Language Learners: Contextualizing Classroom Literacy Practices in Adult ESL'. Unpub. Ph.D. dissertation, UC Berkeley.

—— 2004b. ' "I always had the desire to progress a little": gendered narratives of immigrant language learners'. *Journal of Language, Identity, and Education* 3/4: 295–311.

—— 2005. 'Transgression narratives, dialogic voicing, and cultural change'. *Journal of Sociolinguistics* 9/4: 533–56.

——2009. *Gendered Identities and Immigrant Language Learning*. Clevedon: Multilingual Matters.

Mitchell, W. 2003. *Me++: Cyborg Selves and the Networked City*. Cambridge, Mass.: MIT.

MLA AdHoc Committee on Foreign Languages. 2007. 'Foreign languages and higher education: new structures for a changed world'. *Profession 2007* 234–45.

Molloy, S. 2003. 'Bilingualism, writing, and the feeling of not quite being there' in de Courtivron (2003: 69–78).

Müller-Jacquier, B. 1981. (ed.): *Konfrontative Semantik*. Tübingen: Gunter Narr.

Murray, J. H. 1997. *Hamlet on the Holodeck: The Future of Narrative in Cyberspace*. New York: The Free Press.

Murray, S. J. 2003. 'Myth as critique? Review of Michel Foucault's *Society Must be Defended*'. *Qui parle* 13/2. UC Berkeley.

Muyskens, J. (ed.) 1998. *New Ways of Teaching and Learning: Focus on Technology and Foreign Language Education*. Boston: Heinle & Heinle.

Myers, J., R. Hammett, and A. M. McKillop. 1998. 'Opportunities for critical literacy and pedagogy in student-authored hypermedia in D. Reinking, M. C. McKenna, L. D. Labbo, and R. D. Kieffer (eds.): *Handbook of Literacy and Technology: Transformations in a Post-Typographic World*. Mahwah, NJ: Lawrence Erlbaum, 63–78.

Neisser, U. 1988. 'Five kinds of self-knowledge'. *Philosophical Psychology* 1/1: 35–59.

——(ed.). 1993. *The Perceived Self*. Cambridge: Cambridge University Press.

——and R. Fivush (eds.). 1994. *The Remembering Self*. Cambridge: Cambridge University Press.

——and D. A. Jopling (eds.). 1997. *The Conceptual Self in Context*. Cambridge: Cambridge University Press.

Niemeier, S. and R. Dirven. 2000. *Evidence of Linguistic Relativity*. Amsterdam: John Benjamins.

Noble, D. 1984. *Forces of Production*. New York: Knopf.

Noblitt, J. 1995. 'The electronic language learning environment' in C. Kramsch (ed.): *Redefining the Boundaries of Language Study*. Boston: Heinle & Heinle, 261–90.

Norton, B. 2000. *Identity and Language Learning*. London: Longman.

Nuckolls, C. W. 1997. 'Why Lakoff needs psychoanalysis: on cultural ambivalence and concepts of the self' in Neisser and Jopling (1997: 114–27).

Ochs, E. 1996. 'Linguistic resources for socializing humanity' in J. J. Gumperz and S. C. Levinson (eds.): *Rethinking Linguistic Relativity*. Cambridge: Cambridge University Press, 407–37.

Ortony, A., G. L. Clore, and A. Collins. 1988. *The Cognitive Structure of Emotions*. New York: Cambridge Universithy Press.

Osborn, T. A. 2000. *Critical Reflection and the Foreign Language Classroom*. Westport, Conn.: Bergin & Garvey.

Paton, A. 1960. *Cry the Beloved Country*. New York: Scribner.

Pavlenko, A. 1997. 'Bilingualism and Cognition'. Unpublished Ph.D. dissertation. Cornell University.

——2001a. 'Language learning memoirs as a gendered genre'. *Applied Linguistics* 22/2: 213–40.

——2001b. ' "How am I to become a woman in an American vein?": transformation of gender performance in second language learning', in A. Pavlenko, A. Blackledge, I. Piller, and M. Teutsch-Dwyer (eds.): *Multilingualism, Second Language, and Gender*. New York: Mouton de Gruyter, 133–74.

——2002. 'Emotions and the body in Russian and English'. *Pragmatics and Cognition* 10/1–2: 201–36.

——2005. *Emotions and Multilingualism*. Cambridge: Cambridge University Press.

——and J. Lantolf. 2000. 'Second language learning as participation and the (re)construction of selves' in J. Lantolf (ed.): *Sociocultural Theory and Second Language Learning*. Oxford: Oxford University Press, 155–77.

Peirce, B. N. 1995. 'Social identity, investment, and language learning'. *TESOL Quarterly* 29/1: 9–31.

Peirce, C. S. 1992/8. *Selected Philosophical Writings*. Bloomington: Indiana University Press, i and ii.

Pennycook, A. 1999. 'Introduction: Critical approaches to TESOL'. *TESOL Quarterly* 33/3: 329–48.

——2001. *Critical Applied Linguistics*. Mahwah, NJ: Lawrence Erlbaum.

Perez Firmat, G. 2003. *Tongue Ties: Logo-eroticism in Anglo-Hispanic Literature*. New York: Palgrave.

Phillipson, R. 2003. 'The risks of laissez-faire language policies' in *English-only Europe? Challenging Language Policy*. London: Routledge, 1–23.

Piller, I. 2002. 'Passing for a native speaker: identity and success in second language learning'. *Journal of Sociolinguistics* 6/2: 179–206.

Portman-Tselikas, E. I. 1999. *Dramapädagogik im Sprachunterricht*. Zurich: Orell Fuessli.

Poster, M. 1990. *The Mode of Information*. Chicago: University of Chicago Press.

Powell, M. 2008. 'Native tongues and more'. *New York Times*, 12 July, p. A11.

Pratt, M. L. 1999. 'Arts of the contact zone' in D. Bartholomae and A. Petrofsky (eds.): *Ways of Reading*. 5th edn. New York: Bedford/St Martin's.

——2002. 'The traffic in meaning: translation, contagion, infiltration'. *Profession 2002*. New York: Modern Language Association, 25–36.

Propp, V. 1968. *The Morphology of the Folktale*. Austin: University of Texas Press.

Rampton, B. 1995. *Crossing: Language and Ethnicity among Adolescents*. London: Longman.

——1999. 'Inner London *Deutsch* and the animation of an instructed foreign language'. *Journal of Sociolinguistics* 3: 480–504.

——2002. 'Ritual and foreign language practices at school'. *Language in Society* 31: 491–525.

——2003. 'Hegemony, social class and stylisation'. *Pragmatics* 13/1: 49–83.

Reagan, T. 2002. *Language, Education, and Ideology: Mapping the Linguistic Landscape of US Schools*. Westport, Conn.: Praeger.

——and T. A. Osborn. 2002. *The Foreign Language Educator in Society: Toward a Critical Pedagogy*. Mahwah, NJ: Lawrence Erlbaum.

Reinking, D., M. McKenna, L. Labbo, and R. Kieffer (eds.). 1998. *Handbook of Literacy and Technology*. Mahwah, NJ: Lawrence Erlbaum.

Rheingold, H. 2000. *The Virtual Community: Homesteading on the Electronic Frontier*, rev. edn. Cambridge, Mass.: MIT.

Robinson, D. 2003. *Performative Linguistics*. London: Routledge.

Rodriguez, R. 1982. *Hunger of Memory: The Education of Richard Rodriguez*. New York: Bantam.

Rorty, R. 1998. 'The inspiration value of great works of literature', *Achieving Our Country*. Cambridge, Mass.: Harvard University Press, 125–51.

Rosch, E. and B. B. Lloyd (eds.). 1978. *Cognition and Categorization*. Hillsdale, NJ: Lawrence Erlbaum.

Rosenblatt, L. 1978. *The Reader, the Text, the Poem: The Transactional Theory of the Literary Text*. Carbondale: South Illinois University Press.

Rothenbuhler, E. W. 1998. *Ritual Communication. From Everyday Conversation to Mediated Ceremony*. London: Sage.

Rushdie, S. 1999. *The Ground Beneath Her Feet*. London: Jonathan Cape.

Sacks, H. 1992. *Harvey Sacks: Lectures on Conversation*, ed. G. Jefferson. Oxford: Blackwell.

Sapir, E. 1934/49. 'Symbolism' in D. G. Mandelbaum (ed.): *Selected Writings of Edward Sapir in Language, Culture and Personality*. Berkeley: University of California Press.

Sarraute, N. 1984. *Childhood*, trans. Barbara Wright. New York: George Braziller.

Sartre, J. P. 1981. *The Words: The Autobiography of Jean-Paul Sartre*, trans. Bernard Frechtman. New York: Vintage.

Schegloff, E. A. 1991. 'Reflections on talk and social structure' in D. Boden and D. Zimmerman (eds.): *Talk and Social Structure*. Cambridge: Polity, 44–70.

Scherer, K. R. 1984. 'Emotion as a multi-component process: a model and some cross-cultural data' in P. Shaver (ed.): *Review of Personality and Social Psychology* 5: 37–63.

Schmenk, B. 2008. *Lernerautonomie. Karriere und Sloganisierung des Autonomiebegriffs.* Tübingen: Gunter Narr.

Schoen, D. 1983. *The Reflective Practitioner: How Professionals Think in Action.* New York: Basic Books.

Schumann, J. 1997. *The Neurophysiology of Affect in Language Learning.* Oxford: Blackwell.

Schutz, A. 1967. *The Phenomenology of the Social World,* trans. G. Walsh and F. Lehnert. Evanston, Ill.: Northwestern University Press.

—— 1970. *On Phenomenology and Social Relations,* ed. H. R. Wagner. Chicago: University of Chicago Press.

—— 1973. *Collected Papers,* i. *The Problem of Social Reality,* ed. M. Natanson. The Hague: Mouton.

Schwerdtfeger, I. C.. 1997a. 'Der Unterricht Deutsch als Fremdsprache: Auf der suche nach den verlorenenen Emotionen'. Info-DaF 24:5, 587–606.

—— 1997b. 'Zur (Wieder) Entdeckung von Sehen und Imagination fuer fremsprachliches Lernen–das cognitive Lernmodell auf dem Pruefstand' in A. Wolff et al (eds.): *Materialen Deutsch als Fremdsprache.* Regensburg: Fach ver band Deutsch als Fremdsprache 195–209.

Scollon, R. 2004. 'Teaching language and culture as hegemonic practice'. *Modern Language Journal* 88/2: 271–4.

Siegel, L. and J. Markoff. 1985. *The High Cost of High Tech.* New York: Harper & Row.

Silverstein, M. 1998. 'Commentaries I' in B. Schieffelin, K. Woolard, and P. Kroskrity (eds.): *Language Ideologies.* Oxford: Oxford University Press.

Siskin, J. 2003. 'The native speaker: membership has its privileges' in Carl Blyth (ed.): *The Sociolinguistics of Foreign Language Classrooms.* Boston: Heinle, 277–80.

Slobin, D. 1996. 'From "thought and language" to "thinking for speaking" ' in J. J. Gumperz and S. C. Levinson (eds.): *Rethinking Linguistic Relativity.* Cambridge: Cambridge University Press, 70–96.

Smith, C. A. and P. C. Ellsworth. 1985. 'Patterns of cognitive appraisal in emotion'. *Journal of Personality and Social Psychology* 48: 813–38.

Spivak, G. C. 2002. 'Righting Wrongs' in: Nichols, O. (ed.): *Human Rights, Human Wrongs: The Oxford Amnesty Lectures 2001.* Oxford: Oxford University Press, 164–227.

Spolsky, B. 2000. 'Language motivation revisited'. *Applied Linguistics* 21/2: 157–69.

Sullivan, P. 1996. 'English language teaching in Vietnam: an appropriation of communicative methodologies'. Unpub. Ph.D. dissertation. UC Berkeley.

—— 2000. 'Playfulness as mediation in communicative language teaching in a Vietnamese classroom' in J. Lantolf (ed.): *Sociocultural Theory and Second Language Learning.* Oxford: Oxford University Press, 115–32.

Tawada, Y. 1996. *Talisman. Literarische Essays.* Tübingen: Konkursbuch.

—— 2002. *Überseezungen.* Tübingen: Konkursbuch.

Taylor, C. 1992. *The Ethics of Authenticity.* Cambridge, Mass.: Harvard University Press.

Taylor, M. C. 2001. *The Moment of Complexity: Emerging Network Culture.* Chicago: University of Chicago Press.

Thompson, J. B. 1991. Editor's Introduction in P. Bourdieu *Language & Symbolic Power,* trans. G. Raymond and M. Adamson. Cambridge, Mass.: Harvard University Press, 1–31.

Threadgold, T. 1997. *Feminist Poetics: Poiesis, Performance, Histories.* London: Routledge.

Tomasello, M. 1999. *The Cultural Origins of Human Cognition.* Cambridge, Mass.: Harvard University Press.

Touraine, A. 1992. *Critique de la modernité.* Paris: Fayard.

—— 1995. 'La Formation du sujet', in F. Dubet and M. Wieviorka (eds.): *Penser le sujet.* Paris: Fayard, 21–46.

Turkle, S. 1995. *Life on the Screen: Identity in the Age of the Internet.* New York: Simon & Schuster.

—— 2001. 'Foreword: All MOOs are educational—the experience of "walking through the self" ' in C. Haynes and J. Rune Holmevik (eds.): *Highwired: On the Design, Use, and Theory of Educational MOOs* (2nd edn.). Ann Arbor: University of Michigan Press, pp. ix–xix.

Turner, V. 1969. *The Ritual Process*. Chicago: Aldine.

Valdes, G. 1997. 'Dual language immersion programs: a cautionary note concerning the education of language minority students'. *Harvard Education Review* 67/3: 391–429.

van Lier, L. 1996. *Interaction in the Language Curriculum. Awareness, Autonomy & Authenticity*. London: Longman.

——2002. 'An ecological-semiotic perspective on language and linguistics' in Kramsch (2002c: 140–64).

——2004. *The Ecology and Semiotics of Language Learning: A Sociocultural Perspective*. Dordrecht: Kluwer Academic.

Varela, F. J., E. Thompson, and E. Rosch. 1991. *The Embodied Mind: Cognitive Science and Human Experience*. Cambridge, Mass.: MIT.

Vinge, V. 2001. *True Names and the Opening of the Cyberspace Frontier*, ed. James Frenkel. New York: Tor Books.

von der Emde, S., J. Schneider, and M. Kotter. 2001. 'Technically speaking: transforming language learning through virtual learning environments (MOOs)'. *The Modern Language Journal* 85/2: 210–25.

von Hoene, L. 1995. 'Subjects-in-process: revisioning TA development through psychoanalytic, feminist, and postcolonial theory' in C. Kramsch (ed.) *Redefining the Boundaries of Language Study*. Boston: Heinle & Heinle, pp. 39–57.

Vygotsky, L. S. 1971. *The Psychology of Art*. Cambridge, Mass.: MIT.

Wallace, C. 1992. 'Critical literacy awareness in the EFL classroom' in Norman Fairclough (ed.), 59–92.

——1997. 'The role of language awareness in critical pedagogy' in *Encyclopedia of Language and Education*, vi. *Knowledge about Language*, eds. L.van Lier and D. Corson. Dordrecht: Kluwer, 241–9.

Ware, P. D. 2003. 'From involvement to engagement in online communication: promoting intercultural competence in foreign language education'. Unpub. Ph.D. dissertation. UC Berkeley.

——and C. Kramsch. 2005. 'Toward an intercultural stance: teaching German and English through telecollaboration'. *Modern Language Journal* 89/2: 190–205.

Warner, C. 2001. 'Computer-mediated "chatting": the design and implementation of network-based activities in the German classroom'. *Berkeley Language Center Newsletter* 18/1: 9–10.

Warschauer, M. 1999. *Electronic Literacies: Language, Culture, and Power in Online Education*. Mahwah, NJ: Lawrence Erlbaum.

——2000. Language, identity, and the Internet' in B. Kolko, L. Nakamura, and G. Rodman (eds.): *Race in Cyberspace*. New York: Routledge.

——and R. Kern (eds.). 2000. *Network-Based Language Teaching: Concepts and Practice*. Cambridge: Cambridge University Press.

Watson, R. 1995. *The Philosopher's Demise: Learning French*. Columbia: University of Missouri Press.

Weedon, C. 1987. *Feminist Practice and Poststructuralist Theory* (2nd. edn.). Oxford: Blackwell.

Weizenbaum J. 1976. *Computer Power and Human Reason: From Judgment to Calculation*. San Francisco: W. H. Freeman.

Wells, G. 1981. 'Language as interaction' in *Learning through Interaction: The Study of Language Development*. Cambridge: Cambridge University Press.

Widdowson, H. G. 1994. 'The ownership of English'. *TESOL Quarterly* 28/2: 377–89.

Wolf, A. 2006. *Subjectivity in a Second Language: Conveying the Expression of Self*. New York: Peter Lang.

Wortham, S. 2000. 'Interactional positioning and narrative self-construction' *Narrative Inquiry: Special Issue on Narrative Identity* 10/1: 157–84.

——2001. *Narratives in Action*. New York: Teacher's College.

Wrigley, H. S. 1993. 'Ways of using technology in language and literacy teaching'. *TESOL Quarterly* 27/2: 318–22.

Wylie, L. and J. F. Brière. 1995. *Les Français* (2nd edn.). Englewood Cliffs, NJ: Prentice Hall.

Yurchak, A. 2006. *Everything Was to Last Forever, Until it Was No More*. Princeton: Princeton University Press.

Zarate, G., D. Lévy, and C. Kramsch. 2008. *Précis du plurilinguisme et du pluriculuturalisme*. Paris: Éditions des archives contemporaines.

Index